GIVE ATTENTION TO READING
(1 TIMOTHY 4:13)

Book Reviews Written for the West Virginia Christian

David R. Kenney

COBB

Charleston, AR
COBB PUBLISHING
2024

Published in the United States of America by:
Cobb Publishing
704 E. Main St.
Charleston, AR 72933
CobbPublishing.com
Editor@CobbPublishing.com
479.747.8372

ISBN: 978-1-965789-91-9

Introduction:
A Brief History of the *West Virginia Christian*

The earliest brotherhood paper that I remember reading was the *Gospel Minutes* in the 1950s, edited by brother Dillard Thurman of Fort Worth, Texas. I remember the strong influence that this small, weekly paper had on our family and the congregation. After attending Ohio Valley College (1964-66) and beginning to preach the gospel, I had an early desire to, someday, establish a paper to especially serve the church and the unsaved in West Virginia.

My younger brother, James Edward ("Eddie"), graduated from Freed-Hardeman College in 1978 and was very strong in the faith. He and I often spoke of beginning a paper, but my faith was not strong enough to put plans and dreams into action. In 1980, I wrote to brother Thurman and asked him many questions about things that I thought were important to this type of work. I also spoke with several trusted fellow gospel preachers of my desire.

Finally, after becoming somewhat established in our work with the church of Christ at Salem, WV (1982-2023), and seeing the strong faith that was manifested by a good number of our members, I determined, after much prayer, to face my responsibilities and begin the work. I announced my decision to our family, and they were very supportive.

I contracted with *The Mountain Statesman* in Grafton in the fall of 1993 to begin printing the *West Virginia Christian*. Eddie and I were able to edit and have printed almost 20,000 sample copies of our new paper in the fall and winter of 1993. We distributed them throughout our state and surrounding areas. Soon, single and bundle subscriptions began to be received. Eddie worked diligently to increase our circulation.

The *West Virginia Christian* began publication of numbered issues in January 1994. In the 1993 introductory issue, we referred to our new effort as a "New and Exciting Venture." We wrote, "This sample issue marks the beginning of a private Christian effort which, we earnestly pray, will contribute to the unity, growth, strength, and peace of the churches of Christ in West Virginia." We pray that God has been glorified through Jesus Christ. By His grace, we never missed a month in publishing 369 issues. Our circulation varied and was small in comparison with other brotherhood publications. Over thirty years, many thousands of copies were sent into many states – reaching to the Philippines and to a number of African nations. The circulation of our last issue (February 2024) was 4,106 copies, including 96 bundles sent mostly to churches in WV, OH, KY, and VA, and covering the cities of Pennsboro and Ellenboro.

We were honored to be a part of fifteen annual *West Virginia Christian* lectureships, sponsored and conducted by local congregations: (2000) Mannington church of Christ; (2001) Central church of Christ, Martinsburg; (2002) Central church of Christ, Martinsburg; (2003) Pennsboro church of Christ; (2004) Pumpkin Center church of Christ, Fairview; (2005) Pennsboro church of Christ; (2006) Seth church of Christ; (2007) Pennsboro church of Christ; (2008) Central church of Christ, Martinsburg; (2009) Pennsboro church of Christ; (2010) Weirton Heights church of Christ, Weirton; (2011) Pennsboro church of Christ; (2012) Steer Creek church of Christ, Stumptown; (2013) Pennsboro church of Christ; (2014) Main St. church of Christ, Hurricane. Thousands of lectureship books and/or cassettes and CDs were printed, recorded, and freely distributed in these lectureships.

Also, we were privileged to publish Phil Grear's book, *Probing the Prophets*. Our tract, "In or Out of Christ," written by Dennis Burch, is in its 5th printing, and we also produced his 13-lesson Bible Correspondence Course, "Will I Follow Christ?"

We have not kept a record of the number of faithful men and women – young and old – who submitted articles to us over the years. We are indebted to all of these.

Among our faithful writers was brother David Kenney who especially wrote valuable *Book Reviews* for many years. I am thankful that many of his reviews are now being prepared for publication in book form. I commend this book to everyone and pray for its greatest success in helping readers to become acquainted with many worthwhile books.

Albert E. Farley
August 2024

Foreword

The following work is a collection of book reviews which were written for the *West Virginia Christian* from February 2000 to December 2023 (the paper ceased publication in February 2024). Included are two extended treatments of two related subjects from the *West Virginia Christian* Lectureship. The *West Virginia Christian* Lectureships were designed to be hosted by different congregations in the state of West Virginia. There have been many brotherhood papers that have been published over the years whose stories have become lost with time. It is my hope that this collection of book reviews, along with a history written by the paper's longstanding editor and co-founder, Albert E. Farley, will serve as a lasting record to this paper, which was began by Albert and his brother, James E. Farley. I am indebted to Albert for writing a history of the paper for this book.

My writing of book reviews began with the encouragement of my dad, Warren F. Kenney. We shared a love of shopping for used religious books and restoration history. Upon reflection, I believe my writing of book reviews was planned by my father and Albert Farley. They suggested that it would be a good service to the paper and the brotherhood if I wrote book reviews that brought to the brotherhood's attention certain works that they may not be familiar with in the hopes of stimulating more reading. Many lament that churches of Christ do not have large publishing houses and published works as evangelical publishing houses. This is a function of our purchasing and reading such denominational works, or the lack of our purchasing and reading brotherhood publications. So, I wrote several reviews and began receiving requests for prior reviews, and I began to think about how to provide this service efficiently and economically. Perhaps my number one fan was my dear mother. When dad brought the latest issue of the paper home for her to read, she would ask "Does David have an article in the paper?" After reading a paper without one of my book reviews, she would say to my dad "I don't know why Albert bothered to print this issue without one of David's articles." Please understand, this wasn't a reflection on the paper, but a testament of a mother's love.

I came across a blog by Jonathan Jones II that had some book reviews. I was struck by the blog's appearance and the flexibility it offered to individual interests, as opposed to websites which seemed to be more dominated by organizations. I reached out to Jones, and he graciously gave me a crash course on how to create and maintain a blog. This led to the launch of "The Bully Pulpit" in February 2008. This would be the repository of my book reviews and related writings over the next several years that would facilitate me sharing my writings (and spreading the word about the paper too).

Not surprisingly, the most frequent topic of concern raised was my title, "The Bully Pulpit" and the use of the word "bully." The term "bully" is from Theodore Roosevelt who would use it to describe things that are superb and excellent. The term "pulpit" refers to a platform from which communication is delivered. Often you hear that the President of the United States should use the "bully pulpit" to get the President's message out. So, the "Bully Pulpit," as I use it, is a platform to speak about books that deal with the most sublime, excellent, superb, bully subject— the Christian religion. And the term "pulpit" refers to the platform of delivery, the blog. Sure, the term may be provocative, but I chose it to provoke interest in reading. I did not have to explain it to Albert Farley who cheered "Bully for you!" He recognized it immediately.

Shortly after this, I received a call from the late Hope Shull who was the head librarian at Freed-Hardeman University. She was seeking a complete list of all my book reviews. I inquired as to why, and she explained she periodically receives requests from overseas for such a list to help build religious libraries in preaching schools and churches. While I did not have a list assembled at the time, I offered her a way to obtain all the book reviews via my blog which delighted her.

There have been some controversies along the way with challenges to some of my points. Even those who have challenged some of my recommendations or points I had written about the works were very charitable. These periods helped me focus more intently on writing better. For all those who expressed such interest, I am thankful. There was also some sabotage by some following my blog that allowed them to post subversive pictures and such. Evil never sleeps, but I eventually figured out ways to block much of their nefarious activity.

The thought of compiling these book reviews into an actual book "someday" had crossed my mind, but I always thought it would be some time out in the future. There were years that were extremely difficult for me to submit any writings due to the failing health of my parents and other personal challenges. The last book review I wrote appeared in the December issue of the last full volume of the paper (2023). There were book reviews that did not make the paper for one reason or another, but Albert has been nothing but supportive in my writings. I elected to include all my book reviews I had written for the *West Virginia Christian*, published or unpublished, in this anthology. The bibliography is included in the ones which were printed. I would like to express my tremendous appreciation to Albert E. Farley for giving me the latitude to make these writings available both on the blog and this book. Albert and his dear wife, Nancy, have completed a great work, and I am thankful to have had a small part in it! I am thankful to Bradley Cobb and his Cobb Publishing for his work on this project.

I am also very thankful to my dear wife, Annette, who has helped me each step of the way. She is not only my "extra set of eyes," but my trusted counselor (Proverbs 31:11). It is our prayer that these writings will be a blessing to our children, James and Deborah, and others for time to come.

David R. Kenney
September 22, 2024

Contents

The Value of Church Libraries

In 1995, I preached at a congregation that had existed for over 100 years. I requested to see the church library, thinking it would have some very interesting books. I was saddened to find only a couple of old pew Bibles and a torn-up, incomplete set of Adam Clarke's commentaries. When I returned home, I immediately requested permission to purchase books for the church library.

When I approached the leadership of our congregation about expanding the library, the idea was enthusiastically supported. Even though the funds were limited, the main hindrance was someone willing to make the effort. We were convinced that even purchasing a book a month was a step in the right direction. Interest in the library grew among those seeking to study, but either did not have the resources or lacked knowledge of sound biblical reference materials. One of the results of the library program, we found, was that people's enthusiasm blossomed to where they purchased the same books for their personal library.

Since I am procurer of books for the library, under the oversight of the elders, I have certain goals for the church library. The first is to provide an adult-level reference center. Second is the purchase of religious books of value. Third is to provide a reference source on a variety of topics. Many books exist on any given subject, and some are better than others are. Guy N. Woods estimated that there are over 3,000 books on Romans alone. We want a flexible and strong library. Fourth is to get the input of the congregation. The church can buy a book and put it in the library, but if you do not feel the need for it you may not read it. Fifth is to get the congregation to read and study for themselves. You will never learn all there is to know from a preacher and teacher, no matter how good they are. Consider this appropriate thought from *Leaves of Gold*:

A reading church is an informed church.

An informed church is an interested church.

An interested church is an acting church.

An acting church is a serving church.

A serving church is a Christian church.

No column such as this would be complete without recommending the Book of books - The Holy Bible. The Bible is the only book I can recommend without reservation (provided a good translation is being used). It is complete, authoritative, and furnishes us unto every good work (Jude 3; 2 Peter 1:3; 2 Timothy 3:16-17). The Bible will be the test of the truthfulness of every other book. Read Psalm 119 for the correct attitude we should have toward this wondrous book, its timeless themes, and its eternal message.[1]

The Value of a Religious Library

Guy N. Woods, in *Questions & Answers, Volume 2*, eloquently stated the value of good books when asked to comment on what good books meant to him:

> A good library is truly a fabulous fairyland, a place of genuine delight, affording a happy haven from the swirling currents of restless world. In it we are in the intimate fellowship of the greatest intellectuals, the most profound thinkers and the greatest reasoners of all time. No barriers have been erected to exclude us; here is one of the few areas of human experience where the rich are at no advantage, rich and poor alike being privileged to drink at will from this ever flowing fountain. Into what other select company of distinguished scholars may one appear at will and there

---

[1] Note: The last two paragraphs of this section were not in the original lectureship manuscript, but *were* included in a shorter article on this topic by the same author, which originally appeared in *West Virginia Christian*, Vol. 7, No. 2, February 2000, p. 8. Reprinted by permission.

converse to his heart's content? How else may one in life associate with the spirits of the sainted dead and share in the intellectual and mental labors of their lives on earth? [pp. 327-328]

Focusing his attention on religious books, Guy N. Woods went on to write:

Were I, after a long and eventful life of intense activity as a gospel preacher asked to designate what, in my view, are the most vital aims which should characterize all who teach and preach the word, high on the list would be the accumulation of a useful library, the cultivation of an affection for good books and the formation of regular habits of study. No day should be permitted to pass which does not provide for communion with good books. [p. 328]

Brother Guy N. Woods passed away on December 8, 1993. E. Claude Gardner, writing in the February 1994 issue of the *Gospel Advocate*, mentioned that Guy N. Woods had donated his library to Freed-Hardeman University several years prior to his death. In that issue of the *Gospel Advocate* is a photograph of the more than 7,000 volumes that Guy N. Woods had donated from his personal library.

Principles In Building An Effective Church Library

These principles are ones that I use when purchasing books, whether for the church or my personal religious library.

Appoint Someone Who Loves Books. Ideally someone other than the preacher, perhaps a deacon, should be appointed to the service of maintaining a library. This is not to say the preacher would not be an excellent source of information. One reason is to ensure the work continues when the preacher departs from the local congregation. Another reason is the preacher, if he is worth his salt, already has a love of good religious books. Working among good religious books is contagious and should be allowed to infect others as well. Whoever the person is who is appointed should be the type of individual who shares his experiences with others who may pick up the work in case he has to relinquish it.

The One In Charge Should Be Accountable to the Leadership. Books are inanimate objects and can communicate things that are both good and not so good. The elders are the ones responsible for the shepherding of the flock; it is imperative that they oversee this work. If the congregation does not have an eldership, then the leaders of the congregation should monitor what is being purchased. There is a two-fold purpose of overseeing this work. First, to ensure the content is worthy to be added to the church library. Second, to ensure that funds are not either misappropriated or that there is no opportunity for the appearance of inappropriate behavior.

Determine the Focus. There are nearly as many topics as there are books, so one must determine the parameters of the library. Will it focus only on adults? Will it only contain commentaries? Will it only contain brotherhood material? Will it include videos, audio tapes, or computer programs? Will it include counseling or psychology materials? Will it contain programs of wholesome secular entertainment? These parameters need to be defined early on to avoid getting off track.

Have a Designated Area. Spacing does not always permit a separate room; however, it would be best to have an area that is not part of the preacher's office. The area needs to be one that is accessible to all people at all times the building is open. One of the reasons not to use the preacher's office is to avoid disrupting other church business that is typically done in this office. Another reason is to ensure that the preacher's library does not end up being mixed with the church's library. A preacher's books are his tools and are needed by him. We must respect the preacher's personal property as we would our own (Luke 6:31). The same is true for preachers and members to respect church property. It is sad that such would need to be said, but problems in these areas have been known to occur.

One Does Not Have To Start Big, But One Has To Start. Guy N. Woods' library was not accumulated overnight. He was over 85 years of age when he died and had devoted the majority of his life to tools of study. When we began the building of the library where I attend, we had only one small shelf of books. Starting with an original commitment of adding at least one book a month, over six years the congregation has added far more than just seventy-two volumes (which would be praiseworthy in and of itself). In February of 2001, the church purchased three software programs that have expanded the library by over ninety volumes. The point is that a library does not have to start out big, but it can grow incrementally and exponentially. The key is to start.

Learn What Books Are Especially Good. Many books exist on any given subject and some books are better than others. Guy N. Woods estimated that there are over 3,000 books on Romans alone. You want a library that is strong; however, one does not need 3,000 commentaries on Romans. How does one learn what books are good? First, ask your preacher (or other preachers, teachers, or authors). It takes effort to get the recommendation of good books from others; you must take the initiative to do so. Second, study the reference works cited by books that you have greatly profited from. Third, read periodicals that provide book reviews. Fourth, become familiar with catalogs and those who publish them. For example, if I were searching on a topic involving Christian Evidences, one of the first places I would go would be Apologetics Press' catalog.

A Note About Commentaries. This writer has heard grown men (who should know better) criticize commentaries as if they were creed books. Such broad criticisms of commentaries are not a sign of steadfastness but of ignorance. It thrills me to study of the experiences of Alexander Campbell who was one of the leaders of the Restoration Movement. If he wrote his thoughts about the book of Acts, would it not be grand to know what his studies led him to conclude? Well, he did write a commentary on the book of Acts. Will I ignore this book because it is a "commentary"? Why some think it is any different to go ask a preacher a question rather than look in a commentary for an answer puzzles me. When you consult a commentary, you are consulting the study of the one who wrote the commentary. The commentary is no better than the one who prepared it. Not all of us have time to obtain multiple doctorates in Archaeology, Geography, Restoration History, Greek, Hebrew, Jewish History, Early Church History, Reformation History, etc. Why not read from those who have? Incidentally, one of the men I have heard criticize commentaries is now an elder and values good commentaries now that he recognizes that it is not enough to be persuaded himself but that he must also persuade others (1 Peter 3:15-16).

Kick Aside the Bad. No book made by man is perfect. As my father was told by the senior Tom W. Butterfield in reference to the use of religious books, "You must have the sense of a chicken—to pick out what is food and what is not." It is up to the leadership of each congregation to determine the contents of its library. I would encourage congregations to support brotherhood printed material whenever possible. It is also important to realize that some of the best material on a subject may not even be among the writers of the brotherhood. Avoid the extreme that only brotherhood material will be part of the library. One would eliminate many Bible translations deemed reliable with such a restriction since those among denominations have had part in the work (e.g., KJV, NASB, NKJV, etc.). Also be careful about using material by wolves among us in sheep's clothing. Just because a book is written or published by someone that we think is reliable does not make it true. Not all works in a library necessarily have to teach the truth. Some books may be from a false teaching; e.g., *Book of Mormon*. No one who is true to the Bible can accept the *Book of Mormon*, but it may be in a church library for reference. If something is glaringly wrong with a book, then maybe adding a note card to the front inside cover detailing the error may salvage otherwise good material. We should examine it before adding it to the church library (1 Thessalonians 5:21).

Keep the Congregation Informed. Where I attend we do this in two ways. First, a series of articles is written for the bulletin that tells the congregation about books in the library. Second, whenever someone asks me a religious question I make a determined effort to take them to the library and answer the question using the library rather than my own knowledge. Remember that the concept that the brotherhood should know less than the preacher is the fundamental reason the falling away after the first century occurred and led into Catholicism. Train members to use the library and not to be dependent on you for the answers. Remind them that they will never learn all there is to know from a preacher and teacher, no matter how good they are.

Encourage Participation. Always ask for feedback and suggested topics that could be incorporated in the library. Be careful of requesting specific books because some are still babes and may suggest a work that should not be part of the library. Seeking topics rather than titles would help avoid a hurtful situation. Also, remind the congregation that books can be added to the library in other ways than from the treasury. Remind the congregation that they could purchase a book in honor or memory of someone (provided it is first approved by the leadership). If someone is not familiar with books then they could donate funds to have the person in charge of the library purchase the books. A sign in the book should reflect this dedication. It is a simple gesture, but a high honor. I came across a book dedicated to the memory of Olive Hill whom I have never met. She used to date my grandfather, George W. Kenney, whom I also never met, so I had an interest on what made that book unique. This dedication was actually my introduction to one of the preachers I admire the most - Foy E. Wallace, Jr.

Conclusion

The work of building an effective church library is measured in two ways. The first measurement is the resourcefulness of the contents of the library. A good way to test this is by going to the library to answer questions people ask. Many of the ideas for the church's library are not from suggested books but from people's questions that the library did not have sufficient materials to answer readily. The second measure of effectiveness is the actual use of the library. Some way of determining the utilization of the library would assist in the justification for continuance of the program. One does not need to over engineer the transfer of books which may stifle the traffic to the library, but some sort of measurement of its use would reinforce the need for such a resource. We have a simple sign out form on which members write their name, title of book, date checked out, and date returned. Periodically, we put a reminder to the entire congregation that an inventory is being made of the books and to return any they may have signed out. If a book is lost, then we simply replace it. If someone has the book in their personal library and has not returned it, then what is the real harm just replacing it? The point is to get as much valuable religious material into the hands of the brotherhood as possible. It is their responsibility to read it (1 Timothy 4:13). Finally, keep in mind that books convey messages long after we have passed from this life. The earthly investments today may reap heavenly dividends after we have departed and until Christ returns.

How To Build Interest In Reading & Book Review

When asked how to build interest in reading some say "you either have it or you do not"; however, this fails to consider that our tastes and habits change with time and effort. It may seem odd, but books can be a great source of encouragement. For example, J.W. McGarvey wrote *Lands of the Bible* based on his visit to the Holy Land in 1879. Before he went on his journey he spent time with his books as if they were friends. Guy N. Woods related this incident and agreed that relationships grow between books and those who treasure them.[1]

While it is important to study the Bible, it is also important to realize that there are many books available to enrich our understanding. Dr. T.W. Brents, who wrote *The Gospel Plan of Salvation*, once stated "If you will show us a man who reads nothing but the Bible, we will show you one who reads and understands very little of that."[2] Let's look at how to build interest in reading from two points of view. First, by building interest in reading in ourselves then in others.

Building Interest in Ourselves

The fundamental principle to remember is that you cannot build interest in others if you are not interested yourself. One lesson I learned was that once I started to gather information about religious books, my interest in them grew exponentially. The first step is to commit to cultivate an interest in reading religious books to improve your knowledge of the Bible. The second step is to dedicate time to reading. One of the most avid readers I know is Winford Claiborne who was my professor for General Epistles at FHU and also a friend. When answering the question "Where can I find time to read?" he replied, "You

---

[1] Guy N. Woods, Questions & Answers, Vol. 1, 1976, pp. 327-328.

[2] As quoted by Wayne Jackson, A Study Guide to Greater Bible Knowledge, 1986, p. 83.

cannot find it; you have to make it."[3] If you cannot clear any time, consider getting up earlier. Your mind will less likely be full of things that will break your concentration. These are some suggestions to build interest in reading.

Spend Time With Those Who Love to Read. I am thankful for those who are avid readers; two in particular are Steve Miller and Annette Kenney. Steve and I would shop for books all over Ohio and compare each other's treasured finds. Annette, my wife, makes it easy to read because she cannot help but read. If she has one free moment, you can be sure she is reading something. This makes it easier to schedule time to read and enjoy the company of one with the same interest.

Read Biographies. Biographies can be a good source of information and inspiration about great people and events. For example, if one wanted to learn more about the Restoration Movement, I would suggest *The Fool of God*, a novel based on the life of Alexander Campbell. When I finished reading it, my interest in his life was renewed. Before long I was reading everything I could find on Restoration History.

Read Opposing Works. Sometimes the quickest way to build interest is to read from those on the opposite side of an issue. This should rally us to study the matter further. One great source of building interest along this line is reading public religious debates. Prior to 1820, Alexander Campbell and Barton W. Stone shared negative sentiments about debates. Campbell's attitude changed due to being persuaded to debate John Walker, a Presbyterian, on the issue of baptism at Mount Pleasant, Ohio, on June 19-20, 1820. After the debate Campbell offered a challenge to debate anyone on the subject of infant baptism. W. L. McCalla, Presbyterian from Kentucky, accepted this challenge, in May 1823. After these two debates, Campbell wrote:

There are not a few who deprecate religious controversy as

---

[3] Winford Claiborne, "Read Any Good Books Lately?" Manuscript, p. 8.

an evil of no small magnitude. But these are either ill-in-formed, or those conscious that their principles will not bear investigation. So long as there is good and evil, truth and error in this world, so long will there be opposition; for it is in the nature of good and evil, of truth and error, to oppose each other. We cheerfully confess that it is much to be regretted that controversy amongst Christians should exist; but it is more to be regretted that error, the pro-fessed cause of it should exist.[4]

Campbell's experience led him to believe that "a week's de-bating is worth a year's preaching."[5] He also stated "This is, we are convinced, one of the best means of propagating the truth and exposing error in doctrine or practice."[6] It is also a good way to build interest in reading.

Attend Lectureships. This is a good way to meet many that have written books in our brotherhood. Some may say, "my em-ployer will not let me take time off to attend a Bible Lecture-ship." In that case, why not go to a lectureship on one of your vacations? My family strives to attend the FHU Lectureship each year. One of the highlights for me is to meet individuals who have written some of the books I own such as Leroy Brownlow, Perry Cotham, Curtis Cates, Garland Elkins, Alan Highers, Tom Holland, Wayne Jackson, Jack Lewis, Basil Overton, Bert Thomp-son, Earl West, Clyde Woods, and others.

Shop for Religious Books. One of the greatest tools to build interest in others is getting good religious books in their hands. If one wants to build his interest, then he should go where good books are sold. My father has long been a seeker of good books. We spend nearly every visit together looking for good religious books. Even if we do not find books to purchase, I am always

---

[4] Earl I. West, The Search for the Ancient Order, Vol. 1, 1990, p. 66.
[5] Ibid.
[6] James DeForrest Murch, Christians Only: A History of the Restoration Movement, 1962, p. 77.

rejuvenated. This is not only because he is my father, but also the thrill of hunting books that I can use. A word of caution, purchasing religious books can be habit forming!

Visit Historical Sites. The first weekend in August, the church in Lexington, KY hosts the Cane Ridge Restoration Workshop. This is where the restoration movement spread due to the efforts of Barton W. Stone. I first attended this workshop as a boy. My interest in Restoration History was ignited from that one workshop. I am so thankful that my parents took the family to this workshop. If attending this does not pique one's interest in reading, then I am at a loss for words.

Seek Those With Similar Interests. Most of us are familiar with this passage: "Do not be deceived: 'Evil company corrupts good habits.'" (1 Corinthians 15:33, NKJV). We also need to remember that good company helps cultivate good habits. Be advised that those who appreciate hard to find religious books are sometimes uncomfortable about loaning them. Keep in mind you are sharing information, but you should work to purchase your own books.

Building Interest in Others

The best method to build interest in others is to build interest in yourself. After preparing yourself, you will then be prepared to use the greatest tool to motivate others—enthusiasm.

Ira North was one of the most enthusiastic preachers among churches of Christ. When he was located at the Madison Church of Christ there were approximately 400 members. Within his 32-year ministry, the congregation grew to about 5,100 with a record Sunday School attendance of 8,410 in 1982.[7] He had these words to say about enthusiasm:

Enthusiasm is powerful as dynamite and contagious as measles. Enthusiasm will build buildings and influence people. It will

---

7 Ira North, *Balance: A Tried & Tested Formula For Church Growth*, 1983, Introduction by Willard Collins.

turn multitudes to righteousness. Never underestimate the power of genuine enthusiasm. And it is as contagious as it is powerful. It rubs off on you.[8]

Never underestimate your influence for good—'*Let your light so shine before men, that they may see your good works, and glorify your Father which is in heaven."* (Matthew 5:16, NKJV). The following book review is an attempt to build interest in you based on my preparation.

This material was first presented at the 2001 West Virginia Christian Lectureship.

---

[8] Ira North, *You Can March for the Master*, 1971, p. 19.

A Dictionary of Early Christian Beliefs
(David W. Bercot, Editor)

I became familiar with this volume thanks to Wayne Jackson and the Christian Courier. Brother Jackson was recommending this book for purchase in the column "The Book Shelf" stating, "This is a tremendously valuable reference tool in the area of church history." That was all I needed to hear so I ordered a copy the first opportunity I had. The book indeed is a tremendously valuable research tool into the writings of the early church.

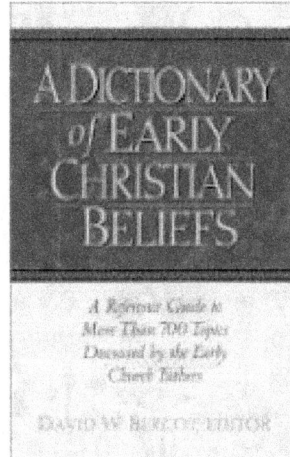

For those unfamiliar with the term Ante-Nicene Fathers, this refers to the period directly after the 1st century but before (or ante) Emperor Constantine assembled the church council of Nicaea in AD 325. The writers of this period include those who were martyred for their faith; e.g., Polycarp, Justin Martyr, Irenaeus, Tertullian and others. A collection of their writings can be purchased in a ten-volume set; however, this volume provides an excellent way to access their writings more efficiently. Then if one wishes to read more about a writer's thoughts, they can follow the citation to read directly from the primary source material that is available. This work provides information from the Bible and early church fathers on over 700 theological and historical topics so one can quickly gather key information on a given topic. Plus, the editor has provided cross-references to other materials in the book that are helpful. Basically this is a topical index to the writings of the early church immediately after the period of the apostles. One should be sure to read the Preface of this book in order to gain valuable insights on how to maximize its use. In addition, the editor has provided a "Who's Who" of the Ante-Nicene Fathers that provides the best estimates of the timeframe the person lived and what we know of their position in the early church. This information is brief but a valuable "snapshot" of the witness.

The adage "Those who ignore history are condemned to repeat it" has again been demonstrated to be true, not only in secular, but church history as well. The firestorm of controversy by the fiction/nonfiction work The DaVinci Code rained longer than it should have because many have neglected church history. This was shown to be true when claims/statements/accusations were not in line with the facts.

A study of this period reveals what the early church did in the years immediately following the apostolic period. One should use caution with this material recalling that these men were not inspired (or guided) by the Holy Spirit as the New Testament writers were. Some afford these men more authority then the apostles and the New Testament, which can be a grave error. Recall the warning Paul gave to the Ephesian elders of the apostasy that they were to watch out for in their lifetime in Acts 20:17ff. This warning would certainly include this period. So one must exercise caution in the use of early church leaders' works after the first century.

A sample of the type of material one will find is an entry under "LORD'S DAY" which includes a statement by Justin Martyr around AD 160. Here is what he wrote:

> And on the day called Sunday, all who live in cities or in the country gather together to one place, and the memoirs of the apostles or the writings of the prophets are read....But Sunday is the day on which we all hold our common assembly, because it is the first day on which God...made the world. And Jesus Christ our Savior rose from the dead on that same day. (Pages 405-406)

This quotation suggests several points: (1) Sunday rather than Saturday was now the day of worship, (2) Saints assembled together in one place rather than splitting into various homes for study, (3) The reading of the Scriptures was prominent during the assembly, and (4) the writings of the apostles were viewed as equally authoritative as those of the prophets. This one entry contains points that could easily be expanded into a lesson on the public worship habits we should have as Christians if we want to be like they were then. And this is just one passage under one entry of over 700 topics.

The Gospel Plan of Salvation
(T.W. Brents)

This particular work was completed in approximately 1874, and it is in its seventeenth edition. This is due to two reasons. First is the greatness of its author. Second is the subject matter of the book and quality with which it deals with its subjects. The book's table of contents reveals the nature of the subject matter: predestination; election and reprobation; foreknowledge of God; hereditary depravity; establishment and identity of the church; faith; repentance; confession; the candidates, design and meaning of baptism; new birth; and the Holy Spirit.

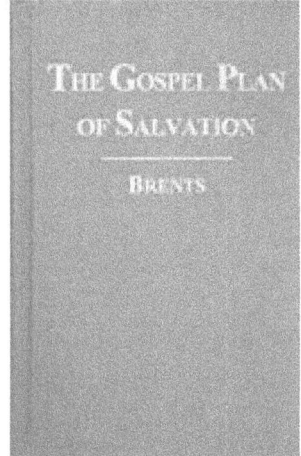

An example of the author's thorough method of refuting error is demonstrated in Dr. Brent's refutation of the Pedobaptist (people who practice infant baptism) belief that baptism replaced circumcision. Pedobaptists argue that circumcision was for male children at eight days; thus, baptism is for children as well. He gives several compelling arguments to show that baptism did not come in place of circumcision. Here are a few:

1). Circumcision was confined to the Jews, and those purchased with money by them; baptism is for all nations.

2). Circumcision was to be performed on native Jews at eight days old; baptism is for any age capable of believing the gospel.

3). Circumcision was confined to males only; baptism is for men and women. If baptism came in the room of circumcision, why baptize females?[1]

In a chapter of Guy N. Woods' final book, Brother Woods had this to say about The Gospel Plan of Salvation:

> ... this excellent work is an encyclopedic presentation of biblical teaching on major topics and a thorough refutation of Calvinistic doctrines that, though not usually recognized as such, are really the foundation of most denominational structures today. It is preeminently biblical in content, tersely and simply written in the best tradition of Victorian English and its conclusions are therefore irresistible.[2]

T.W. Brents was a medical doctor and considered worthy of three doctorate degrees. His writing style in Victorian English alone is worth reading the book. Read it and you will understand why this book is one of the most respected works in the brotherhood.

Originally printed in *West Virginia Christian*, Vol. 7, No. 10, October 2000, p. 4. Reprinted by permission.

---

[1] T.W. Brents, The Gospel Plan of Salvation, Bowling Green, KY: Guardian of Truth Foundation, 1987, pp 341-342.

[2] Guy N. Woods, How to Study the New Testament Effectively, Nashville, TN: Gospel Advocate Company, 1992, p. 125.

Brigance's Outlines
(E. Claude Gardner, Editor)

Several factors go into the success of any book, and books of sermon outlines are no exception. Some have differing attitudes toward sermon outline books. Some naively think that all a preacher needs is a book of sermon outlines, while others find very little use for them. Incidentally, L.L. Brigance himself was reported to have the opinion that sermon outlines by others were of very little value to his preparation. So what would make these sermon outlines unique?

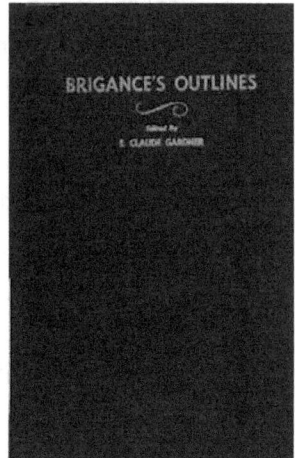

L.L. Brigance was a humble man. In fact, many today know very little about him, which is sad. The fact that E. Claude Gardner would edit these sermons himself for DeHoff Publications so others could have them at their fingertips shows that Brigance's contributions were viewed greater by those who were recipients of his scholarship. Some may not realize that L.L. Brigance prepared some of the sermons that were preached by N.B. Hardeman in his famed Hardeman Tabernacle Sermons. Never seeking to take anything away from the contributions of others, he would comment when asked, "I cannot preach like brother Hardeman, but I did help load his gun."

L.L. Brigance was born in Scotts Hill, TN. He attended what was then Georgie Robertson Christian College, which would eventually become Freed-Hardeman University (the change of an institution once operated by the Christian Church to one operated by churches of Christ is a story of interest all by itself). A.G. Freed was the President of the school. Brigance's teachers included A.G. Freed, N.B. Hardeman and others. He earned both the B.A. and M.A. degrees there, was valedictorian of his undergraduate class, and received the oratory medal. He was baptized by the same man who baptized N.B. Hardeman, who was R.P. Meeks. He was a restoration history student, scholar and teacher and wrote an excellent series of articles for The Gospel Advocate back in the 1930s and 1940s which has been reprinted in book form by Hester Publication. Brigance spent the vast majority of his work teaching at Freed-Hardeman College (now University) and preaching on appointment basis. Some of his students included E. Claude Gardner, Hugo McCord, George W. DeHoff and others. His students urged him to publish his outlines which he intended to complete but failing health and other pressing demands prohibited him from completing the task. Brother Gardner described Brigance's outlines as "...Scriptural, fundamental, simple, logical and usable. For decades the small and great have preached effectively his outlines." (Preface). Leonard Lee Brigance passed away February 4, 1950. His body lies in Henderson Cemetery with other great men and women of the past. As a student at Freed-Hardeman University, I lived most of my dorm life in Brigance Hall which was named in his honor in 1971.

The book contains a brief biographical sketch written by Brigance at some point in his life and a Preface written by E. Claude Gardner. Brother Gardner wrote the Preface on February 23, 1951, which was just over a year from Brigance's passing. These outlines were ones that Brigance freely shared with his students and others. Thankfully, brother Gardner compiled these and preserved them for future generations. If you are looking for an excellent book of sermon outlines to help a young preacher, then you should give serious consideration to this book. It is filled with 100 scriptural sermons, the type which we need to have preached in our brotherhood today.

Originally printed in the *West Virginia Christian*, Vol. 21, No. 7, July 2014, p. 8. *Reprinted by permission.*

Theology of Three Early Restoration Documents
(L.L. Brigance)

My father and I were able to enjoy the 2014 Freed-Hardeman University Bible Lectureship together, which is a great blessing! I always enjoy the presentations coordinated by the Friends of the Restoration Movement. This year, I was delighted to hear Sam Hester of Hester Publications announce the near completion of a new book. For those unfamiliar with Hester Publications, they reprint books, particularly restoration works that are difficult to find. The book is a compilation of articles by L.L. Brigance written for the *Gospel Advocate* in the 1930s. The book is entitled *Theology of Three Restoration Documents* and analyzes *The Last Will and Testament of the Springfield Presbytery*, *The Declaration and Address*, and *The Sermon on the Law*. Sam Hester agreed to send me one of the first copies available.

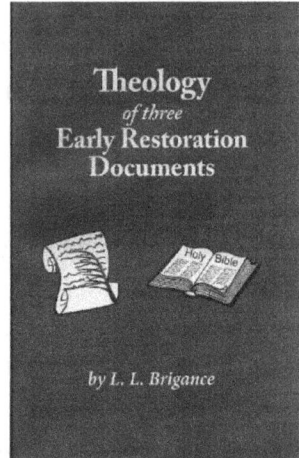

E. Claude Gardner studied under L.L. Brigance, and he was at the announcement. Sam Hester asked Gardner to comment on Brigance. Gardner's comments match his statement on the back cover of the book:

> L.L. Brigance was known as one of the top Bible teachers and scholars of Freed-Hardeman College the first half of the 20th century....He was recognized for being balanced and free of extremism. His writings and teachings on the Restoration Movement had a far-reaching impact on influential preachers.... I counted him as the best Bible teacher of my college career. Because of my admiration and appreciation of him, I edited a volume of his sermons.

Brother Gardner did more than edit the sermons, he typed them himself!

I have enjoyed reading Brigance's analysis of *The Declaration and Address* which he considered the greatest religious document since inspiration. Now, one may find Brigance's assessment excessive; however, I suggest reserving one's verdict until reading Brigance's case. Here is a sample from "The Right to Private Judgment":

> "Intolerance has ever been one of humanity's greatest weaknesses. We want others to agree with us—to see things like we see them, to believe, think, and act like we do. And if they do not, we do not like it nor them. We want to suspect their motives, declare them unsound, interdict them, 'read them out of the party.' Of course it is not only our right, but our duty, to insist upon the plain teaching of God's word—to urge all men to follow it. It is the divine standard, the infallible standard, the only standard of truth and duty. But our opinions, preferences, prejudices, and judgments are an entirely different matter. We have no right to insist upon anyone conforming to them. To do so is to deny to men 'the right of private judgment.' Suppose that after diligent study I am in doubt as to the meaning of a passage of Scriptures. I search the commentaries. I find that 'able men' differ about it. And 'what shall we do when the doctors disagree?' We must decide for ourselves..." (L.L. Brigance, Theology of Three Restoration Documents, p. 22)

Many are familiar with N.B. Hardeman but may be unaware that Brigance assisted in the preparation of material for the *Hardeman Tabernacle Sermons*. Hugo McCord, who was baptized and taught by Brigance, told me Brigance stated "I cannot preach like brother Hardeman, but I helped load his gun." Be sure and do not overlook this keen analysis of three major works which moved many toward "a restoration of the ancient order of things."

Theological Dictionary of the New Testament – Abridged in One Volume (Geoffrey W. Bromily)

This is an abridgment of the highly regarded ten-volume set edited by Gerhard Kittel and Gerhard Friedrich which was originally in German as a nine volume set with Kittle overseeing volumes 1-4 and Freidrich volumes 5-9. Geoffrey Bromily translated the work into English, but he also prepared a single volume abridged. People often refer to the full volume set as "Kittel" and the abridged volume as "Little Kittel." According to the dust jacket, this volume contains 1,400 rather than 8,420 pages of the full set. One should look at both the price and size of these volumes before determining which option suits their situation best. If space and money are a factor, then one may decide the abridged volume is the better option. Either choice, one would do well to include the work of Kittel in their library.

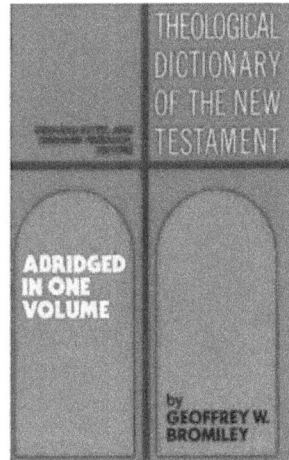

This work provides information regarding how a Greek word was used both by secular writers such as Homer, Aristotle, Plato, et al. and how the term is used within the New Testament. The abridged work focus' is more on NT usage. If one is interested learning more about the details surrounding a term's etymology and linguistic use, then consulting the entry in the full set may be of value. (The volume and page number from the unabridged set is included at the end of each entry.) There is a Table of Greek Keywords which contains a listing of all the Greek terms in the transliterated English format the editor deemed theologically significant and the corresponding page number. There is also a Table of English Keywords as well so one can locate the terms rather easily. Please note, this is not an exhaustive treatment; i.e., it does not cover all the words in the Greek New Testament.

An additional value of this abridgment is the work was completed by the one who translated the original work. Ideally it would be nice to have the original editor do this work, but having the one who translated each word from German to English complete the abridgment is a significant benefit when switching from one volume to another. There will be those who will cite weaknesses of this set as to technical matters relating to Greek language or indexing to Strong's Numbering System. Some of their arguments may have merit; however, I have not found any of these to keep me from profiting from the work.

Also, one may want to be aware that Gerhard Kittel was arrested after WW2 for his support of Adolph Hitler and the Nazi Party. One critic stated that they hoped the original dictionary would be revised by a team including Jewish scholars. With all sincere respect to all those who suffered much under Hitler, the validity of the work should not be measured by the ethnicity of the contributors but how the work stands from a scholarship perspective. Geoffrey Bromily, born in England, saw enough value in this research to translate it so others could profit from it as well. This set is treasured by many who appreciate the insights it provides while abhorring the political views that Kittel himself held. One wonders how the product could be improved simply by having those from Jewish descent contribute to its revision? Of course, some are never satisfied, and I have even seen claims that the NIV is the "Nazis Inspired Version" simply because Kittel's work was listed as a reference source. While the NIV is not my first choice for a Bible translation, I certainly would not argue the NIV is a product of Nazism! It seems to me that this line of thinking does more to impugn the work of the linguistic expert Geoffrey Bromily, who translated the work into

English, rather than protest one of the more evil regimes to rise upon the earth.

As with other works, a good rule of thumb is to use comparative works as much as possible. The study of words of the New Testament and their occurrence by writers outside the NT is an enriching experience, but one must be careful not to overly rely on arguments from linguistics alone. For example, those who rightfully argue that *baptizo* [to baptize], including this writer, must be translated "to immerse" (or some synonym) should be able to support this argument with other supporting facts such as immersion being congruent with a burial which baptism depicts plus NT examples in Acts which clearly implies full immersion. Basing an argument on linguistics alone has led some into doctrines contrary to the Bible because words of differing meanings in their respective contexts. This work will assist one in a full discussion of a word's etymology and theology in the New Testament and is an extremely valuable resource.

Why I am a Member of
the Church of Christ
(Leroy Brownlow)

The church constantly needs a firm understanding of the fundamentals of Christianity. One of the best tools to explain the distinctive identifying marks of the church of Christ in the New Testament is this book by brother Brownlow. When I have a religious discussion with someone and they have expressed an interest in learning more about churches of Christ then I give them a copy of this book. I recommend a copy of this book be given to each new convert and that this book is used in the teenage class regularly so that every teenager is taught from this book. We are losing people to apostasy and one of the reasons is because people do not fully understand what they are leaving and exchanging for the church of Christ.

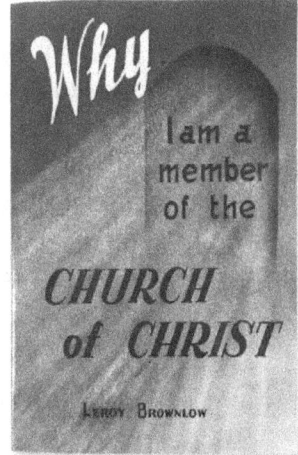

This book is best explained by a listing of the table of contents. Why I am a member of the church of Christ:

- Because if was founded by the scriptural builder—Christ.
- Because it was founded on the scriptural foundation.
- Because it was founded at the scriptural place—Jerusalem.
- Because it was founded at the scriptural time—The Pentecost following the resurrection of Christ.
- Because Christ is the founder of only one church—His church.
- Because it is scriptural in name.

- Because it is scriptural in organization.
- Because it has the Bible at is only creed, confession of faith or church manual.
- Because it believes the Bible to be the inspired word of God.
- Because it believes the Bible is a book to be rightly divided.
- Because it is undenominational.
- Because it is scriptural in doing missionary work.
- Because it teaches the kingdom has been established and Christ is now reigning.
- Because it gives scriptural answers to the question— What must I do to be saved?
- Because it teaches that man is saved by faith but not by faith only.
- Because it teaches that man is saved by the blood of Christ.
- Because it teaches that a change of heart is indispensable to man's salvation.
- Because of its teaching and practice concerning prayer.
- Because it teaches and administers scriptural baptism.
- Because it teaches that a child of God can so sin as to be eternally lost.
- Because it teaches that infants are born pure and innocent rather than depraved.
- Because it teaches that the miraculous manifestations of the Spirit have ceased.
- Because of its scriptural teaching and observance of the Lord's supper.
- Because it has scriptural music in the worship.
- Because salvation is in Christ's church.

It was thrilling to hear brother Brownlow at the FHU Bible Lectureship speak on the same topic. I wish everyone would have had the opportunity to hear him that day. In 1991, my wife and I graduated from FHU and brother Brownlow was awarded the Doctor of Laws degree. So, brother Brownlow was in my graduating class at FHU, which was one of the highlights of that great day.

When 2,000 copies of the first edition of this book were printed in 1945, Brownlow wrote in the forward: "The hope is now entertained that this volume of reasons for being a member of the church of Christ will be a source of light to those in darkness; a source of aid to those seeking Bible helps; and a source of glory to Him who will deal with all books according to their merits." It is estimated that this book has sold over 1 million copies since its publication. I believe his hope has been realized. I was fortunate to have him sign a copy for me. One source I came across states he had written and sold more books in Texas than any other author. He has authored 30 books. Brother Brownlow passed away at the age of 88 on November 8, 2002. He will be greatly missed.

Originally printed in the *West Virginia Christian*, Vol. 10, No. 4, April 2003, p. 8. Reprinted by permission.

12 Compelling Truths —
Why Biblical Faith is Completely Reasonable
(Dewayne Bryant)

That Christianity is under assault in our society is no secret to even the casual observer today. The assault I speak of is not with carnal weapons, but intellectual and philosophical attacks. Our young people are being told through mass media that believing in Jesus Christ or being a follower of Jesus the Christ; i.e., a Christian, is not only irrational but also anti-intellectual. The parade of those who willingly trumpet such a mantra is steady and loud; however, steady and loud does not always equate to sound and balanced! In *12 Compelling Truths — Why Biblical Faith is Completely Reasonable*, Dewayne Bryant takes us on an expedition of apologetic defenses in response to 12 points of attack against Christianity. These points are:

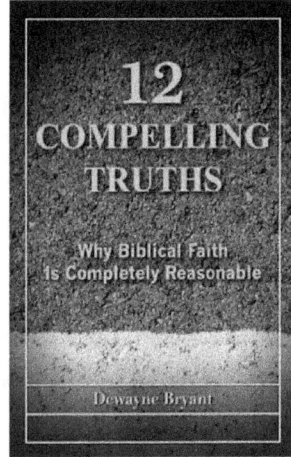

(1) Truth can be known,
(2) The universe had a creator,
(3) God does exist,
(4) The biblical record is historically accurate,
(5) Archaeology provides collaborative testimony to Bible's reliability,
(6) Jesus of Nazareth really lived,
(7) Jesus was raised from the dead,
(8) Evil, pain and suffering do not disprove God's existence,
(9) The Bible is inspired,
(10) Christianity is unique from other religions,

(11) Early writers of the new testament were not plagiarists, and

(12) God truly loves sinners.

There is also an insightful appendix which challenges the modern atheistic movement as not so modern. This is an important point that we need to continually be aware of—these truths need a steady and effective defense because evil does not sleep. Evil is constantly preying upon our children and grandchildren. If our young people are not taught a proper, rational, logical, and reasonable defense by the home or at church, then where will they be taught these truths?

This book is an excellent modern-day apologetic defense that would be well worth our young people's study, both young in body and at heart too. There is a study guide provided to help stimulate thought and discussion which makes the book very adaptable to classroom study. Dewayne Bryant is a recognized archaeologist, professor and preacher. He has been published in the *Gospel Advocate*, *Reason and Revelation*, *Bible and Spade* and other periodicals. One must be very careful about the types of literature one reads, and we all must be critical thinkers. For example, I have seen members of the church read archaeological magazines by those who rejected the inspiration of the Scriptures. There are those who claim to be biblical archaeologists; however, sometimes this statement is made from a historical standpoint rather than a theological one. In other words, there are some who use the Bible as a historical reference but reject the Bible as the inspired word of God. One must be careful about the theological viewpoint of such journals. Dewayne Bryant is currently Professor of Bible and Biblical Languages at the Southwest School of Bible Studies, and he is an adjunct professor of Bible and Biblical Archaeology at Amridge University. I was delighted to hear Dewayne Bryant give a series of lectures on Biblical Archaeology at Polishing the Pulpit. He is also the son-in-law of Phil Sanders, Speaker on "In Search of the Lord's Way." I have had a few personal interactions with Dewayne Bryant, and

I look forward to more writing from him to come. Read his book and see if you do not want your children and grandchildren to do the same.

Originally printed in the *West Virginia Christian*, Vol. 22, No. 11, November 2015, p. 8. *Reprinted by permission.*

Defending the Faith Study Bible
(Kyle Butt & Dave Miller, Executive Editors)

Study Bibles can be a great resource; however, the reliability of a Study Bible is contingent on the company and editors that are publishing it. Some members of the church have been waiting for a Study Bible they could rely on, one published by faithful members of the Lord's church. Well, here it is! Apologetics Press has done the brotherhood an inestimable value in using their team to collaborate and publish the *Defending The Faith Study Bible*. I was excited about this Study Bible from the moment I heard that it was coming to fruition. It will serve as a tremendous resource for years to come. Looking over the contents of its pages, it is as if the editors assembled some of the greatest writings from Apologetics Press that relate to defending the Christian faith and collated them within a Bible one can open and both learn and use to defend the faith.

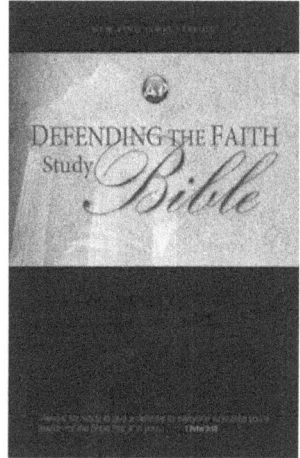

The editors of this work include Kyle Butt, Dave Miller, Eric Lyons, and Jeff Miller. These names should not be strangers to those among churches of Christ who appreciate sound apologetics. In addition to the editorial work, several well respected writers' names whose articles have been included will be readily recognized by many: Wayne Jackson, Justin Rogers, Dewayne Bryant, Caleb Colley, Mike Houts, and Brandon May.

I am a bit skeptical about Study Bibles and some of the new materials being published by denominational publishing houses. While I have great confidence in this team, I still wanted to examine the Study Bible first hand before I recommended it. For me, a Study Bible that is claiming to be apologetic in scope must deal with several vital topics effectively before I would recommend it. One of the topics that served as my "litmus test" for this Study Bible is its treatment of the Day-Age Theory and Age of the Earth. Theism is a big tent, and many do not realize this and assume that if someone is a theist then they view the days of creation the same way as all those who believe the Bible. This is *not* the case. Theist is a "big tent" term embracing various and conflicting approaches to the Genesis account. Apologetics Press has long been a defender of the 24-hour creation days, but I wanted to be sure that position was held within the pages of this Study Bible. On page 10 begins a 7-page scholarly work on the question "Does Genesis Allow For Billions of Years?" The conclusion, in part:

> Many apparently well-meaning Christians have felt pressure to compromise Scripture in an attempt to accommodate modern naturalistic theories. Neither Moses, Paul, the underlying Hebrew of Genesis, the chronology of Genesis 1, nor the statements of Jesus Himself will allow for such compromises (16).

The translation utilized is the New King James. There are many explanatory notes and scholarly articles to supplement the apologetic thrust of this study Bible. Major apologetic themes are designated with a color-coded key and include: Creation, Bible Inspiration, Existence of God, Deity of Christ, Alleged Bible Discrepancies, and World Religions. Keep in mind that there are many Study Bibles with various themes; e.g., *Archaeology Study Bible*. This Study Bible is devoted to the theme of apologetics or defending the faith. This is a Study Bible you will want for yourself, for your children, and your grandchildren. Do not miss obtaining your copy of the *Defending The Faith Study Bible* by Apologetics Press!

Originally printed in the *West Virginia Christian*, Vol. 27, No. 1, January 2020, p. 8. *Reprinted by permission.*

A Matter of Fact –
A Look At More Evidence for Christianity
(Kyle Butt)

This book is a follow-up to *Out With Doubt*. Recently we utilized this book with our teenagers in Bible Class. Although I did not teach the class, I followed up with the teacher and students to gather their feedback on the material. Those familiar with talking with teenagers are not surprised to hear the "it was alright," "Okay," or some in vogue expression these days. This was different. Our teenagers were enthusiastic supporters of the study, and the teacher was eager to search for other materials on subjects that intrigued them. If you have not included studies in Christian Evidences with your young people, then you need to remedy that deficiency immediately. Our young people are constantly bombarded by the philosophies of atheists, agnostics, ungodly and a host of other threats to New Testament Christianity. We need to do all that we are able while we have opportunity before our children leave our care and enter a sometimes dark world where their faith will be tested. Have we fortified them to withstand these attacks? If you are not supplying them with materials from Apologetics Press (or other faithful proponents of Christian apologetics), then you may be unaware of some excellent teaching tools available today.

In this book, brother Butt dispels the common falsehood that faith is some "leap in the dark." Tragically many are taught due to a distorted view of faith. I can recall hearing it said that the difference between belief and faith is whether the object is

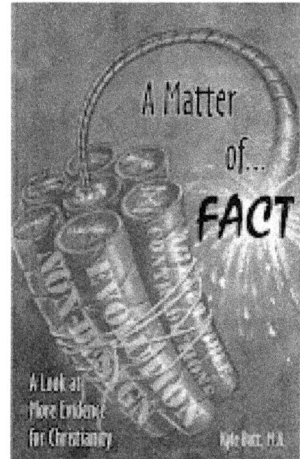

seen or unseen. If you can see it, then it is belief. If you cannot, then it is faith. That is partially true but misses a key component. Some extrapolate the unseen into no proof to back it up. Sadly, that is what many Christians are sometimes left to believe—that there is no evidence for their beliefs. What they fail to realize is the scientific method is only one measure of evidence. Some become so narrow in their definition of evidence that they fail to realize that testimony constitutes evidence. The book points out that faith in the Bible is not a "leap in the dark" (suggesting no proof), but is based on testimony that can be substantiated.

The book also deals with substantiating the testimony with a discussion of archaeology. There are many events in the Bible that have been mocked at by skeptics until the spade proved their attacks wrong—in spades! The Bible is unique in that it has been used as a guide by archaeologists to explore great treasures that would boggle the mind. That is solid testimony to the accuracy of the Bible. Skeptics such as William Ramsay set out to disprove the Bible by using archaeology and other tools to check the accuracy of books such as Acts and have come away converted to the accuracy of the sacred record.

A Matter of Fact also hits on key points that evolutionist would like to call trite but these are really unanswerable truths. For example, no rational person can deny that there is design in the world. The clear implication is that where there is design there must be a designer. The truism has spawned a movement known as "Intelligent Design Movement" where scientists have acknowledged that even though one may be uncertain about the Designer's identity there certainly is design. Christians already know who the identity of the Designer is.

The book also calls to the attention of young people, that while all these facts are great and powerful, they must recognize that they are accountable to the God of heaven. It relays a story of one teenagers transition from the faith of a child to that of a young adult who submits to God by being united in Jesus' death, burial and resurrection in baptism.

I highly recommend it for the church library. If possible, I suggest you purchase a copy of the book for each of the members of the teenage class for them to keep. There are challenging Study Questions at the end of each chapter to help the student review and ensure they have grasped the key points of the material. This is an excellent book to supply to your teenagers. Our teenagers were eager to keep their copy for their future reference.

Out With Doubt –
A Look at the Evidence for Christianity
(Kyle Butt)

Looking for an excellent book to begin a study of Christian Evidences with teenagers? This is a good place to start. The book deals with various topics relating to Christian Evidences: the existence of God, the inspired word of God, pain & suffering, creation and age of the earth, evolution and theistic evolution, dinosaurs, and facts surrounding the life of Jesus Christ—his existence, the miracles performed and his resurrection. I appreciated Butt's rebuttal of the compromise with evolution often called "theistic evolution." Efforts to harmonize the Bible with macroevolution per Darwin and such are not possible. The sooner our teenager realize this the better in order to protect them from an untenable compromise. All of these topics could be expanded to additional books with a greater degree of detail; however, this book is designed for those unfamiliar with these areas so as to encourage a life-long study of these great themes.

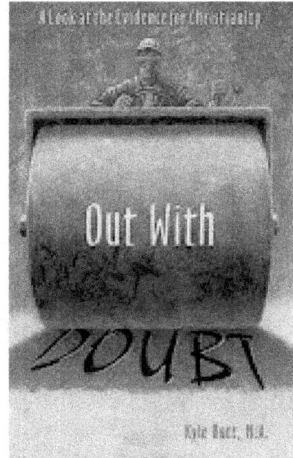

Christian Evidences (or Apologetics) is an exciting field of study. I have been a student of this field of study since my teenage years and have never grown weary of it. I know that young people's faith and resolve have been strengthened by studies along these lines. Often when I am looking to begin studying on a complex issue, I seek out literature that seeks to make the "complex understandable." This is what this book does.

In this book, brother Butt dispels the common falsehood that faith is some "leap in the dark." Tragically many are taught due to a distorted view of faith. I can recall hearing it said that the difference between belief and faith is whether the object is seen or unseen. If you can see it, then it is belief. If you cannot, then it is faith. That is partially true but misses a key component. Some extrapolate the unseen into no proof to back it up. Sadly, that is what many Christians are sometimes left to believe—that there is no evidence for their beliefs. What they fail to realize is the scientific method is only one measure of evidence. Some become so narrow in their definition of evidence that they fail to realize that testimony constitutes evidence. The book points out that faith in the Bible is not a "leap in the dark" (suggesting no proof), but is based on testimony that can be substantiated.

An aspect of the book that I also appreciate is the Afterward. I have several books by Josh McDowell which are excellent reading. One of my criticism of McDowell's work is his explanation of the plan to be saved as reciting the "sinner's prayer." One should be careful to think critically and validate material in books. Even the Bible demands to be tested (1 Thessalonians 5:21). When one compares the "sinner's prayer" with the Biblical plan, one realizes that the "sinner's prayer" is nowhere found in the Scriptures, but baptism for the remission of sins is clearly taught in the New Testament. Brother Butt makes an appeal to young people to consider the biblical plan of salvation and obey it.

I became more familiar with this book thanks to our teenage class. The teacher and I were looking for an idea of how to generate interest in the teenage class. When we examined this book, we decided it would be a useful tool to teach a subject that we had not taught as much as we would have liked. . The discussion questions helped stimulate the critical thinking for both the students and the teacher. The church decided that a book would be given to each teenager to keep for his or her own personal libraries for future reference. At the conclusion of the class, I spoke to the teenagers and the teacher about the class to see what the results were. The teenagers I spoke to were eager to keep the book (plus there were none sitting around unused later). The teacher and students thought it would be a good idea to have a follow-up class on the material. The study was viewed as very profitable to the point that we are seeking to maintain in the curriculum so no young person who goes through the teen years attending our classes will miss this vital material. I highly recommend it for the church library since it makes excellent reading for new Christians who may be unfamiliar with the field of Christian Apologetics as well.

Defending God: His Existence and Creation
(Kyle Butt and Eric Lyons)

I am excited to have young people to teach in Bible Class! I am not always blessed to have a class of young people, so I try not to take them for granted. I have not taught a teenage class several years as I had worked with a small congregation and had to teach the adult class. I was looking for something new to teach our young people and came across a new series of book by Apologetics Press and World Video Bible School. The Defender Series is yet in production, but the first three volumes are complete in what will be a four-volume set. The four books include a defense of God, a defense of the Bible, a defense of Christ, and a defense of one's faith. These books are little hardback books that remind me of a series that was very popular a few years ago, *A Series of Unfortunate Events*. These are similar in appearance, but not in content. Even though I have never read the Unfortunate Events series, I always find these "eye-catching" in bookstores. So, the Defender Series "caught my eye" and the content caught my attention.

Each chapter of these books includes video links supporting the lessons taught. The website is provided in the book utilizing a QR code. Don't know what that is? Ask a young person! There are so many things we can learn from one another. Please don't allow generational differences to create barriers! Each chapter has a few pages for notes which would be ideal for the videos that are supplied on the Internet. The videos are taught by Kyle Butt and Eric Lyons. These are produced by World Video Bible

School. We have been posting the links to these videos on our church Facebook Page so all members can view the supplemental videos (which are not dependent on the contents of the book itself).

Our goal is to provide each one of our young people a copy of a book that they complete in class with us. These four volumes will not only be nice looking on the shelf, but these will also be rich in content that will serve them well in the days ahead. In addition, it is our hope that when our young people look for more information that they will consult organizations such as Apologetics Press rather than denominational organizations which may lure them away.

The first book in the Defender Series is entitled *Defending God: His Existence and Creation*. It provides discussion on arguments for God's existence including First Cause, Morality, Design, and challenges to God's existence. In addition, the book discusses some of the major issues relating to the creation such as the age of the Earth, the fossil record, and the existence of dinosaurs. Perhaps many of the points in these books are more than familiar to us who have benefited from the work of Apologetics Press and other such institutions, but do our or your young people know these things? Are you sure? Many young people are lost through a series of unfortunate events. Be sure a lack of apologetics training is not one of those reasons.

Originally printed in the *West Virginia Christian*, Vol. 30, No. 5, May 2023, p. 8. *Reprinted by permission.*

The Christian System
(Alexander Campbell)

This book is challenging. As my father says, "You better have your thinkin' cap on when you read Alexander Campbell's books." The book is a structured look at Christianity and its major tenets including baptism, communion, faith, the kingdom, and the Godhead. Campbell structures much of his writings on propositions which lead to a conclusion, then substantiates the propositions which lead to that conclusion. Particularly illuminating is this technique used in his discussion of the Lord's Supper and remission of sins. His book analyzes certain biblical principles and practices which some have nearly forgotten as such. For example, Campbell's comments on baptism for the remission of sins need to be heeded by some of the liberal elements among us:

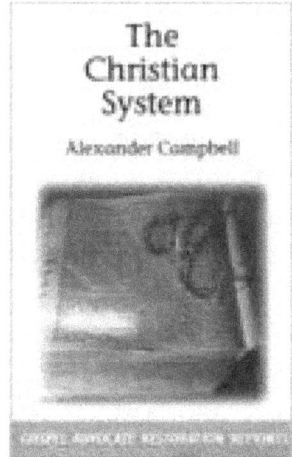

> The doctrine of remission is the doctrine of salvation; for to talk of salvation without the knowledge of the remission of sins is to talk without meaning. To give to the Jews 'a knowledge of salvation by the remission of their sins' was the mission of John the Immerser, as said by the Holy Spirit. In this way he prepared a people for the Lord. This doctrine of forgiveness was gradually opened to the people during the ministry of John and Jesus, but was not fully developed until Pentecost, when the secrets of the reign of heaven

were fully open.[1]

Alexander Campbell was one of the greatest leaders during the Restoration Movement from the blinders of denominationalism to pure Bible-centered Christianity. So popular was this man that we were called "Campbellites" in disdain. Now Campbell did not establish the church, Christ did; but he made many valuable contributions which I feel we neglect for fear of being associated with the man as the Lutherans are with Martin Luther. It is my fear with the arrival of the information age of computers and the entertainment craze to be visually stimulated, we as members will forget the significant contributions of men like Alexander Campbell, Barton W. Stone, and J.W. McGarvey to the cause we plead. In an excellent novel based on the life of Campbell, the then current President of Bethany College (which Campbell founded) had this to say about the accomplishments of Campbell:

Mr. Campbell has not received simple justice at the hands of American History. The fact that he was chiefly responsible for the development of the largest religious body of American origin, which now numbers more than 3,000,000 adult communicants in all its branches, is in itself enough to place him in the American Hall of Fame. His relationship with James Madison, John Marshall, Thomas Jefferson, and Henry Clay is significant. His influence of the Virginia Constitutional Convention in 1829 began the movement that later founded the State of West Virginia. His debates were national events of great importance.[2]

One will not agree with every position Alexander Campbell holds, but we should not treat the opinions and views of this great scholar lightly.

---

[1] Alexander Campbell, The Christian System, Tennessee: Gospel Advocate Company, 1980, p. 153.

[2] Louis Cochran, The Fool of God, New York: Duel, Sloan and Pearce, 1958, Jacket.

Originally printed in *West Virginia Christian*, Vol. 8, No. 4, April 2001, p. 8. Reprinted by permission.

Sounding Brass and Clanging Cymbals: The History and Significance of Instrumental Music in the Restoration Movement (1827-1968) (J.E. Choate and William Woodson)

Once I was listening to some discussion following a sermon on the subject of instrumental music. A comment was made that they were weary of hearing lessons on the sin of using instrumental music in worship since they had heard many lessons on the subject. What this person failed to realize (at the time) was the lesson was not just about what type of music we are to use in worship but by what authority are we going to govern our lives in religion—the teachings of the New Testament or of men. Several years followed and this writer was able to see the same evangelist deliver another lesson on the same subject. The same person commented "I am so thankful that you have delivered such an important lesson." What had changed? In my opinion the change was the listener had seen the wider lesson to be learned—the authority of the Scriptures. The person has seen the effects of the change agents and the agenda they are pushing with success in large part because people are ignorant of Bible authority. The person again realized one of the great principles of hermeneutics that is often ignored—the silence of the scriptures. Instrumental music is a great illustration of what happens to the church when it ignores Bible authority. This is the subject of the book.

The book begins with a valuable record of early hymns among churches of Christ. There is not much material in existence on this subject. One point that I learned from the book was

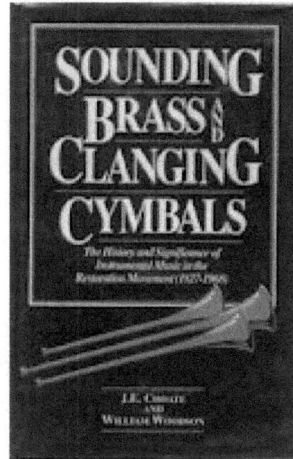

why Alexander Campbell did not speak out more against instrumental music in worship. The reason was because it was not an issue during his day. It was not until the last five years of Campbell's life did the instrument become a source of controversy. Alexander Campbell published a very popular hymnbook of his own and refused to print the music notes in the book, considering it wrong. He preferred to have just the words with his hymns to be sung to a few familiar melodies.

This book takes the reader on a journey through history of the departure of the Christian Church from churches of Christ over the issues of the instrument and missionary societies. It discusses key historical people and events over the past as it relates to these two groups. It shows the ugliness of division that occurred because people were more concerned for their pleasure rather than the pleasure of God.

An illustration of how ugly the instrument issue became was the treatment toward J.W. McGarvey. In 1902, the church where McGarvey was an elder voted to have the organ brought in over his clear objections. McGarvey and his wife promptly left and removed their membership. At his funeral the instrument was brought in and played for three hymns. Was this a sign of ignorance or disrespect toward the man? Possibly this was a consequence of his continued practice to preach at congregations which used the instrument even though he himself was opposed to it. This was a mistake he realized and stated as such; c.f., Burl Curtis, "McGarvey's Mistake," Gospel Advocate, September 2002, pp. 28-29.

The book chronicles several efforts to reunite the two groups that had divided. The result would always be the same. As long as those who craved the innovations would not relinquish them, then there would not be a reunification. One effort was a Murch-Witty Unity Session in 1939 in Indianapolis, IN.H. Leo Boles spoke forcefully about the real crux of the matter:

Brethren, this is where the churches of Christ stand today;

it is where unity may be found now; it is where you left the New Testament; it is where you left the churches of Christ, and it is where you can find them when you come back. On this ground and teaching, and only on this, can scriptural unity be had now; on these basic principles of the New Testament Christian unity may always be had... Brethren put away the organ and you will be where the pioneers stood when the unity of God's people was enjoyed. The churches of Christ are stand on this item just where the pioneers stood before its introduction in 1859; there was unity then on this point and there can be unity now at this point when the organ is pushed aside.

The words of Moses Lard recorded in the book are shown to be true:

The day on which a church sets up an organ in its house is the day on which it reaches the first station on the road to apostasy. From this it would proceed to other innovations; and the work of innovation once fairly commenced, no stop can be put to it till ruin ensues.

We should all read this history and remain committed to stand where the pioneers stood—solely on authority of the Scriptures.

Originally printed in the *West Virginia Christian*, Vol. 10, No. 7, July 2003, p. 8. Reprinted by permission.

Books, Books and More Books
(Winford Claiborne)

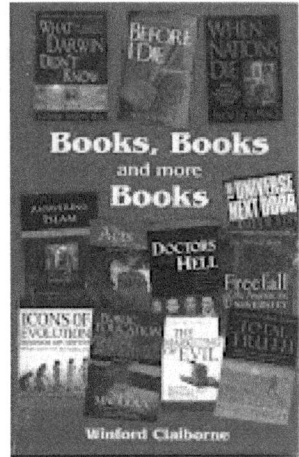

Through the encouragement of my father, several others, and kindness of Albert Farley, the editor of *The West Virginia Christian*, I have been honored to have both written and lectured on recommending books of value for church libraries for over 12 years now. R.R. Bowker, a specialist in Bibliographic material, estimated there are some 479 books published *daily*. True are the words of Solomon— *"The words of the wise are like goads, and the words of scholars are like well-driven nails, given by one Shepherd. And further, my son, be admonished by these. Of making many books there is no end, and much study is wearisome to the flesh"* (Ecclesiastes 12:11-13, NKJV). Recognizing that the vast majority of books published today would provide little to any value to a church library, one is still faced with the daunting challenge of keeping abreast of the issues impacting the church in the large number of books required. One has to prioritize their reading in order to come close to keeping up, but how does one know which books are the better books on a given subject? If you are a slow reader, as I am, then prioritizing is essential! One of the resources I use is brother Winford Claiborne's digest of books, *Books, Books and More Books*.

Brother Claiborne was a Professor of Bible at Freed-Hardeman University, Lectureship Director for the highly acclaimed Freed-Hardeman University Bible Lectureship and is now Director and Speaker for the International Gospel Hour. One could not conduct such great responsibilities effectively without being an effective reader—on all kinds of subjects. In an interview for the Huntsville Times, the late Wallace Skipper stated that Winford reads approximately 125 books each year and retains what he reads. Winford was my teacher for General Epistles. When my future wife and I had him for General Epistles, he would come to class with an arm full of books. He would spend a few moments using the books in illustration of the material when appropriate. Today, I cannot recall the title of any of those books; however, I can tell you that each class period was a totally different set of books.

The church in Duluth, Georgia, invited Claiborne for a gospel meeting. This congregation's gospel meetings included preaching at night but also classes in the day time too. They requested brother Claiborne spend all the time in the day classes speaking about the importance of reading and recommending various books on an array of topics. Thankfully, Paul Sain bound Winford's notes from this meeting into a small book format that we all can profit from. The book, *Books, Books and more Books* is available from International Gospel Hour (gospelhour.net) for a donation.

One of my favorite quotations in this book is the one by Mark Twain—"The man who does not read good books has no advantage over the man who cannot read." We need to be readers of *good* books, ones which can be used in the proclamation and defense of the gospel. This book contains a listing of books under various subjects: Abortion, Apologetics, Character, Cultic Groups, Ethical Issues, Modesty, New Age Movement, Suicide, Racism, Homosexuality, Evolution, Islam, Pluralism, Post Modernism, and others. Someone once told me that they needed to be a better reader and just did not know where to begin. When I heard that, I handed them this book and in an encouraging way said "Start by reading every book in this book. When you have completed that, you will never have to ask that question again." Whenever I am blessed to hear Winford lecture or preach, I always make it a practice to jot down the title of any book he recommends. I hope someday to be able to say I have read all those titles! Now, back to my reading.

Originally printed in *West Virginia Christian*, Vol. 19, No. 11, November 2012, p. 8. Reprinted by permission.

Christ: Prophet, Priest and King
(An Analysis of Hebrews)
(Winford Claiborne)

While attending Freed-Hardeman University I became friends with two great men of our brotherhood, Winford Claiborne and E. Claude Gardner. Brother Claiborne was one of my professors and brother Gardner was president of the school. I see them regularly at the lectureship and look forward to any opportunity to be in their presence. This book is dedicated to brother Gardner by Winford Claiborne. So the book is precious to me for various reasons, but the subject of Hebrews is important to every man, woman, and child. The subject of Hebrews is the superiority of Jesus Christ over every other being—men, beasts, and angels. It stresses the superiority of Jesus and Christianity over every other religion. Yes, Jesus is superior to Mohammed, Confucius, Buddha, Moses, Abraham, Luther, and any other man you can name. Yes, Christianity is superior to Islam, Buddhism, Catholicism, Hinduism, Satanism, Judaism, the New Age Movement, and any other religion you can name.

Winford Claiborne is a very meticulous student of the Scriptures. I know this because he was a very meticulous teacher in class. As an illustration, my wife and I had to write a term paper for his class. Upon returning the graded papers he asked me if he should penalize a student who had spelled his name incorrectly. Now, I had looked in the FHU Catalog to make 100% sure I had spelled his name correctly, but I considered there could be a misprint in the catalog. So I said that he should be lenient since

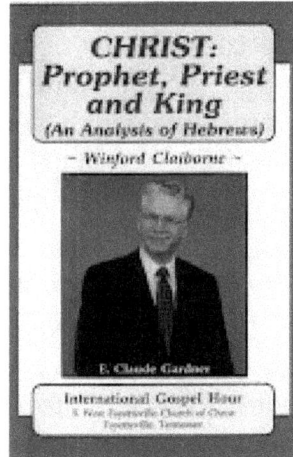

his name could be easily misspelled. (In fact, he explained they had misspelled his last name on his birth certificate.) His reply was, "Well, I agree. That is why I am giving your girlfriend an A even though she misspelled my name." When I looked at my paper it received a lower grade. I had made the mistake of not capitalizing "Greek" and misspelled judgment as "judgement." Being a religious paper one can imagine how many times those two words can show up on a term paper. Well, he discounted my grade for the same error at every occurrence of these two words. I can laugh about it now, but it sure was not funny then! It was a lesson in being meticulous and illustrates the high level of performance he expected and strove for in his studies.

This book is an analytical outline of the epistle of Hebrews. It contains a well-written introduction, brief but poignant commentary, illustrative quotations from modern day writers and observers, and very appropriate application for our lives. The book is divided into chapters corresponding to the chapters in Hebrews and is for assisting in study to prepare and teach a class on Hebrews. Each chapter closes with review questions, which makes the book a suitable tool for use in the classroom as the student's book.

Brother Gardner and Max Patterson kept encouraging Winford Claiborne to publish this manuscript on the epistle of Hebrews. I was hesitant to buy another book on Hebrews since I have several excellent books on this wonderful epistle, but because of my deep admiration for brothers Gardner and Claiborne I decided to purchase a copy. Reading through the book has been very rewarding and exciting. I highly recommend using this book to study one of the greatest pieces of writing from the greatest book man has ever been given. A study of the book of Hebrews will strengthen your faith.

Winford Claiborne delivers a regular radio address on the International Gospel Hour. This is his fourth book published by the International Gospel Hour. All proceeds from the sale of his book are used solely to support the gospel radio program. The

International Gospel Hour also has a website gospelhour.net that contain sermon texts and audio lessons. If you enjoy great "true to the Book" gospel preaching that is direct and plain, then you will not be disappointed. Tell your friends about the program.

Originally printed in the *West Virginia Christian*, Vol. 13, No. 4, April 2006, p. 8. Reprinted by permission.

Divine Relationships
(Five Minute Gospel Messages From 1 Peter)
(Winford Claiborne)

Attending Freed-Hardeman University was a great blessing to my life for many reasons. Not only did I meet my Christian spouse there (which is sufficient reason for all Christian young people to attend a Christian college), but we also established relationships that will last for eternity. I attended a state university for my graduate degree and the difference in environment between the Christian campus and secular campus is striking. Not only can relationships be established between students, but relationships can be established with professors who show such dedication to their students. One of the blessings my wife and I received was establishing a relationship with Winford Claiborne as our professor for General Epistles. We had the privilege of listening to his instruction on 1 Peter first-hand. I remember his emphasis on 1 Peter being an epistle emphasizing divine relationships so the title of this book is very appropriate. Brother Claiborne also served as Director of the Freed-Hardeman Bible Lectureship for several years.

The book contains 155 chapters that represent five-minute messages brother Claiborne delivered on the International Gospel Hour. Brother Claiborne became the main speaker for the program in 1995 after retiring from teaching at Freed-Hardeman after the aging V.E. Howard was looking to turn over the longest continuously produced radio broadcast program in the world. The chapters of the book follow the verses of 1 Peter for easy

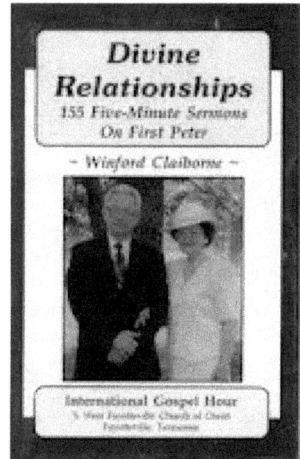

reference. The amount of information that can be expounded from 1 Peter is astonishing. The depth of the subject matter of 1 Peter was impressive in the classroom and just as impressive in this book. The book deals with great themes such as our relationship to Jesus, the Gentiles' relationship to God in the church, our relationship to government, the relationship between husbands and wives, defending the faith, suffering as a Christian, relationship with worldly friends, and our relationship with our adversary the devil, to name a few subjects.

The chapters are brief which allows for reading during brief intervals. The chapters are very informative including relating texts, word studies, moral applications, and thought provoking questions. Due to the great esteem and love that my family has for Winford Claiborne, it may appear that I am being biased in favor of brother Claiborne. My response is that my great respect for Winford Claiborne was formed as I sat and listened to him deliver the gospel truths from 1 Peter first-hand in the spring of 1990. I am thankful that God has preserved brother Claiborne so he could prepare this volume and you have the opportunity to see why brother Claiborne is worthy of your respect and attention. If you have an opportunity to tune into the International Gospel Hour then do so and encourage others to listen. International Gospel Hour also has a website (gospelhour.net) that contains sermon texts and audio files of previous lessons. If you enjoy great "true to the Book" gospel preaching that is direct and plain, then you will not be disappointed.

Originally printed in the *West Virginia Christian*, Vol. 14, No. 7, July 2007, p. 8. Reprinted by permission.

General Epistles
(Winford Claiborne)

While a student at Freed-Hardeman University, I was blessed to have the opportunity to study the general epistles directly from brother Claiborne in his General Epistles class. Brother Claiborne and I have developed a close friendship over the years but do not think this review has been impacted by personal bias. One of the many reasons for our enduring friendship is a love of books and serious study of the Scriptures.

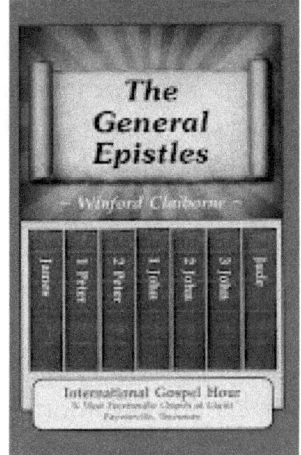

I was captivated by the material presented in class and took copious notes. In fact, I have taught the adult Bible class on James, 1 Peter and 2 Peter relying largely on a review of my notes from class. I plan on using the material from this book for the epistles of John and Jude as well. When brother Claiborne began publishing books to support the International Gospel Hour, I reminded him that I was still interested in the rest of the material we did not cover in class due to time. (My class notes stop at 1 John 2:11.) Occasionally I would go further and tease brother Claiborne that he should produce this book so I would get the full value for the tuition I paid for the class. When he told me that he had completed the book I became anxious for my copy. Bother Claiborne is a serious student of the Scriptures and his lecture on the general epistles was deep and meaningful. This book fulfills my request and then some! Thanks brother Claiborne!

For those who have his book CHRIST—Prophet, Priest & King, you will recognize the same outline form in this material as well.

It includes treatment of the epistles of James; 1, 2 Peter; 1, 2, 3 John & Jude. As I read the pages of the book it takes me back to the days I had him in class. It is excellent for preparation of lessons to teach classes for high school, college and adult classes. I plan on recommending the book to Christian men who have yet to teach an adult-level Bible class because they do not have as much time to spend in preparation. This book allows a person to quickly grasp the material on a deeper level so as to enrich any class. In addition, the general epistles (sometimes called catholic epistles) are rich in lessons, which need to be preached from the pulpit. This book does an excellent job of presenting expository material for preaching. Plus, brother Claiborne provides examples from modern theologians that help enrich one's study (including those who he takes serious issue with). Those who are familiar with brother Claiborne will recognize his style in his chapter "Jude: An Addendum" where he details some false concepts some have espoused relating to the epistle of Jude. His methodic treatment in thoroughly refuting their error is so reminiscent of the times I have spent with him that I can literally hear his voice as I read through the material. I wholeheartedly agree with brother Sain's words in the Preface:

> ...Winford Claiborne is a dedicated student of God's Word. Thus, when he speaks, whether orally or in print, he will know his subject well. And, with a fine command of the English language, he knows how to communicate effectively. Not everyone who hears him will agree with him, but all who listen will know what the truth is, and that he will not compromise the truth. (Page 7)

This book is a product of teaching the material at the college level for at least fourteen years so it has been tried and tested! This is a book to be added to all libraries—members, preachers and churches. Do not miss this invaluable resource to help equip future teachers and preachers of God's word!

Restoring God's Pattern for the Home
(Winford Claiborne)

Many know of brother Claiborne's teaching on controversial issues and textual lessons at Freed-Hardeman College. Some may not realize he also taught "Marriage and the Family" for fourteen years at Freed-Hardeman College. He comes from a family of twelve children. His Christian wife, Molly, passed away in 2002. They had been married for over fifty years. They have two sons, Doron and Danny, who are faithful to the church and their families. I often remember brother Claiborne speaking excitedly of the grandchildren. In fact, the paperback version of this book includes pictures of his grandchildren on the cover. So, brother Claiborne has lived and knows the principles that make a sound family and has taught these principles to others.

The main element that makes this book on the family superior to others is Winford Claiborne's respect for both the authority and all sufficiency of the Scriptures. He realizes that the family was not created by politicians, educators, committees, or focus groups. Who better to teach us the proper functioning of the family then the Creator of the family? Where else can we go to learn the principles of successful family then the Bible in which God taught the proper roles and functions of the family? So a book that calls us back to God's pattern for the home is worth consideration. There are destructive books on the family with supposed "experts" with perverted ideas on how the family ought to operate. Restoring God's Pattern for the Home reveals some of those who would destroy the family as God has

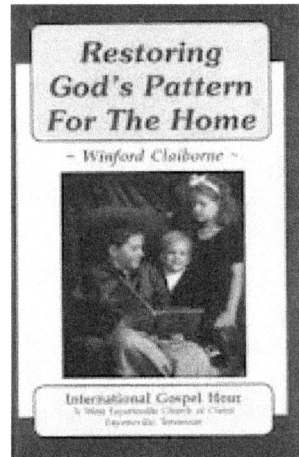

designed it. Brother Claiborne then speaks from his knowledge of the Scriptures, family experience, and keen mind to expose the utter folly of the bizarre ideas that some have for the family.

The book discusses God's pattern for the home, for husbands, and wives. It discusses the relationship of the church and the home. It also discusses the fact that marriage is for mature adults, not the immature. Too many people enter into marriage too flippantly which is reflected in the statistics on divorce and broken homes. As my father often says "Love is blind, but marriage is the eye opener." Every couple considering marriage should seek a qualified premarital counselor who is a Christian.

Some in the church think it is unnecessary to have lessons on the home. These speak from ignorance and not from examination of the condition of families among the brotherhood. We need strong lessons on God's pattern for the family from pulpits, class lecterns, college campuses, and in the home. My father recommends for every Christian married couple to attend the Brecheen-Faulkner Marriage Enrichment Seminar whenever possible. This is good advice. My wife and I have been able to attend the seminar (not to mention taking Marriage and the Family at Freed-Hardeman University as taught by Mike Cravens). I made the same suggestion to a married man and he stated that he did not need any marriage enrichment. I, jokingly, suggested that maybe he should get a second opinion from his wife. We all can use teaching or reminding on the fundamentals relating to the family.

Winford Claiborne delivers a regular radio address on the International Gospel Hour. There is also a website gospelhour.net that contain sermon texts and audio lessons. Tell your friends about the program and the website.

Originally printed in the *West Virginia Christian*, Vol. 11, No. 4, April 2004, p. 8. Reprinted by permission.

Silence Can Be Sinful, Vol. 1
(Winford Claiborne)

As a former student of Winford Claiborne at Freed-Hardeman University, I was impressed by brother Claiborne's reading habits. Twice a week he would come in with at least a half dozen books under his arm. Occasionally, he would refer to the books he was reading. I was noticed two things about his reading. First, the books were diverse in subject matter. Second, the reading was voluminous. He had a completely different stack of books each class period. One estimate I read was that he reads at least 125 book a year!

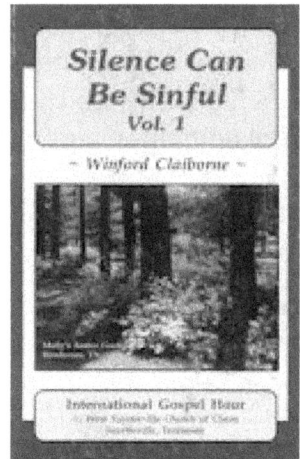

Brother Claiborne commented on the importance of reading in an outline entitled "Read Any Good Books Lately":

> How much time do you have—or rather—how much time do you make for reading—not studying your Bible or preparing your next Lord's Day's sermon—but reading? The single most common complaint I hear from preachers is: We do not have enough time for study. Reading time will not come easy—especially if you have a young family which needs and deserves your attention. You should have a book located wherever you are—in the bathroom, in your automobile, at your office, in the living room, in the bedroom. A few minutes here and there can make a difference.
>
> Why should we spend so much time reading? To prevent a major American problem: ignorance. I know there are positive reasons for reading, but we should strive to keep from

being ignorant. Many people in our communities will judge our effectiveness by our reading habits. People who come to hear us preach can tell if we read regularly and widely...

Through the years I have made a commitment to reading widely in a number of different fields—sociology, psychology, medicine, bioethics, law, criminology, politics, family studies, etc. When I begin to read in a given field, I buy a number of books in the field so I can have a pretty comprehensive view of what is involved. I have read dozens of books on abortion, on the Women's Liberation Movement, on our legal system, etc. It is incumbent that we read both sides of every issue. I have read numbers of books by the feminists because I want to know what they actually teach—not what they are accused of teaching.

From reading brother Claiborne's articles, hearing him teach class, attending his lectures at the FHU Bible Lectureship, listening to him on the International Gospel Hour, and attending gospel meetings in which he was preaching, I can tell you first hand that Winford Claiborne is a great source on a great many subjects threatening the morality of our nation today. That is what Silence Can Be Sinful is about—issues that we as Christians must speak out against in order to save our nation. This book is written to equip us with information we can use to speak out against such evils as homosexuality, abortion, hate groups, gambling, civil disobedience, assisted suicides, Planned Parenthood, prostitution, immoral government leaders, and a host of other related issues. The book contains background information about the issues, explanations of unfamiliar concepts, and teaching from the Bible relating to these subjects.

Our beloved country is in serious trouble. Read about the conditions of Israel before their downfalls and you will see a striking parallel to our day. Unless we speak out against evil in every medium available to us, a book may soon be written entitled the "Decline and Fall of the United States" with the same contributing factors which led to the collapse from the inside out of another great empire as recorded in The Decline and Fall of the Roman Empire.

Winford Claiborne delivers a regular radio address on the International Gospel Hour. The International Gospel Hour also has a website gospelhour.net that contain sermon texts and audio lessons. If you enjoy great "true to the Book" gospel preaching that is direct and plain, then you will not be disappointed. Tell your friends about the program.

Originally printed in the *West Virginia Christian*, Vol. 11, No. 6, June 2004, p. 8. Reprinted by permission.

Silence Can Be Sinful, Vol. 2
(Winford Claiborne)

Oliver Goldsmith wrote "Silence gives consent." This is the thrust of this follow-up work to Claiborne's *Silence Can Be Sinful* (2002). Are we speaking out against the evils in our society and promoting Christian views? If we are not, who do we think will? If one needs fortification to motivate them to speak out for Christianity, then the Introduction of this book should be read and meditated upon. If one needs fortification to equip himself to do so, then this volume is a must for reading.

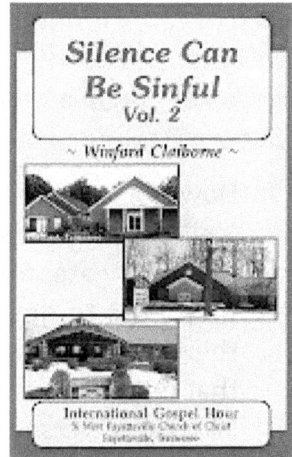

Brother Claiborne is well known for his vast reading and research on a variety of social, religious, history and other pertinent issues. The fruits of his labors are manifested on each radio broadcast he makes on the International Gospel Hour. (There is also a website, gospelhour.net, that contains manuscripts and audio files from the program as well.)

This work addresses several challenges we face as a nation. Issues such as: macroevolution, eugenics, racism, illegal immigration, cohabitation, alcohol, abortion, infanticide, euthanasia, homosexuality, government corruption, media corruption, marriage, and the sanctity of life. This volume provides excellent material that is well worth the effort to read and share with others when we have opportunity to discuss these issues. My concern is that we are more apt to remain silent than speak out as we have opportunity. Think how much better our nation could be if people spoke out more for God. I have heard reports of a "silent majority" which was believed to be morally conservative. This is sad, not that they are conservative, but that they are silent. Hopefully that will change. This work will well equip one to speak more effectively.

One of my favorite chapters is "Pesky Bible Verses" where Claiborne quotes a religious advocate for homosexuality attacking scriptures forbidding their chosen lifestyle as "those pesky Bible verses." Brother Claiborne uses the concept of "pesky Bible verses" against other areas of concern. For example, brother Claiborne writes concerning the Sermon on the Mount:

> How do you suppose a liberal theologian reacts to these well-known words from Christ's great sermon? "Enter in at the strait gate: for wide is the gate, and broad is the way, that leads to destruction, and many there are who go in thereat: because strait is the gate, and narrow is the way, that leads to life, and few there are who find it (Mt. 7:13-14). These verses give bushels of trouble to liberal theologians like Robin Meyers. They are unquestionably 'pesky Bible verses' for all Universalists. (Page 75).

Another suggested use for this material—share with our young people. Parents want to shield their children from the harsh and evil realities of the world for as long as they can; however, there comes a time when they must be equipped to face the world. They need to be made aware of the issues they will encounter, how to respond to them, and how to fight efforts to move such evils into the mainstream in various ways including proposed laws. They need to have the resources to make effective arguments against the forces which would destroy our nation.

Originally printed in the *West Virginia Christian*, Vol. 17, No. 8, August 2010, p. 8. Reprinted by permission.

Chart Sermons: Flannel-graph Bible Lessons (Artie Collins)

It is difficult for some to imagine just how great the age of transparencies were in this modern PowerPoint Age! However, there was a time where flannel boards, bed sheets and chalkboards were used to add a visual component to sermons. I can recall my mother using a hoop, stencils and various colors of liquid embroidery ink in tubes to add major points, scripture references and even artwork to a bed sheet that would be hung behind the pulpit and utilized by my father in his preaching. My mother tells me that a bed sheet chart would take her a couple of days to complete. My father still has those "bed sheet" sermons and has agreed to let me have them one day. While not convenient to display, these will remain a respected heirloom of days when first principles were preached, preached, preached from the pulpit. One knew that a bed sheet sermon was something special just by the amount of work it took to produce one! Many of these charts are not just a labor of love but required time and talent to create these works of art.

I recently had the opportunity to hear brother John Moore at the Polishing the Pulpit Workshop present a session on the value of bed sheet sermons. He was able to collect several of these from various preachers utilizing a digital camera. He made a very important point that we should remember. We often like to use multiple slides in PowerPoint because we think that it will keep the audience's attention. While it may do that, consider this about a single chart displayed for over 30 minutes—it has a

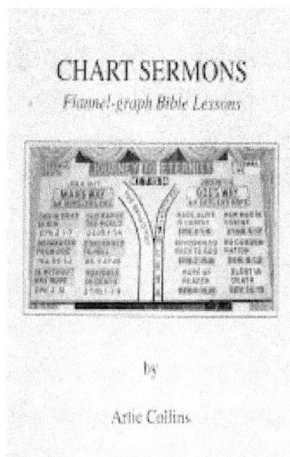

way of sticking in your mind. Brother Moore placed charts on the screen that I immediately recognized even though I had not seen them for several years. Something for us to consider in preparing our lessons—maybe less is more!

Sermon Charts is a collection of photographs of flannel board sermons that were prepared by Artie Collins of Hohenwald, TN. Artie has been a friend of our family since I was a little boy when my dad attended the Nashville School of Preaching in the late 1960s. Visits with Artie and his wife Marie are always a treasure for our family. Artie would regularly attend the Freed-Hardeman Bible Lectureship with my father when I was growing up. While they were away, I would often imagine how great it would be to go with them to enjoy in the friendship and fellowship. Not so ironically, these memories propelled me to attend Freed-Hardeman University. In fact, I told my parents quite bluntly the only Christian college I would even consider was Freed-Hardeman University even though I had never been on the campus. One year, Artie came to hold a gospel meeting for the church in New Philadelphia, OH where we were located at the time. I can recall very well his use of charts in his sermons. (The picture with this article is from that meeting.)

Charts are wonderful devices to help us learn and retain information. I have collected a few books of sermon charts and am always interested in looking at them. I never grow weary of just leafing through the pages of them. For the past few months I have been editing the church bulletin here at Streetsboro and one of the goals I accomplished was to be able include an instructional sermon chart on the back page of each week's bulletin. Whether the congregation liked it or not, I sure enjoyed it! Having a few sermon chart books in a church library is a good tool to help young men to sketch in their minds a sermon that they might want to deliver from a pulpit someday. Something we should probably do more of—encouraging our young men and boys to prepare lessons to preach. By being an inspiration to young boys, they will grow up to be aspiring preachers and elders!

Originally printed in *West Virginia Christian*, Vol. 18, No. 11, November 2011, p. 8. Reprinted by permission.

A Harmony of Samuel, Kings and Chronicles
(William Day Crockett)

Harmonies of the gospels are interesting to study and the efforts to harmonize the gospel accounts is a formidable challenge since some events are difficult to put in chronological order. One student of the Scriptures sought to create another harmony of the gospels, but decided that the work had been done by other scholarly men. The thought occurred to him that there were no harmonies of the books of history for the nation of Israel. The books of Samuel, Kings and Chronicles, similarly to the gospels, have overlapping accounts. The person thought this would be a more profitable venture to concentrate his efforts of study in this area. That person was William Day Crockett, and he published A Harmony of Samuel, Kings and Chronicles in 1951 which has gone through numerous printings. As he completed the first draft he discovered there were other similar works but those were out of print and largely unavailable in his day. This book remains in print and is a profitable study of the exciting era of the kings of Israel.

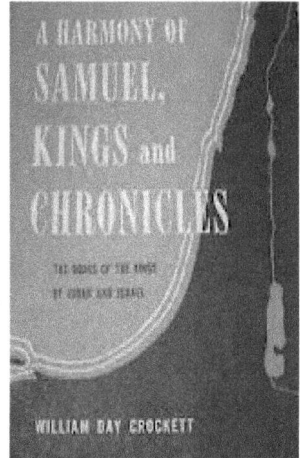

The book begins with the genealogies from Adam to Noah found in 1 Chronicles and ends with the proclamation of Cyrus permitting the Jews to return from Babylonian Captivity recorded in 2 Chronicles 36. In between are all the events of Samuel, Kings and Chronicles in chronological order as best determined by Crockett. This includes the lives of Samuel, Saul, David, Solomon and others during the divided kingdom and captivities. It covers events relating to the close of the period of the judges,

84

the time of the kings, the break of the kingdom and the subsequent Assyrian and Babylonian captivities. It covers the change in worship from the tabernacle to the temple and the destruction of Israel due to its idolatry. Many exciting events occur during this period. I thrill to read about the lives of David and Jonathan. In fact, I hope to go someday to Mount Gilboa where Jonathan made his final stand with Saul, resulting in the subsequent heartbreak David felt at the loss of his dear friend and his father. These are stories that have never lost their appeal to me and I often turn to them to read these again and again.

Indeed, much history is recorded in these books. The book begins with an analytical outline of the books, outlined in major events. Texts from the historical accounts are cited so one can turn and read the text. The outline splits into two side-by-side columns to cover the divided kingdom so one can see what was occurring at the time in the other kingdom more easily. One might be interested to know that originally there were three, not six, books of history—Samuel, Kings & Chronicles in the Hebrew Bible. Each of these books was divided in two (to make six books) during the translation of the Septuagint. The reason for the division was the difference between the languages of Hebrew and Greek. Hebrew does not require vowels so it was easier to condense the material onto one scroll. Greek; however, does have vowels and requires much more space to translate the same Hebrew material. In fact, one estimate states the size of the text doubled with the translation to Greek. The translators divided these books in order to accommodate the amount of writing space available on a scroll.

Then Crockett takes this outline and expands it to include the Revised Version of 1884 including many footnotes pertinent to the study. In this layout one can quickly read the parallel accounts. If three books cover the same event, then three columns are used to preserve the reader's ability to read in parallel. The book concludes with an appendix showing other books of the Bible which cite passages from Samuel, Kings and Chronicles.

There is also an index in the back that allows a person to find a certain passage within the harmony with ease.

While one may not agree with certain sequence of events, the reference work is extremely valuable study to a thrilling section of scripture from a different approach.

Originally printed in *West Virginia Christian*, Vol. 18, No. 2, February 2011, p. 8. Reprinted by permission.

"I See My Time Is Up"
(George DeHoff, Sr.)

This book is the autobiography of George W. Dehoff, Sr. (1913-1993). I first came across this book while visiting with my good friend Don Cooper, the minister at Wadsworth in Ohio. I was skimming the book and found many interesting sections I read immediately. A couple of years later (after doing a book review of a biography on Hugo McCord, The Enchanted Knight) Don Cooper asked me if I would do a book review for the area preachers' meeting. I suggested "I See My Time Is Up" and Don graciously let me borrow his copy to read. So I have been in the process of reading this very informative book about a preacher, Christian college administrator, business leader, politician, and publisher of Christian class literature.

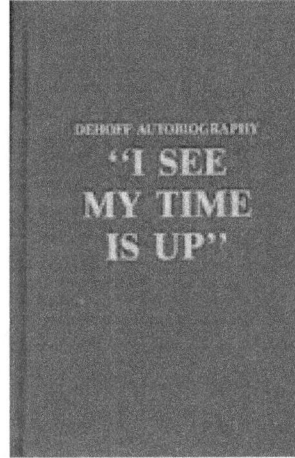

When I read a biography I sometimes wish I had all the major writings relating to the subject. That appears to be what his assistant and daughter, Bonnie DeHoff Fakes, has done. As a consequence, some of the material is repetitive (maybe even redundant). Of course, this will not concern those who want to know all they can about George Dehoff.

George DeHoff has a rich family heritage. He was a frequent traveler to the Holy Land and was highly regarded for his knowledge relating to these travels. He was very active in the Rotary International and was recognized for the many contributions he made. He served as President of Magic Valley Christian College in Idaho. He also served as Vice President at Freed-Hardeman College. He founded DeHoff Publications and has contributed widely to Christian literature. He also wrote one of the first commentaries on the whole Bible in the brotherhood. He conducted several public debates on topics relating to Bible classes & women teachers (DeHoff-Head Debate), located preachers (DeHoff-Garrett Debate), orphan homes (DeHoff-Holt Debate), Calvinism (DeHoff-Davis Debate), and marijuana (DeHoff - Barrett Debate).

Two of my favorite sections in the book are reflections written by prominent preachers about their relationship with DeHoff and DeHoff writing about preachers he knew. He also includes a short church history from 1929 to 1988 that is informative. Articles, sermons, and speeches also are supplied in the book including a popular address "What Made America Great?" that received several requests to be repeated. There are several excellent sermons printed in the book including "What the Pioneers Preached," "The Providence of God," and "The Final Authority in Religion." DeHoff had begun preaching in 1929 and was known as the "boy evangelist" because he began at the age of sixteen. He had reportedly baptized over 2,300 people by the time he was 25 years of age, and it is estimated he baptized 8-10,000 people during his entire career.

When I finished reading the book, I reviewed the book to see what I would include in this review. It is astonishing just how much George H. DeHoff accomplished for the cause of Christ. The book is excellent reading for everyone for its sound teaching and to become more familiar with the brotherhood of the recent past.

One of the personal traits that shines throughout the book is George DeHoff's sense of humor. In a chapter entitled "Incidents Along The Way" DeHoff relates an encounter he had after a sermon entitled "What Will it Be Like In Hell?" A Jehovah Witness spoke up stating there was no hell and God would not punish anyone. DeHoff waited to see if a visiting preacher in the meeting would answer, but there was none and the members were looking at DeHoff to respond. DeHoff asked the man to read from Revelation 23. The man turned in his Bible and told DeHoff, apologizing for embarrassing DeHoff, that there are only 22 chapters in Revelation. DeHoff's response is classic:

> Thank you very much, that is a load off my mind. I have read Revelation 22, and it leaves all of the wicked people in hell. I thought maybe you had another chapter to get them out.

DeHoff was a forceful proclaimer of the truth and could hold his own under fire. We need more Christians like George H. DeHoff, Sr. His grave is located in Evergreen Cemetery in Murfreesboro, TN where he served several years as an evangelist.

Originally printed in the *West Virginia Christian*, Vol. 12, No. 5, May 2005, p. 8. Reprinted by permission.

Restoring New Testament Christianity
(Adron Doran)

On November 22, 2001 Adron Doran departed from this life at the age of 92. I have a tremendous amount of respect for him due to his many accomplishments for the cause of Christ. He had preached the gospel for nearly 70 years, was president of Morehead State University, member of the Kentucky State Legislature including Speaker of the House, member of FHU Board of Directors, married for over 70 years, and an avid student/scholar of Restoration History. There are several other accomplishments that this great man achieved, but I want to focus on his efforts in the field of Restoration History. He spent the last twenty years of his life focused on the study of Restoration History and wrote several articles from his research.

It seems, to this reviewer, that many congregations have set themselves doctrinally adrift in an effort to meet felt needs in an effort to drive their attendance numbers up. They have lost sight of the plea that brought churches of Christ in accordance with God's word and have given preference to being in accordance with the fads of the day. Church growth by trying to meet the whims of the public, compared to obtaining the favor of God by obedience to His Word, is a shallow, vain, and futile pursuit. Men need to be reminded of Samuel's words about the sin of Saul that cost him the kingdom—"Has the Lord as great delight in burnt offerings and sacrifices, as in obeying the voice of the Lord? Behold, to obey is better than sacrifice, And to heed than the fat of rams. For rebellion is as the sin of witchcraft, And

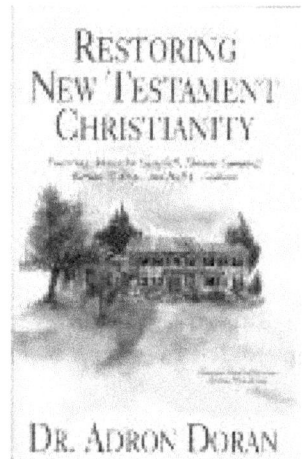

stubbornness is as iniquity and idolatry. Because you have rejected the word of the Lord, He also has rejected you from being king" (1 Samuel 15:22-23). Saul sinned in thinking God would be more pleased with the sacrifices rather than obedience. Imagine how God feels when churches have pursued the pleasure of the masses rather than obedience to God! Abandoning the Biblical pattern will take churches down the same road to apostasy that has taken prior generations who abandoned the Restoration Plea to "Speak where the Bible speaks and to be silent where the Bible is silent." We desperately need to examine the events of Restoration History to avoid the mistakes of the past. In times like this one needs the wisdom of men who have dedicated their lives to the pursuit of obeying God's word. Adron Doran was such a man who pursued this and studied others who had dedicated their lives to the same pursuit. Sadly, we cannot call him before us to tell us about restoring New Testament Christianity any longer. However, we are blessed in that he delivered a series of sermons that address this very subject.

This work discusses the New Testament church, the departure of men from the New Testament pattern, and efforts of men to return to the Bible in order to restore their worship and practices in accordance to the original New Testament pattern. It discusses the efforts of Restoration leaders such as Alexander Campbell and Barton W. Stone. These men (and others) accomplished so much toward restoring New Testament Christianity. As brother Doran wrote in his book:

> In retrospect we ponder what if these courageous, loyal, dedicated, and devoted men had not labored tirelessly to bring us out of denominationalism and into the church of our Lord? What if they had not taught what they did, when the outcome seemed, at times, in question? Had Stone and Campbell not accomplished what they did, we know not what the situation would be like today. We have accepted the teaching of Stone and Campbell wherein they taught the word of God. One things is certain; it would be a pitiable

situation indeed if these men, and hordes of unnamed supporters, had not given themselves to the leadership of this
great movement. Thank God for their lives and their efforts! Let us attach the same significance to the Bible and
to the church as they did. God rest their weary souls. (Page
38.)

It also discusses several of the difficulties that Restoration
leaders experienced along their journey. It is these lessons that
we desperately need to be taught today.

This book is a transcription of six lectures delivered in Nashville, TN in 1996. There are copies of these lectures available that
can be ordered for viewing. I encourage congregations to have
these lectures presented to the assembly by men who have
equipped themselves to fulfill the work of an evangelist.

Originally printed in the *West Virginia Christian*, Vol. 10, No.
6, June 2003, p. 8. Reprinted by permission.

The Elders Which Are Among You:
The Qualifications, Selection, and Appointment
of Elders (Bobby Duncan)

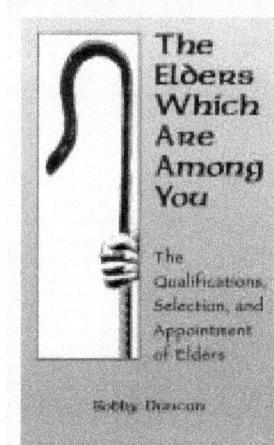

Working for a Fortune 500 company, I have seen that the need for leadership is apparent to ensure the organization is focused and on course. The same is true for the best organization in the world—the Lord's church. One of the major reasons cited for a company's bankruptcy is the lack of sound leadership. One wonders at the state of congregations of Christ due to the lack of sound leadership. A word of caution—the leadership to run a Fortune 500 company is not the same as the leadership to shepherd the Lord's church.

I have experienced the effects of sound and unsound leadership among churches. Choosing sound leaderships is critical. The Lord intends for congregations to have shepherds—biblical shepherds. It is my opinion that some congregations have suffered from unqualified men serving as elders to the point that they have become sour on the eldership as a whole. While it is true that it is better to have no eldership than to have an unscriptural one, it is not God's plan for churches to go without the leadership provided by qualified elders. Possibly one of the reasons elders are called "shepherds" is to understand that the danger of not having elders is similar to the danger for sheep not to have shepherds to guide and protect them. I serve as a deacon in the congregation where we worship. There was a time when the congregation did not have elders so the men did the best they could. Today, the congregation is stronger and tensions are less due to the fruits of the search for elders. The effort was laborious but worth every minute. While we may not get our way all the time, I have never heard anyone express a return to the period before elders were appointed!

Bobby Duncan produced a very worthwhile study of the New Testament qualifications for elders. The book is a product from the encouragement of several in response to a series of articles brother Duncan had written. Brother Duncan worked with elderships and was often consulted by congregations and elderships to assist them in their work.

All of the qualifications for the eldership are important and vital for our study. I have heard of congregations glossing over one of the qualifications to their regret. Do not make this mistake. The Lord did not provide these qualifications for us to minimize or disregard! This book is divided into chapters where each qualification is discussed at length. There are also important chapters on the relationship between the elders, the preacher, and the congregation.

There are many wise points in this book for all to consider. For example, writing about "Desire the Office" brother Duncan shows the selection process is not a political campaign where the candidate has to introduce himself for consideration:

> How does one...become an elder in the Lord's church? Certainly not in the same way one might seek some political office by campaigning for the office. One who would do such likely is demonstrating by that very act that he is not the kind of man needed in the eldership. In fact, one who has reached the point at which he is qualified to serve as an elder in a congregation will not have to call to the attention of the membership his qualifications; they will know about them already. And when they are ready to select and install elders, this man will not be overlooked. One cannot possess the characteristics that would qualify him as an elder, and yet possess them in secret for very long. (Pages 11-12).

This is an excellent book that should be read and studied by Christians. If we do not have men in congregations preparing themselves for the office James Garfield referred to as stepping down from and into the Presidency of the United States of America then we need to be encouraging men and boys to prepare themselves for the highest level of service known to mankind—shepherd of the Lord's church.

Originally printed in the *West Virginia Christian*, Vol. 12, No. 9, September 2005, p. 4. Reprinted by permission.

Protecting Our "Blind Side" – A Discussion of Contemporary Concern in churches of Christ (Earl Edwards)

Would it not be a wonderful thing to not have to deal with controversies among those in the Lord's church and focus solely on evangelism? Unfortunately, as wonderful as that would be, such is not the case in this life. Controversies exist and how we handle these can have a profound impact on the future of the church. Sometimes controversies come out of nowhere like a car can appear out of our "blind spot." Having good materials on hand to help someone sort through some of these issues is a valuable way to present material in a way that helps reduce the personal element in dealing with controversy.

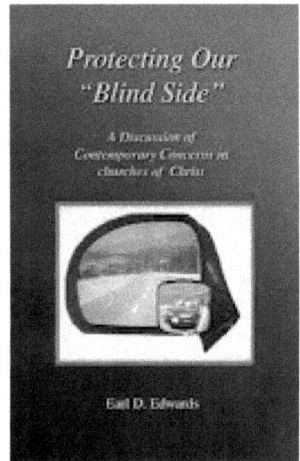

One book that is worthwhile to have on hand is Protecting Our "Blind Side" by Earl Edwards. Brother Edwards is the Director of Graduate Studies in Bible at the School of Biblical Studies at Freed-Hardeman University. He has been a teacher at Freed-Hardeman University since 1982. He has been a faithful gospel preacher since 1952. His experience and love for the truth makes a volume of this nature weigh heavily with wisdom that should be given serious consideration.

In this book, brother Edwards deals with such issues as the essentiality of Baptism, divorce & remarriage, Bible authority, the new hermeneutic, eternal punishment in hell, the work of the Holy Spirit, the restoration plea, role of women in the church, and instrumental music in worship. He provides things to think about relating to hand clapping and other matters relating to the worship of the church.

I have seen brother Edwards deliver lectures and appreciate his comments at the Open Forum at Freed-Hardeman University. I have seen him introduce someone very graciously at the FHU Bible Lectureship, but not hesitate to take issue with the content of someone's statement in a lecture in order to make sure the truth is upheld. In order to give you a flavor of the writing that brother Edwards displays, a quotation from his chapter on "Divorce and Remarriage" will be provided. Brother Earl does a fine job describing the background of this subject as it relates to the law of Moses and the Jewish schools of thought about divorce during the days of Jesus' ministry on the earth. He makes a very salient point that all should keep in mind when discussing this matter. Speaking of Matthew 19:9, he writes:

> Jesus is contrasting the teaching of Moses in verse 8 with what "I say unto you" here in this verse. Were Jesus merely trying to make clear the true meaning of the Seventh Commandment and restore it to its proper place, He would have also made it clear that He was restoring the death penalty for unchastity (Deut. 22:22) rather than suggesting that the guilty woman might be put away without blame. The truth is He is contrasting His own teaching for His coming kingdom with what Moses had taught (pp. 70-71).

Brother Edwards deals with issues in a very direct and kind way. You will find this work a valuable resource when facing or preparing to face the issues of our day.

Each One Reach One – A Study of Church Growth & Personal Evangelism (Andrew D. Erwin)

At the 2014 Ohio Winter Lecture-ship I was invited to speak on the topic "The Christian and Opportunities for Outreach." When I research a topic, I like to consult a variety of sources. Of course, I always place a premium on brotherhood materials. One year at the Freed-Hardeman University Lecture-ship I was introduced to the new editor of *The Gospel Gleaner*, Andrew D. Er-win. I obtained a copy of his book as we got acquainted. When I was preparing for my lecture, this book is one that I found to be very practical and helpful without all the unscriptural approaches and false-hoods of church growth groups outside of the church. For exam-ple, I read one book from a denominational/community church author. The writer did not mention baptism a single time, *ever*. There was an emphasis on loving the Lord, how to help develop this love in others who need to obey the gospel, but no refer-ence to baptism at all. One wonders if they have not read what Jesus said on more than one occasion— *"If you love Me, keep My commandments"* (John 14:15, NKJV). Perhaps they have read this, but they failed to notice that baptism is a command given by Jesus Christ just prior to His ascension— *"He who believes and is baptized will be saved; but he who does not believe will be condemned"* (Mark 16:16, NKJV).

Another of the books I read spoke of a national survey that concluded two surprising statistics. One was that 82 percent of the "unchurched" would be "somewhat likely" to come to

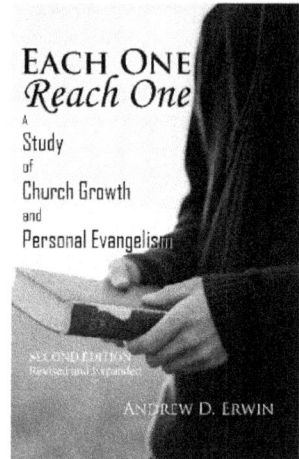

worship if they received a personal invitation. The other statistic found that only 21 percent of people invited anyone to church within a year. Someone commented to me that they thought these numbers were too high, but I asked which number—the people who would come if asked or the people who were doing asking? The point remains—when is the last time you *personally* invited someone to church! Sometimes we can become pessimistic. Now, the person who commented to me about these numbers was not asking out of pessimism; however, we sometimes allow ourselves to become pessimistic. One of the quotes I wanted to read during my lecture from Erwin's book, but was unable to because of time, was this one:

> Pessimism is never kept quiet. When a brother is pessimistic, he will no doubt discourage another brother (see Numbers 13—14). As Christians, we are commanded to encourage and provoke one another unto love and good works (Hebrews 10:24). When a brother discourages another brother because of his lack of faith in things good, he is sinning against God. It is no doubt disturbing and discouraging to Christians who want to see the church grow and yet are privy to the many times their congregation's eldership's business meetings are filled with discussions critiquing why good work(s) cannot work. We ask, instead of thinking about all the reason why a good work cannot work, why not discuss all the reasons why a good work can work? (p. 41).

The question remains on the table—when was the last time you personally invited someone to worship services? By personal, this does mean the sign out front, the service times in the bulletin or on the website. Those are impersonal invitations. We are speaking of *personal* invitations. Of course, the more you know the person, the greater the *personal* invitation has of succeeding!

Erwin's *Each One Reach One* contains several excellent chapters with discussions questions at the end of each chapter. There are also five lessons in the back of the book to assist a person to do a personal Bible Study with someone. This book would make an excellent Bible Class study to train workers for the vineyard. Beware—personal evangelism involves you, personally. I always have appreciated the title of Ivan Stewart's book, *Go Ye Means Go Me*. We must go!

Baptism in the Early Church – History, Theology and Liturgy in the First Five Centuries (Everett Ferguson)

A few years ago, the congregation where I was attending was looking for a reputable building contractor. I offered to consult with the head of the construction department where I worked to see if he could make some recommendations. His first question was "Are you a Baptist?" I replied, "No, but why?" He said "Because Baptists practice full body immersion, and I wanted to make sure you didn't need a baptistery." I stated that while I was not a Baptist, we did follow the New Testament pattern of the early church pattern of full body immersion. He made a very significant point that I wonder if many have given thought to. He stated that congregations which practice full body immersion; i.e., baptism, seek to install a baptistery which is a building's worst nightmare, since a constant presence of heated water is detrimental to a building's integrity. One wonders if people have given much thought to the "convenience factor" when studying whether or not "baptism" is by sprinkling, pouring or immersing? Certainly one recognizes that either sprinkling or pouring is far more convenient than immersing! What does the practice of the early church reveal about the mode of baptism? Certainly if the matter was up to matters of convenience, then their practice would reflect such.

When considering the "convenience factor" I came across this information in brother Ferguson's research:

The literary sources give two principal symbolisms for the baptismal font—the tomb of the death and resurrection and the womb of new birth. The former symbolism was reinforced by variations on a cross shape, which became fairly common in the fifth and sixth centuries. Both baptisteries and basins in the shape of a hexagon may have alluded to Jesus' death on the sixth day of the week; the octagon to his resurrection on the eighth day or at any rate to the idea of resurrection and eternal life. The latter was explicit in the case of the octagonal baptismal font in Milan. Even the frequency of three steps for the entrance and three for the exit of pools may have had symbolic worth (three days in the tomb), and the practice of sinking the font below floor level may have enhanced the association with a tomb. The rectangle may have alluded to a tomb, and the circle may have alluded to the womb or to eternity; or they could have been merely utilitarian. Often symbolic considerations must finally remain in the realm of speculation. (pp. 819-820)

Clearly the early church practiced full body immersion and went to great lengths to construct baptisteries for their buildings. This would be of no surprise to men such as Luther, Wesley, Calvin and the Catholic Church. These authorities readily admit that immersion was the practice of the early church. The salient question remains—who gave their followers the authority to substitute sprinkling or pouring for the New Testament teaching and early church practice? Dr. Everett Ferguson provides a monumental amount of research on the subject of baptism in his work *Baptism in the Early Church*. This volume will be a standard reference work on this subject for years to come. He has rendered the church an invaluable service with this research. Be sure to include this volume in your church library for researchers.

Early Christians Speak
(Everett Ferguson)

The study of early church history after the close of the apostolic age has been a little intimidating since I have not taken the opportunity to study under a teacher on this subject. But, I have always been intrigued to read about the views of those after the days of the apostles to see what they said in regards to the New Testament books and practices of the early church. We would do well to learn more of this material to help fortify our faith and be able to resist modern day attacks against Christianity by such works as The DaVinci Code or others that seek to erode our faith in Christianity. Of course one always needs to keep in mind that the apostles warned of an apostasy in the church that had already begun in their lifetime. So it is imperative that one does not allow what happened in later centuries to overrule what happened in the first century.

Brother Ferguson makes a valuable point about the Christians in the second century,

> All who strive to be New Testament Christians in the present age are in a way second-century Christians. Not that we have, consciously or unconsciously, followed the second-century church or taken it as an authority. But, at best, we stand in relation to the first-century Christians as did the second-century Christians. We can never hope to reproduce the circumstances of the first century with its living apostolic witness, miraculous works of the Spirit, and specific historical setting. Apart from the second century's

103

geographical and chronological proximity to the first century, we sand in the same relation to the first century as did the second century. Our faith is dependent on the first-century testimony, and we try to carry that faith over into a new setting. So, we can hope to be, in a sense, only "second-century Christians." Therefore it is of value to see what that second-century church was—what was its life, what were its successes and failures. That will say something to us about our efforts in our derivative and secondary situation to be faith to the first-century message. (Page viii)

The book begins with an overview of church history from various vantage points: geographical expansion, relationship to Roman Empire, organizational development, and doctrinal controversies. Then the book provides a topical guide to the writings of early Christians and is structured as:

- **Chapters II – V** discusses baptism
- **Chapters VI – XIII** discusses worship
- **Chapters XIV – XV** discusses organization and discipline
- **Chapters XVI – XIX** discusses the Christian lifestyle

The book also includes indices to the materials quoted from the early Christian writers, a scripture index and a general index as well. There is an important Glossary of Terms in the back that is helpful in learning various items as it relates to this period. Plus, there is a listing of the early writers and brief overview of who they were. Also, there is a time chart showing how these writers relate to one another over time. The time chart shows in parallel columns the Christian writers, Non-Christian writers, the Roman Emperors, and key events relating to the material.

Everett Ferguson is Professor of Church History Emeritus at Abilene Christian University. He earned a Ph.D. from Harvard University "with distinction." His works are highly respected and utilized in various religious circles. I had the pleasure of hearing and meeting brother Ferguson and his wife at the Freed-

Hardeman University Bible Lectureship. He written and edited several books that are worthy of study.

Thinking-Living-Dying:
Early Apologists Speak to the 21st Century
(Everett Ferguson)

When judges review prior court decisions when deciding their judgments, they are said to be looking for precedence or past pattern to guide their decision. It should be obvious that clear and consistent teaching and practice formulates a strong precedence while inconsistencies in teaching, practice, or both weaken precedence.

While the Bible is clear on God's great love for mankind as demonstrated by sending His Son to redeem humanity (John 3:16), it is also plain that God has standards for acceptable moral behavior. For example, God designed marriage to be one man and one woman for life (Genesis 1:24) and homosexuality is contrary to that design. God codified this design in both the Law of Moses (Deuteronomy 20:7) and the New Testament (Matthew 19:4-5; Mark 10:6-7). The Bible also documented His abhorrence for various sexual practices contrary to the design of marriage such as homosexuality, bestiality, *et al.* (Leviticus 18:22-23). In addition, God has demonstrated His commitment to those standards by punishing those who flagrantly disregarded Him and His standards of morality; e.g. Sodom (Jude 1:7). He has also promised to do so in the future (Revelation 21:7-8). So, His design in creation, His laws across generations, His actions in the past and His promises in the future have been consistent in what constitutes moral rightness and immorality. One should not overlook God's precedence in these matters!

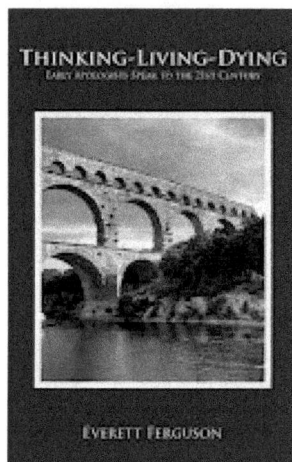

There are religions claiming Christianity who have historically opposed homosexuality, but recently have not only tolerated this lifestyle but have promoted those who practice it into leadership ranks. One wonders how faithful churches are going to hold to God's standards of morality in our legal system with so many other religions compromising God's standards? I am convinced that one of the determining legal factors for churches who have consistently attempted to save those engaged in homosexuality by helping them cease the activity and become sanctified (1 Corinthians 6:8-10) will be the teaching and practice of churches across the centuries. In other words, what will precedence reveal?

This is where *Thinking-Living-Dying* becomes such an important study. The study is a fascinating one, especially for those who appreciate both early church history and apologetics. I was privileged to hear brother Ferguson deliver these lectures, and as I listened to him explain the early apologists' debates with pagan philosophers on subjects such as celibacy, marriage, extra-marital sex, abortion, infanticide, and homosexuality, I was struck by how explicit and contextual these issues were in our society today. For example, Celsus, who was a pagan philosopher, attacked Christians in his writing *True Discourse* (or *True Reason* or *True Doctrine*) around AD 178. Origen defended Christianity in his apologetic work *Against Celsus* around AD 248. Origen's work was viewed to be one of the strongest apologies in early church history. Interestingly, the attacks of Celsus were only preserved because of the extensive quotations and refutation by Origen. Origen lost his father due to persecution under the reign of Septimius Severus. Some fifty years later, Origen would also be imprisoned, persecuted and die in AD 253 at Tyre. Origen answered the call both in his defense of Christianity in thinking, living and even dying. What will our commitment be when we are put to the test?

Living With Depression
(Dowell Flatt)

While a student at Freed-Hardeman University, I attended the 1991 FHU Bible Lectureship and was fortunate to hear an outstanding lecture on "Myths About Depression" by Charles White. I attended this lecture for one reason: to learn more about depression that had attacked a fellow student and a teacher I highly respected— Dowell Flatt. I was intrigued that depression would take hold of the Chairman of the Bible Department and leave him nearly unable to continue his work.

Brother White, who suffers from clinical depression, is a minister among churches of Christ so his background was similar to brother Flatt. White explained that there are two basic types of depression: exogenous (situational) and endogenous (clinical or biological). The difference was very vividly portrayed by brother White as he relayed his personal battle to identify the source of his depression. At first he thought it was situational. After a physical exam his regular doctor agreed and chastised him for an apparent lack of faith. As I recall, he stated one day the depression nearly caused him to commit suicide. At this point he checked into a hospital since he knew there was no logical reason for having thoughts of suicide. After extensive examinations by a more qualified doctor, he learned that he had a severe case of biological depression. He uses medication to combat this disease and probably will for the rest of his life.

Depression is not rare. According to the National Institute of Mental Health, 18.8 million American adults (9.5% of the adult population) suffer from clinical depression. Christians are to be compassionate for those who suffer from both types of

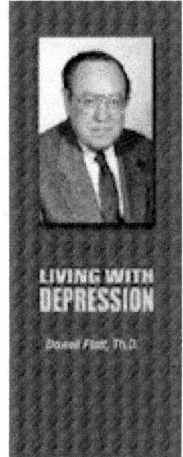

depression; however, it is important to realize the difference be-tween situational and biological depression. Reading brother Flatt's booklet will give a person a glimpse of the battle those who suffer from biological depression are fighting. It also dis-cusses myths of depression from a Christian's perspective. Un-derstanding the types of depression will assist in our ability to show greater compassion.

Note: This is a booklet of 16 pages and would also make a valuable addition to the tract rack in addition to keeping a copy in the church library.

Originally printed in the *West Virginia Christian*, Vol. 10, No. 5, May 2003, p. 8. Reprinted by permission.

There Is A God:
How the World's Most Notorious Atheist Changed His Mind
(Antony Flew)

There are a few things I would like to point out or suggest prior to discussing this book. First, one should read (also available on DVD) *The Warren-Flew Debate* and Thomas B. Warren's book *Have Atheists Proven There is no God?* prior to reading this book. Garland Elkins, close friend and coworker with brother Warren reported:

> Brother Warren told me that during his debate with Mr. Flew he walked over to his table and saw that Mr. Flew had a copy of brother Warren's book entitled, Have Atheists Proved There Is No God? Brother Warren said that the book was very worn around the edges indicating that Mr. Flew had used it much in his studying. Mr. Flew's change is a devastating blow to atheism. He is to be congratulated and commended for his change. He now needs to learn the identity of the God of the Bible, and obey Him and become a Christian. — Garland Elkins, "A Renowned Atheist Renounces Atheism," Yokefellow, Vol. 32, No. 1, January 2005, p. 2.

Second, one will not agree with everything written in Flew's book, but it is very valuable as will be observed. Third, be aware that while Flew did change his mind about the existence of God, he remained unchanged about his rejection of an afterlife—also called a "mortalist." Tragic as that is, this provides an important

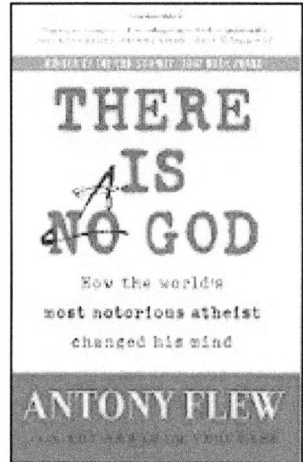

point—he did not make a "deathbed confession or conversion" as some of his atheist associates attempted to excuse or deflect his change with. Tragically, he ran out of time to either recognize or accept the truth on matters pertaining to the afterlife. Sadly, he remained a "mortalist" until April 8, 2010 when he passed away.

Interestingly, when Warren debated Flew, Flew had accepted a debate proposition that was unique among atheists— he affirmed (rather than just denied) that "I Know That God Does Not Exist." This is far different than other debates with atheists who attempt to shift the burden of proof to the theist. Flew mentions the 1976 debate with Warren although briefly. Flew states Warren "wielded an impressive array of charts and slides." Interestingly, according to Warren's assistant Roy Deaver, Warren presented 75 charts during the debate, but he had prepared over 400 detailed charts for the debate. (David Lipe who helped create many of the charts has the total number at 500.)

There are several important matters Flew brings to light in this book that are worth reflecting on.

First, how many times has an atheist challenged theists to produce observable, empirical data or proof via the scientific method for the existence of God? Flew discusses this tactic which was called "logical positivism." Flew points out that while he was an atheist, he had written a devastating refutation, "Theology and Falsification," to the man credited with logical positivism, Alfred Ayer. In fact, Ayer himself renounced his work, Language, Truth and Logic, and stated: "Logical positivism died a long time ago. I don't think much of Language, Truth and Logic is true. I think it is full of mistakes...I think it is full of mistakes which I spent the last fifty years correcting or trying to correct." (Pages xiv-xv). Also, Albert Einstein's statement on the demand for empirical data or positivism is intriguing:

I am not a positivist. Positivism states that what cannot be observed does not exist. This conception is scientifically in-defensible, for it is impossible to make valid affirmations of what people 'can' or 'cannot' observe. One would have to say 'only what we observe exists,' which is obviously false." Flew also counters the modern militant atheists of today who attempt to change the subject by pointing out the abuses of adherents of Christianity by stating "But the ex-cesses and atrocities of organized religion have no bearing whatsoever on the existence of God, just as the threat of nuclear proliferation has no bearing on the question of whether E = mc2. (Page xxiv)

Second, Flew points out that some atheists attempt to claim that Einstein was an atheist. Flew records this important and powerful statement by Einstein to the contrary—

I'm not an atheist, and I don't think I can call myself a pan-theist. We are in the position of a little child entering a huge library filled with books in many languages. The child knows someone must have written those books. It does not know how. It does not understand the language in which they are written. The child dimly suspects a mysterious order in the arrangement of the books but doesn't know what it is. That, it seems to me, is the attitude of even the most intelligent human being toward God. We see the universe marvel-ously arranged and obeying certain laws but only dimly un-derstand these laws. Our limited minds grasp the mysteri-ous force that moves constellations. (Page 99)

Also in the appendix is a critique of some of popular atheists of today by Roy Abraham Varghese who assisted Flew with the writing of this book.

Third, Flew was able to open his mind to omnipotence from the evidence gleamed in the field of science. He states:

Science qua science cannot furnish an argument for God's existence. But the three items of evidence we have consid-ered in this volume—the laws of nature, life with its teleological organization, and the existence of the universe—can only be explained in light of an Intelligence that explains both its own existence and that of the world. Such a discovery of the Divine does not come through experiments and equations, but through an understanding of the structures they unveil or map. (Page 155)

Or as others have so argued—where there is design, there must be a designer that is at least equal to or greater than the design. This admission by Flew is interesting since in his debate with Warren he attempted to skirt arguments from biology pressed by Warren since he was not a biologist.

Sadly, Flew ran out of time to completely "follow the evidence wherever it leads," but he did provide a hint to where the evidence was leading him at the writing of his book. He places in the appendix of his book a defense by Anglican N.T. Wright of the revelation of God in the person of Jesus Christ. Flew states of Christianity—

As I have said more than once, no other religion enjoys anything like the combination of a charismatic figure like Jesus and a first-class intellectual like St. Paul. If you're wanting omnipotence to set up a religion, it seems to me that this is the one to beat! (Page 157)

Hopefully this work will save some atheists or agnostic from wasting time to get their "thinking straight" (a title of another book on logic by Antony Flew—which, perhaps ironically, Thomas B. Warren recommended). Flew stated he tried to do what Socrates advised—"follow the evidence to wherever it leads." This work provides an excellent piece of evidence for parents to share with their children. The lesson is obvious—if Flew, a son of a Methodist minister, can go so far away from Christianity as to affirm in public discourse that there is no God, make an academic career as a philosophical atheist, but be turned to theism based on evidence, then the case for God is far stronger than many may have considered. Perhaps it will save some from the thought expressed in the hymn—"'Almost per-suaded' now to believe...'Almost'—but lost!'"

Life and Times of Benjamin Franklin
(Joseph Franklin)

When people hear the name "Benjamin Franklin" the patriot quickly comes to mind; however, some are surprised to learn of a preacher by the same name. He was the great, great, great nephew of the signer of the Declaration of Independence but was far more than that. For example, David Lipscomb wrote :

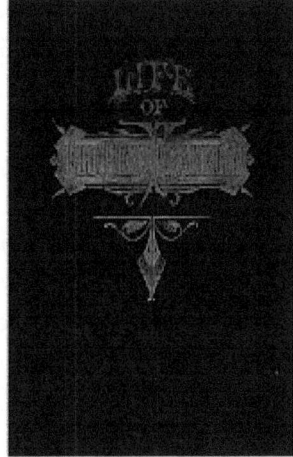

> The cause loses its most able and indefatigable defender since the days of Alexander Campbell, and his loss is simply irreparable. Earnestness, clearness, simplicity, with a strong reverence for and determination to know nothing in religion save what the Bible teaches was the striking characteristic of his discourses (Gospel Advocate, December 5, 1878).

Benjamin Franklin was born February 1, 1812 in Belmont County, OH. As a young man, Benjamin went to live in Henry County, IN, and his parents would soon follow him to live in Indiana. Benjamin married Mary Personnett and had eleven children. While in Indiana, the Franklins had a new neighbor—restoration preacher Samuel Rogers. While the Franklins were Methodist, they liked Rogers and studied the Bible together. Ultimately the family was converted and four of the boys became preachers. Benjamin was committed to the Bible, sold his business interests, and became a preacher.

With little formal education, Franklin became a very effective evangelist, debater and editor. He often dealt with controversies of the day including: included the missionary society, instrumental music, Civil War & slavery, open communion, the name a Christian should wear, and the operation of the Holy Spirit. While he edited several papers, his most enduring work was the American Christian Review which he founded in 1856 and edited until his death in 1878 (the paper did not cease with his death). While the Gospel Advocate was nicknamed "Old Reliable" the American Christian Review was called "Old Faithful." He often defended the truth against various forms of false teaching and conducted at least 30 religious discussions. Franklin was loyal to the truth and would even reverse a course if convinced the prior was unsound. For example, Franklin approved the missionary society and served in both the American Christian Missionary Society and the Ohio Missionary Society. He eventually "studied himself out of it" and then opposed these types of organizations in spite of criticism for changing his position. Benjamin Franklin was a protracted meeting preacher rather than doing located work. Consequently, he would be away for weeks and even months at a time to preach. The family made tremendous sacrifices for the cause of Christ. The son of Benjamin Franklin chronicles some of these in this biography.

Benjamin Franklin eventually settled in Anderson, IN during 1864 where his son Joseph and family lived although he continued meeting work. He wrote two books of sermons: Gospel Preacher, Vol. 1 and Gospel Preacher, Vol. 2 which sold very well and remains in print to this day. He also authored a tract "Sincerity Seeking the Way to Heaven" which sold widely and was considered the best selling publication among churches for several years. Benjamin Franklin preached his last sermon in Anderson two days before he died of a heart attack on October 22, 1878. He was buried in West Maplewood Cemetery in Anderson. Joseph Franklin wrote this biography; which was released shortly after Benjamin's death in 1879. It chronicles the life of a frontier preacher and those who likewise made tremendous sacrifices for the kingdom. Benjamin Franklin's life and commitment reminds me of Paul's words *"Imitate me, just as I also imitate Christ."* (I Corinthians 11:1, NKJV).

Hardeman: Preacher, Professor, President
(E. Claude Gardner)

Sometimes people whom we never met can influence the trajectory of our lives. When I had graduated from Centralia High School, my father spoke to the President of Freed-Hardeman College about my needing to attend the college there but not having the money. The President told him to send me and they would find a way to enable me to attend. The school song has the line "A debt we owe to thee" which some sang with punctuated emphasis, but the truth points to the spiritual balance sheet of my life. That President was E. Claude Gardner who has written a book about a man who greatly influenced the trajectory of his life and mine too, Nicholas Brodie Hardeman or N.B. Hardeman.

HARDEMAN:
PREACHER, PROFESSOR, PRESIDENT

E. CLAUDE GARDNER

One of the objectives I have in mind when I prepare to teach or preach restoration history is how to make rather mundane details such as dates and places "come off the page" and take on renewed meaning. One of the ways to do that is to have anecdotal stories about the person or timeframe that help an audience connect with the subject. Ironically, I became "connected" to the life of N.B. Hardeman through an article E. Claude Gardner had written about Hardeman in the paper *The Messenger*. It sparked an interest in the life of two men who created an institution that would lead to Gardner being President and my being a student, A.G. Freed and N.B. Hardeman. N.B. Hardeman hired E. Claude Gardner through a letter. There was no interview in the traditional manner common today. In the offer letter to Gardner on March 31, 1949, Hardeman wrote "I believe this will be a fine opportunity for you and that you would never have occasion to regret accepting this position." (p. 85) At the writing of this review, brother Gardner is still a walking testament to the truth of that assessment by Hardeman; although N.B. Hardeman would leave the school never to return a few short months later. In fact, Gardner is the last surviving person N.B. Hardeman hired for the school.

Brother Gardner's latest work *Hardeman: Preacher, Professor, President* is unique in that it is written about a powerful preacher of the gospel, a popular professor and president of one of the finest Christian colleges in the brotherhood by one who has shared in those roles as well. Brother Gardner kept a regular correspondence with N.B. Hardeman through the years, so this work contains several remembrances that are uniquely told by one "who was there." N.B. Hardeman was considered by many to be "The Prince of Preachers" so it is fitting that one of his sermons is included in this biography too. There are also biographical articles written by brother Gardner over the years and family relations over the years included in the book.

In my possession is among the last diplomas that N.B. Hardeman signed as President. It bears a distinctive blue ink signature that matches the letters reproduced in the book. Freed-Hardeman College became Freed-Hardeman University while I was a student. It still bears the names of its two founders. E. Claude Gardner served this institution for six decades. He came to the school as teacher but also served in several positions before being appointed President. Other works about the life of N.B. Hardeman are available and are excellent reading, but you will not want to miss this fine work by one who walked in Hardeman's shoes. Also, all proceeds from the sale of *Hardeman: Preacher, Professor, President* will be used for the E. Claude Gardner Bible Scholarship Fund at the Freed-Hardeman University School of Biblical Studies.

Instrumental Music in the Public Worship
(John L. Girardeau)

There are history books that may mistakenly state the use of the organ began in worship, which is an unauthorized addition to Christian worship, as late as 600-AD 700. Further studies in church history as found that this date is too early by as much as 200 to 300 years since these incidents referred to court proceedings and not actual worship services. Dr. Everett Ferguson, noted church historian, wrote in *A Cappella Music in the Public Worship of the Church*:

> It was perhaps as late as the tenth century when the organ was played as part of the service. This makes instrumental music one of the late innovations of the medieval Catholic Church. (Page 74).

When people who are unfamiliar with New Testament worship first visit worship services of churches of Christ, they often comment on the lack of mechanical instruments or how much they enjoy congregational singing. Some think this is rather odd; however, what they fail to realize is the use of mechanical instruments is truly the oddity. Some may be astonished to learn that the mainline denominations also once opposed the use of instrumental music in worship. They perhaps fail to realize that acapella does not just mean "without instrumental accompaniment" but is an Italian word meaning "in the style of the chapel." The very word itself speaks to the fact that the early worship of the church was without mechanical instruments!

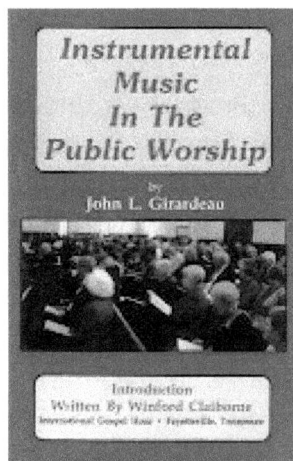

The International Gospel Hour has reprinted a classic work by a John L. Girardeau. A Presbyterian professor of Columbia Theological Seminary, he was repeatedly asked by his students why he *opposed* the use of mechanical instruments of music in worship. This book was his response. The book was originally published in 1888 and remains a classic reference work on this subject. Brother Winford Claiborne includes a valuable introduction in the book which includes some vital points relating to some errors made by Girardeau regarding denominationalism and such. The book is divided into several sections: The General Argument from Scripture; Arguments from the Old Testament, Argument from the New Testament, Argument from the Presbyterian Standards, Historical Argument, and Arguments in Favor of Instrumental Music. Included are valuable references showing that the early church did not utilize instrumental music and the early denominations recognized this and excluded likewise, at first.

Consider these words by Dr. Girardeau which he wrote in warning to the Presbyterian Church about the adoption of instrumental music in its worship. A similar warning could be made for us today:

> Those of us who protest against this revolution in Presbyterian worship are by some pitied, by others ridiculed, and by others still denounced as fanatics. If we are, we share the company of an innumerable host of fanatics extending from the day of Pentecost to the middle of the nineteenth century. We refuse not to be classed, although consciously unworthy of the honor, with apostles, martyrs and reformers. But neither were they mad, nor are we. We 'speak the words of truth and soberness.' Mindful of the apostolic injunction, 'Prove all things,' we submit arguments derived from Scripture, from the formularies of our church and from the consensus of Christ's people, and respectfully invoke for them the attention of our brethren. We call upon them to examine these arguments, and either disprove or

adopt them. But should they be dismissed without notice, and our faithful remonstrances be unheeded, we humbly, but earnestly, warn the church of the evil and bitter consequences which will, we verily believe, be entailed by that corruption of public worship which has been pointed out; and against it, in the name of the framers of our venerable standards, in the name of the reformers, divines and martyrs of the Presbyterian Church, in the name of Christ's true witnesses in the centuries past, in the name of our glorious King and Head, we erect this solemn PROTEST. (Page 200).

Here is an excellent resource to give to someone who mistakenly believes this is a "Church of Christ view." We should give this work lovingly and state this is the New Testament view! Churches of Christ aim to follow the New Testament in her worship to God. We have no man-made creeds, confessions of faith, or church manuals. The church belongs to Christ, and it is imperative that we worship according to the will (testament) of Christ.

Halley's Bible Handbook
(Henry H. Halley)

There are several handbooks on the market these days, but this is one that has endured. The book began in 1924 as a 16-page leaflet that Henry Halley would hand out to friends & students. It quickly turned into a 32-page booklet that he would continue to expand. At first the book was called *Halley's Pocket Bible Handbook*, but it soon outgrew the pocket! Since then, it has gone through numerous expansions to where it is now over 850 pages. The book has gone through numerous editions (at least twenty-five), multiple copyright renewals, translations into at least 13 foreign languages, and has sold over 5 million copies—a testament to its popularity and enduring value.

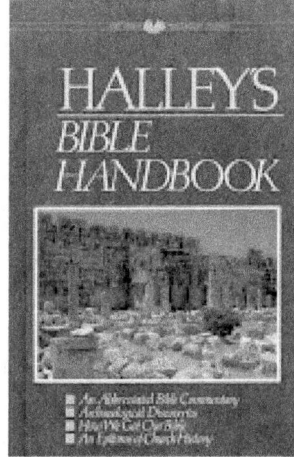

My first introduction to this book was from Don Baugh, one of my high school Bible class teachers. He would bring it to class and often use it to expand on the material covered in class. I can still remember him saying "I don't know exactly who he is or how to precisely pronounce his last name, but his material is often, not always, right on."

Henry Halley was taught by a man who is perhaps more well-known than his teacher, Alexander Campbell, and that is J.W. McGarvey. Halley graduated from McGarvey's College of the Bible in 1895 with Associate and Bachelor degrees. He taught at the school for a year, then the following year he taught for the Women's Missionary College in Hazel Green, KY. In 1897 Halley became the Pastor for the Disciples of Christ in Michigan. His study in the College of the Bible prepared him to assemble such a valuable handbook. Due to an illness, Halley had to suspend his pulpit work so he spent hours in memorization of the Bible. One report is that he could quote the Bible for as long as 25 hours without stopping! He applied effort to the study of Bible History, Bible Geography and other key Bible subjects. It is reported that he would often weave these points in his sermons so that he was in great demand as a speaker.

The book is organized to provide insights into each book of the Bible. It is supplemented with maps, charts, illustrations and pictures to better understand the subject matter. Often there are photographs of artifacts and biblical places with explanations that are of interest. There are also articles relating to how we got the Bible and how to read it more effectively. Halley also includes articles that are worthy of thought including reflections on the importance of worship, reading the Bible, and preaching the gospel. There is also an interesting overview of church history with key characters during each period of history. While space is provided to discuss the Reformation Movement, sadly there is no mention of the far greater movement—The Restoration Movement. This is most unfortunate since Halley would have been very familiar with the plea of returning back to the Bible.

Certainly one will not agree with every point in the book; however, three factors need to be kept in mind. First, Henry Halley was not a member of churches of Christ and was influenced by the digressive element. Second, there have been archaeological discoveries since the days of Henry Halley that are not incorporated in the book. Third, the book is no longer under Halley's oversight since selling the rights to Zondervan Publishing so future editions may include/exclude information Halley would not support. When giving this book as a gift, one would do well to bring these points to the recipient's attention. In fact, the copy my parents gave me includes the words "Read Carefully." With these points in mind, it remains a very useful reference work. So much so, that in 1961 Henry Halley received the Gutenberg

Award from the Chicago Bible Society in acknowledgment for this reference tool.

Henry Hampton Halley died in 1965 and is buried in Lexington Cemetery, which also is the final resting place for other notable restoration preachers such as J.W. McGarvey, John T. Johnson, Raccoon John Smith and others.

Waking the Sleeping Giant
(David W. Hamrick)

While working in industry, I had the opportunity to plan various budgets and forecasts. One forecast of particular interest was the sales forecast because an organization bases much of its operating budget on what they project their sales will be in the coming year. Often two terms would be used during the planning process—"organic growth" and "inorganic growth." Inorganic growth came primarily from mergers and acquisitions; i.e., growing your organization by purchasing other companies. Organic growth is what we generally think of as "growth"—increasing the number of customers or persuading existing customers to purchase more. In the church, it seems, sometimes we lump these two terms organic and inorganic growth together, but maybe we should ponder on this. I often remind members that having Christians move into our area and transfer membership is not exactly growth. It would be similar to inorganic growth perhaps, but it would not be organic growth. Organic growth would be finding those who are lost and persuading them to obey the gospel or getting existing members to do more in the service to the Lord. One wonders how our growth numbers would look like if we merely looked at the number of baptisms or restorations in a year compared to the attendance board?

Achieving growth is challenging! One of the challenges is getting a congregation to think seriously about growth. Some are good at talking about growing, but do their actions reflect the talk? Have you ever met someone that said "We are happy

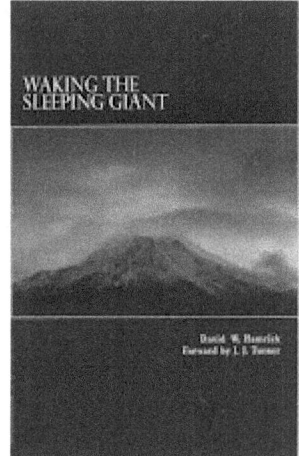

126

with the size our congregation. We do not need to grow." That is a very dangerous attitude! We are commanded to evangelize, to save souls - in other words, grow in number! But how do we get a congregation to think about growth, much less be energized into action? Once they are energized and motivated to action, how do we convert this energy into action plans? One resource I would like you to consider is David W. Hamrick's latest book *Waking the Sleeping Giant – Proven Church Growth Principles and Strategies For Reviving Struggling Churches*. David and I have known each other for several years, and I have been very impressed with his work in missions. Currently, David is the President of the World Bible Institute (worldBibleinstitute.com) which offers online training for preachers and church leaders. He also served nine years with Bear Valley Institute as their Director of Extension which set up satellite schools. Perhaps you are unfamiliar with World Bible Institute but have heard the name of J.J. Turner. J.J. Turner is on the Board of Directors of World Bible Institute. David Hamrick has helped establish preaching schools and colleges on six continents. He has done local work for several years. David's credentials are well worth your consideration of his book! He also designed a study guide for the book, which may be used to facilitate a class at your congregation. David also has some availability to conduct a Church Growth Workshop. Knowing David Hamrick, I am certain you will appreciate the time spent with him and be able to tap into his experience to help the congregation where you are. David's words ring true when he wrote:

> There is no doubt that every Christian who loves the church has a burning desire to see her grow. You want the borders of God's kingdom to expand worldwide. Though you cannot convert the world by yourself, you can, however, turn things around where you are. (p. 11.)

The book is filled with scriptural references and applications. As brother J.J. Turner wrote in the Forward:

This dynamic book should be read, studied, and applied by every congregation. It will be a blueprint for igniting a revival fire as the sleeping giant wakes up. If you want to help the church grow, this is the book for you.

Perhaps this book and study guide will help start the congregation thinking, talking and then working towards growing the body of Christ where you are.

Originally printed in the *West Virginia Christian,* Vol. 21, No. 2, February 2014, p. 8. *Reprinted by permission.*

The Bible Searchlight and the Holy Land &
One Dozen Sermons
(N.B. Hardeman)

This review includes two separate books since the material from these books is very similar to the material in the *Hardeman's Tabernacle Sermons* volumes. One should keep in mind the amount of labor and expense it took to print a book prior to today. Indeed, God has blessed this generation with so many means of spreading the gospel today.

The Bible Searchlight and the Holy Land was copyrighted 1924. It appears that the book is a compilation of sermons from the first and second Tabernacle meetings conducted in 1922 & 1923. The book also includes lectures on Hardeman's tour of the Holy Land. These lectures would later appear in print from the fifth volume of *Hardeman's Tabernacle Sermons*; however, this meeting did not occur until 1942. So, *The Bible Searchlight* contains the earliest known printing of the Holy Land tour.

In 1919, the Board of Directors agreed to purchase the National Teachers' Normal and Business College from brothers A.G. Freed and N.B. Hardeman. Over Freed and Hardeman's protest, the board renamed the school "Freed-Hardeman College." In 1923, both Freed and Hardeman left the school. Freed would go to work in

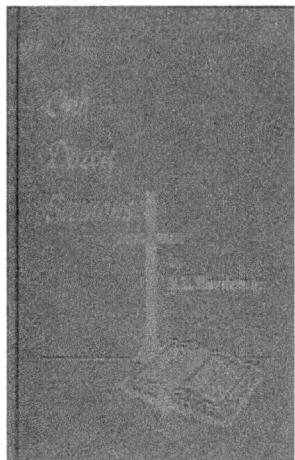

Christian education in Nashville, TN, and Hardeman traveled to Europe and the Holy Lands for three months. While a trip to the Holy Land is considered a "trip of a lifetime" today with the political uncertainty, in Hardeman's day with the political uncertainty and more difficult means of travel, the expression "trip of a lifetime" becomes closer to its original meaning. Upon his return, the town of Henderson filled Chester County Courthouse to hear him speak of his travels. In 1925, Hardeman returned to Freed-Hardeman College as president and would continue with the school until 1950. (Note that the school included Hardeman's name before he served as president in 1925. Freed and Hardeman made many significant contributions to the school prior to Hardeman's extended presidency. The Holy Land Tour was also a popular subject at Freed-Hardeman College. In fact, N.B. Hardeman received more requests for these lessons that he was willing to fulfill, being concerned he would feel "gorged."

One Dozen Sermons, copyright 1956, is a compilation of sermons: two delivered in Glasgow, KY; seven near Gallatin, TN; and three from *The Bible Searchlight*. N.B. Hardeman states in the Preface that some of the sermons come from the *Hardeman Tabernacle Sermons* that were largely out-of-print at the time. Hardeman's correctly stated, "If a sermon is worth preaching once, it should be told over and over." This book is the smallest of the books authored by brother N.B. Hardeman. It would make a fine addition to any library. The sermon "The Hardening of Pharaoh's Heart" (which appears in both second *Hardeman's Tabernacles Sermons* and *The Bible Searchlight*) is indeed a classic. Anyone who has been perplexed by this subject apparently has not had the opportunity to read this sermon (or hear it preached by a preacher who has so profited).

In conclusion, assuming one has a set of the *Hardeman Tabernacle Sermons*, one will find the material in these two works repetitive. That does not diminish the value of the books. It could be that one comes across these two works and seek to add them to the church library since one is out of print at the time.

Whether supplementary to a library or not, these two books of sermons are very valuable to those who love the gospel of the kingdom. As I have been reading and researching the material for the series of reviews on the written works on or by N.B. Hardeman and reading about the current events of the church today, I am convinced that the brotherhood would profit greatly from encouraging the continued proclamation of the material contained in these lessons. E. Claude Gardner, retired president of Freed-Hardeman University who also worked with N.B. Hardeman, stated the *Hardeman Tabernacle Sermons* had a stabilizing influence among the brotherhood.

We need this type of stabilizing influence today!

Boswell-Hardeman Discussion
(N.B. Hardeman)

The use of mechanical instruments of music in worship is a topic that has been debated and discussed so frequently in years past that some have mistakenly thought the issue could be dropped from teaching in churches of Christ. Tragically, we are seeing the results of this mistake today. While attending a worship service in California this summer, we selected a congregation whose website seemed satisfactory enough to attend. While this congregation stated they were committed to singing acapella (meaning "in the style of the chapel or church), they played a modern pop song that included instrumental accompaniment during the sermon. Did they not realize that this violated their claim? Did they mistakenly think the sermon is not part of worship and they could therefore do whatever they saw fit at that time?

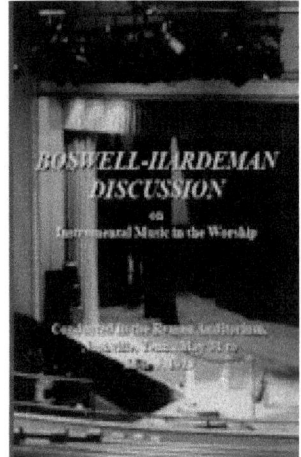

In the early 1920s, the Christian Church was attempting to make inroads into Tennessee and other areas of the South. The Commission on Unity, an organization of the Christian Churches headquartered in Nashville, TN had been distributing O.E. Payne's book "Instrumental Music is Scriptural" as a refutation to M.C. Kurfees classic book "Instrumental Music in Worship." The Commission was so sure of itself that they sent a copy to the editor of the Gospel Advocate, F.B. Srygley. When Srygley did not give Payne's book notice, the Commission questioned him on the matter. Srygley suggested a debate between two individuals from both sides to discuss the matter publicly in Nashville. The Commission quickly agreed and selected Ira M. Boswell to represent them. N.B. Hardeman was selected to represent churches of Christ and Srygley moderated for Hardeman. N.B. Hardeman was not only preparing for this discussion but was to deliver the first of the Tabernacle Sermons in the famous Ryman Auditorium as well. So, N.B. Hardeman had two grand events to be engaged in at roughly the same time.

The discussion on instrumental music was also held at the Ryman Auditorium in , Nashville, TN from May 31 – June 5, 1923. Boswell's primary "trump card" was the Greek word *psallo*. The psallo argument is still being parroted by those among us clamoring for instrumental music today even though it has been answered and defeated even before Hardeman's discussion of the matter. N.B. Hardeman's treatment of psallo needs to be read by every member of the church. The following is a portion of brother Hardeman's treatment of the Christian Church's misuse of psallo:

> Now, the question between us is this, and can be reduced to a matter of the utmost simplicity: Brother Boswell, is the instrument the hair?...Is the instrument the bowstring? Is the instrument the strings of the heart? Let us allow the Bible to forever settle that. Paul, what do you say about that? It is not the plucking or the psalloing of the hair; it is not the twitching of a cord or the plucking of the carpenter's line; it is not the twanging or the twitching of an instrument of artificial mechanism; but it is the touching or the twanging or psalloing of the heart, and that is the thing upon which the psalloing is done. But may I submit to you this idea: In the five times used in the New Testament, the word psallo not one single, solitary time, is ever translated by the King James or by the Revised Version "to play." These translators, about one hundred and fifty in number, represented the scholarship of the world. They were selected and appointed because of their scholarship; and when they came to the rendition of the word psallo and to the translation thereof, without exception, without

dissenting voice, they rendered it "to sing, to make melody." Where? In the human heart. (pp. 44-45).

Hardeman's response to the psallo argument was devastating to Boswell. The debate was a victory for the Truth and the advance by the Christian Church was turned back. Some 20 years after the debate, Hardeman met Boswell in Louisville, KY. Hardeman had heard the pastor of the Vine Street Christian Church in Nashville say that Boswell and his team was up all night trying to assemble an effective reply to Hardeman's logic on psallo.

One stated, "Hardeman did for the Instrumental Music question with Boswell, what Alexander Campbell did with Rice on the baptism question." Guy N. Woods stated it was the greatest debate on Instrumental Music ever conducted and it is still regarded as one of the finest to be read even to this day. I was recently discussing this topic with a coworker (who is a preacher for the Christian Church as well). He stated "I think the word psallo authorizes the instrument; although I know your response is the word refers to the plucking of the strings of the heart." He could not contradict the point. The truth stands the test of time!

Originally printed in the *West Virginia Christian*, Vol. 13, No. 7, July 2006, Reprinted by permission.

Hardeman-Bogard Debate
(N.B. Hardeman)

N.B. Hardeman, president of Freed-Hardeman College and Ben Bogard, Dean of Antioch Missionary Baptist Institute, debated at Little Rock, Arkansas, April 19-22, 1938. Subjects discussed included: The Work of the Holy Spirit, The Necessity of Baptism, the Establishment of the Church, and the Possibility of Apostasy. This is one of the two debates printed by brother Hardeman although he held several debates. Hardeman's debate skills were developed largely by his instructor and mentor, A.G. Freed. The church has been blessed by the efforts of Freed and Hardeman in so many ways that there is no way to calculate the good they accomplished. Ben Bogard had debated many of the prominent men in the brotherhood including Foy Wallace (son of Foy E. Wallace), Joe Warlick, G.C. Brewer, A.G. Freed, and J.D. Tant. He was considered the most prominent Baptist debater of the period. The relationship between these men was not ugly as some who criticize debating often assume is the case. The issues can be discussed openly and in a friendly manner.

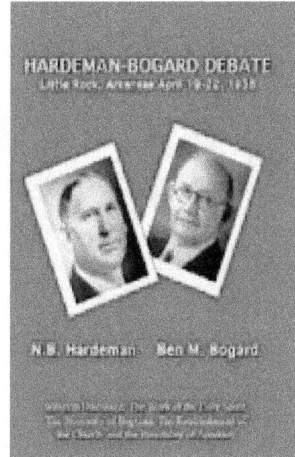

There is much material that could be presented in this review for consideration. One of the passages quoted frequently relates to the operation of the Holy Spirit. Based on the reported confusion on this matter, the quote should be brought to our remembrance:

> But how does the Spirit operate? That is the question. My answer, first, last and all the time, is that he influences through the gospel, which is God's power. The word is the

medium through which the Spirit accomplishes his work. If that book there were the sinners heart and this hand were the Holy Spirit (placing hand on book) there is direct and immediate contact; if you put something between, the hand will operate on the book, but this time it is through the medium of this tablet. That represents the only two ideas that can be had from this proposition. That represents the difference between Dr. Bogard and me, the difference between error and truth! (p. 21).

It is tragic that some today feel more comfortable with the position of Ben Bogard on this matter. Some even think it strange that one would claim that the Holy Spirit operates on man solely through the word of God in conversion and sanctification; however, that is the position faithful members of the past and present have held. Any position that degrades the all sufficiency of the scriptures either directly or implicitly is to be reviewed cautiously. This debate will provide much to think about along these lines. A question for the recent publishers of the concept of the Holy Spirit operating in a supra-literary way to preserve the Christian—would not the greater effort be required in the conversion of the alien sinner than keeping the converted saved? If the Holy Spirit is using only the word of God to save the sinner, why would He require more resources to keep the Christian saved?

A humorous incident occurred in this debate. Ben Bogard had bragged to E.R. Harper (who was the minister where the debate was to be held) that he was going to present the negative on the possibility of apostasy. Bogard boldly exclaimed "...your folks haven't introduced a new argument in forty years on the question of apostasy. I intend to write my first negative speech and read it, for I know every argument Professor Hardeman will make." E.R. Harper advised N.B. Hardeman of Bogard's plan. So, brother Hardeman organized a complete new line of arguments that caught Bogard off guard and unable to effectively reply to the affirmatives Hardeman made. The impact was devastating to Bogard's effectiveness in the debate since his negative was written to respond to what he thought surely would be the affirmative material. Hundreds if not thousands have been converted to the truth during the various debates Bogard has had with our brethren. It is sad that Ben Bogard could (or would) not recognize and accept the truth. This is a lesson for us in that it shows the difficulty of those entrenched in false doctrine to see the truth clearly.

This debate has been widely recommended since its publication in 1938. Many who attended the debate (or read the book) consider it worthy of required reading prior to allowing a preacher to graduate from school. Hopefully, we are encouraging our young people to read this material prior to going to some of our schools since some schools seem to have wandered off track.

Originally printed in the *West Virginia Christian*, Vol. 13, No. 8, August 2006, p. 3. Reprinted by permission.

Hardeman Tabernacle Sermons Vol. 1 (N.B. Hardeman)

One of the more successful evange-listic efforts of the 20th century would have to be the cooperative gospel meetings in Nashville, TN at Ryman Au-ditorium preached by N.B. Hardeman who was president of Freed-Hardeman College. This reviewer's intention is to present a review of brother N.B. Harde-man's sermons (and other works) over the next few articles. There are several reasons why this is being done, but the most prominent reason is the need for these lessons to be read by every member of the church. The lessons are fundamental and are considered classics in the style of preaching. Writing on the quality of these sermons, Guy N. Woods stated:

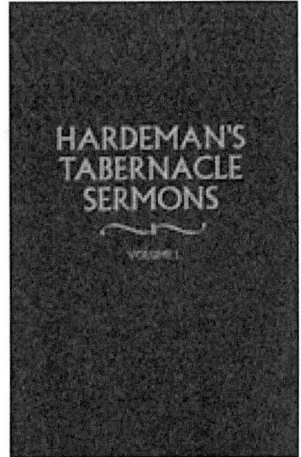

> The Hardeman Tabernacle Sermons, all things considered, is the finest series of sermons ever published in the English Language. As long as the world stands, they will never be surpassed for their amazing simplicity of style, striking clar-ity of diction, and widest possible inclusion of basic and fun-damental truth. The Gospel Advocate Company is perform-ing a service of inestimable value in making available this marvelous material to a younger generation of preachers who may profit greatly not only from the study of the truth presented, and the principles embodied, but who should also master the sermons as models of homiletic skill. All who would be informed in a mode and method of preach-ing now altogether too rare, whether preachers or not, should obtain these sermons.

The first Hardeman Tabernacle Sermons were delivered from March 28 to April 16, 1922. N.B. Hardeman was chosen as the preacher rather than C.M. Pullias who was also a very effective evangelist being considered for the meetings. When the leaders approached brother Pullias about leading the congregational singing rather than preaching, his response was that he would be willing to sweep the floors in order to assist moving the meeting forward. L.L. Brigance assisted in some of the research and outlines of material used by brother Hardeman. It has been reported that L.L. Brigance stated "I cannot preach like brother Hardeman, but I can load his gun."

Attendance figures were estimated to be 6-8,000 people with as many as 2-3,000 being turned away. Two prominent newspapers in Tennessee, The Tennessean and the Nashville Banner printed texts of entire sermons in their coverage of these meetings and the impact on the church abroad was substantial. At the time, and probably since, it was believed that no other preacher of churches of Christ was so extensively quoted or had sermons printed in full by secular papers. Thankfully, these sermons were compiled into a book which has continued to bless countless others.

A list sermon titles include the following: The Bible; Rightly Dividing the Word of Truth; The Power of God's Word; Federalist and Antifederalists; Conversion; The Great Commission; The Conversion of a Civil Officer; The Conversion of a Military Officer; God's Immutable Laws; God's Foolishness vs. Man's Wisdom; What Must I Do To Be Saved?; The Savior's Invitation; Repentance; Baptism; What Church to Join?; Reconciliation; The Terror of the Lord; Reformers and Restorers; Theory and Practice; and The Bible in Business (by C.M. Pullias).

The sermon on Federalists & Antifederalists is an excellent example of a past political controversy that continues to resurface in our nation's courts—does the Constitution's silence on a matter indicate permission or restriction? This principle we often discuss in this manner—does the silence of the scriptures authorize an action or restrictions an action? N.B. Hardeman expressed it this way:

> Do I look upon it [word of God] as a law granting me the liberty to do anything not specifically forbidden therein? Or, on the other hand, have I accepted God's constitution and do I propose to be governed by what it says rather than by what it does not say? [N.B. Hardeman, Hardeman Tabernacle Sermons, Vol. 1, p. 80].

If your preacher is not preaching these types of fundamental lessons, you should insist that he does so. If he refuses, then you need to find a gospel preacher. Preachers should not hesitate to preach these fundamentals because the spiritually mature will always love to hear them, the spiritually immature need to hear them, and the lost must hear these fundamental truths. The Gospel Advocate has reprinted these sermons in paperback and these are currently available.

Hardeman Tabernacle Sermons Vol. 2 (N.B. Hardeman)

As mentioned in the review of Volume 1, one of the more successful evangelistic efforts of the 20th century would have to be Hardeman Tabernacle Sermons delivered at Ryman Auditorium in Nashville, TN at Ryman Auditorium by N.B. Hardeman. The first series of sermons were so well received that the churches made provisions to repeat the effort the following year. The printing of the first volume of sermons had sold nearly 5,000 copies before the second meeting, which was a remarkable result.

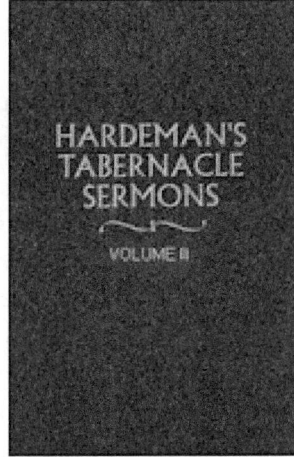

The second series of Hardeman Tabernacle Sermons were delivered from April 1 to April 22, 1923. The media exposure for the second series of lessons was comparable to the first meeting. Between these meetings, brother Hardeman conducted one of the more famous debates on the subject of mechanical instruments of music in worship with Ira Boswell (which was also held in Nashville, TN).

This volume includes biographical information about N.B. Hardeman that discusses his early life, education, marriage, religious background, and various aspects of this multi-talented educator & evangelist. In N.B. H., brother Hardeman explains just how he came to be a preacher of the gospel:

> Brother Freed had an appointment out about sixteen miles east of Henderson, at Enville, right close to my old home, and he decided he couldn't go. Along about Friday or Saturday before the third Sunday (April 18, 1897), he told me

to go out there and make a little talk. Of course I tried to get out of it, but he insisted, so I went, and got along pretty well.

About a month or six weeks after that, he had scheduled a meeting in Juno, TN, out from Lexington. I have always felt there was a trick in this, for he came to me at the last of the week just preceding his appointment and said "I have a meeting commencing Sunday morning and I am not able to go. I want you to go and start it and I will be over right soon, possibly Monday." Well, I went over there and preached Sunday morning & night. Monday morning—no brother Freed! Night came and still he did not arrive. Well, I felt sure he would be there Tuesday. That hope kept on until Thursday. I only had one or two sermons, but I had to preach both day and night till Thursday. When finally Brother Freed came in, a little sheepishly, he said the meeting was doing so well he would go on back home. So I finished out until the following Sunday. That's my start. That was in 1897, and I haven't missed preaching many Sunday's since.

I just drifted into preaching—with some fatherly propulsion from Brother Freed. (N.B. H., p. 155)

This illustrates the importance of encouraging or using "fatherly" (or motherly) propulsion in encouraging our young boys and men to equip themselves to preach the gospel and strive for greater degrees of service in the kingdom.

The following is a list of topics from this volume of sermons: Bible History; Three Great Religions; Believing a Lie; Man's Accountability; The Gospel; Evolution of the Gospel; The Gospel in Earthen Vessels; The Lost Christ; The Rich Fool; Hardening of Pharaoh's Heart; Prayer; The Holy Spirit and His Work; The Blood of Christ; The Church—Its Establishment; The Church—Its Unity; The Church—Its Identity; The Church—Its Work; The Church— Its Worship; Christ and the Church; Why a Member of the

Church of Christ; A Summary and Review; and Instrumental Music.

Hopefully you are hearing these types of lessons from the pulpit where you worship. If not, encourage your preacher to do so immediately. We have many who have failed to heed the warning of the Hebrew writer:

> *For though by this time you ought to be teachers, you need someone to teach you again the first principles of the oracles of God; and you have come to need milk and not solid food. For everyone who partakes only of milk is unskilled in the word of righteousness, for he is a babe. But solid food belongs to those who are of full age, that is, those who by reason of use have their senses exercised to discern both good and evil (Hebrews 5:12-14, NKJV).*

As stated in the review of Volume One, the Gospel Advocate has reprinted these sermons in paperback and these are currently available.

Hardeman Tabernacle Sermons Vol. 3
(N.B. Hardeman)

While I was a student at Freed-Hardeman College (soon to be University), brother E. Claude Gardner (then President) worked with brother Hardeman's grandson, Joe Hardeman Foy, to reprint volumes 1-3 and distribute to preaching students at Freed-Hardeman University. I read an article where brother Gardner was told by an admirer of N.B. Hardeman, "The young preachers will not buy them. Many do not preach these fundamental sermons." Refusing to preach the types of lessons taught in these volumes is an excellent diagnosis of the problem we are facing today. As brother Gardner wrote in the Foreword of Volume 3,

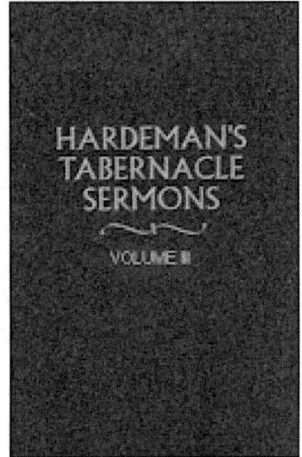

> The sermons N.B. Hardeman preached are the kind which enabled the church to grow and prosper. Because of current conditions both in and out of the brotherhood the sermons brother Hardeman preached should live again. Today the church sorely stands in need of this kind of preaching.

The third Hardeman Tabernacle Gospel Meeting was March 18 – April 1, 1928 again at the famous Ryman Auditorium in Nashville, TN. The following is a list of topics from this volume of sermons:

- Remembering
- Establishment of the Church
- Christ on David's Throne
- Church History of First Century
- The Development of Ecclesiasticism

144

- Catholic Church of Sixteenth Century
- The Primacy of Peter
- The Reformation, No. 1 & 2
- The Restoration; Unity, No. 1, 2 & 3
- Vowing, No. 1 & 2
- The Way
- Authority
- Is the Bible Credible
- Three Prayers
- The Cost of Discipleship
- The Crucifixion of Christ.

Notice the emphasis on church history from the falling away of the church into Roman Catholicism, to the earlier attempt to reform the Roman Catholic Church, to the final plea to return to the Bible and restore the church of the New Testament. Apparently this created quite a sensation among those who prefer sectarianism over what Alexander Campbell often called "New Testament-ism." In the original Foreword of the book, F.W. Smith speaks to the reaction of the sectarians to the preaching of N.B. Hardeman:

> From both sacred and profane history, with which N.B. Hardeman shows himself to be perfectly familiar, it was shown how the church established by the Lord Jesus Christ had departed from the truth. He showed the origin, creed, doctrine, and practice of all the denominations as purely the work of uninspired men, and how far they were from the word of God.
>
> This unusual presentation of historical facts stirred the defenders of sectarianism as they have not been for generations, and many criticisms were hurled at the preacher. However, these only served to emphasize the far-reaching and revolutionary effects of the truth so ably, earnestly, courteously, and kindly presented by N.B. Hardeman, who, modest, unassuming, and void of egotistical mannerisms, is

one of the greatest preachers of the age.

I particularly profited from Hardeman's use of topography to illuminate the misinterpretation of Matthew 16:13-19 by Catholics in the sermon "The Primacy of Peter." Here is what N.B. Hardeman proclaimed:

> Here they are at Caesarea Philippi, a city builded upon a rock and surrounded by a rock wall in which there are gates with a keeper holding the keys. The very stability of this rock founded, rock bounded, and rock surrounded city suggested the idea of the church of our Lord. Hence he said, "Thou art Peter, and upon this rock I will build my church." Now get it. In that imagery Christ is the builder. The rock, which is the great foundation truth that Jesus is the Christ, the Son of God, is the foundation, and Peter is out yonder at the gate holding the keys admitting those who would pass in and out.

> Now, here is a general proposition. It is a violation of the principles of every language, for one character to occupy two different positions in the same illustration at the same time. I repudiate therefore the idea that Peter can play a two-fold part in this scenery. He cannot be represented as a keeper of the gate with the keys in his hand, and at the same time be the foundation upon which the thing rests.

> But that is not all. Paul said, 1 Corinthians 3:10-11, "As a wise master builder, I have laid the foundation, and another buildeth thereon. But let every man take heed how he buildeth thereon. For other foundation can no man lay than that is laid, which

> is Jesus Christ." Therefore, instead of the possibility of Peter's being the foundation of the church to be built by Christ, the exact reverse is true and Peter's position, I want to insist, in this tropical language, is not underneath the structure. His is the gatekeeper and holds the keys in his

hands. The beautiful imagery is destroyed if the Catholic idea were correct. (Page 80-81)

Based on what I hear reported, it seems that some have become either too timid or ashamed of the gospel to have the truth proclaimed along these lines. Jesus taught that the truth would be divisive, but we have others who think they know better in trying to compromise the truth to avoid the possibility of offending others. Accepting religious error at the expense of the truth is not unity but union. Jesus desires unity based upon, not the compromise of, the word of God.

As stated in the review of Volume One, the Gospel Advocate has reprinted these sermons in paperback and these are currently available.

Hardeman Tabernacle Sermons Vol. 4 (N.B. Hardeman)

The fourth Hardeman Tabernacle Gospel Meeting was October 16 – 31, 1938. It would be the last series delivered at the famous Ryman Auditorium in Nashville, TN by N.B. Hardeman. The focus of this series of meetings was more for members of the church. Concern had arisen that congregations in the Nashville, TN area were sliding with digression and some wanted to alert them to the danger and encourage them to return to solid ground. The church had been troubled by efforts of the premillennialists, which is a subject that is dealt with in this series of sermons. It was reported that interest among other congregations outside of Nashville and even Tennessee itself was reflected in the attendance.

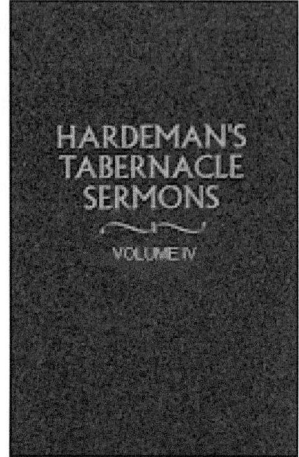

The following is a list of topics from this volume of sermons:

- The Purpose of This Meeting
- Is the Bible the Word of God?
- The Reception of Any Truth Depends Upon Our Attitude Toward It
- Teaching the Word of God
- Is the Gospel, as God Gave It, Adapted to Man, as God Made Him?
- Unity Among Brethren
- Cost of Discipleship
- Essentials and Non-Essentials
- "The Spirit of Christ"
- The Blood-Bought Institution of the New Testament

- The Establishment of the Kingdom
- Premillennialism
- How God Speaks to Man
- The First Sermon Under the Commission
- The Church
- The Vine and the Branches
- Is Christ With Us?
- The Final Exhortation

N.B. Hardeman addressed a concept advocated among those who would deny importance of the penitent believer being immersed in water for remission of sins—essential commands & non-essential commands. In his sermon "Essential and Non-Essentials" he explains:

> Those words [Essential & Non-Essential] are quite common among many professed Christians. Some things are Essentials, some things Non-essentials. The fact is, I came up under expressions of that kind. The implication was that God had commanded lots of things, some of them were important and obligatory upon man; others, while in the Bible, and plainly taught, were just commands. The idea was that we can be saved as well without them as with them. Hence, they are Non-essentials. I think that is the idea of the world in general now. Of course, say they, there are things mentioned in the Bible, but you don't have to respect all of them. Therefore, there are Essentials and Non-essentials. (Pages 99-100)

Hardeman then turns to the Great Commission and shows that God does not give non-essential commands. This is a message the religious world needs to be reminded of (even ones who are not part of the New Testament church). It has been reported that the reporter Ted Koppel stated that the Ten Commandments are commandments, not suggestions. Another way of phrasing that would be—Ten Essentials not Ten Non-Essentials. My concern is that those who claim allegiance to Jesus are minimizing, deflecting, reducing, ridiculing, detracting, and avoiding His teaching. We cannot say we love Christ and ignore his commandments by labeling some as "non-essential" (John 14:15).

Brother E. Claude Gardner wrote this in regards to the Hardeman Tabernacle Sermons, "His five Tabernacle Sermons conducted between 1922 and 1943 had a stabilizing influence in Nashville and in the brotherhood. He dealt with issues facing the church and he called for a return to New Testament Christianity." As stated in prior reviews, the Gospel Advocate has reprinted the Hardeman Tabernacle Sermons in paperback and these are currently available.

Works Cited:

Gardner, E. Claude, "N.B. Hardeman 1874-1965," *The Messenger*, Knoxville, TN: East Tennessee School of Preaching & Missions, November 1997.

Hardeman Tabernacle Sermons Vol. 5 (N.B. Hardeman)

The fifth and final Hardeman Tabernacle Gospel Meeting was November 1-8, 1942. It was delivered at the War Memorial Building and Central Church of Christ. The Ryman Auditorium was not used for this meeting for two reasons. The first was the focus on internal brotherhood lessons. The second was the lean years of WWII had made it less affordable. H. Leo Boles suggested this series of meetings be conducted. Brother Hardeman also preached lessons daily on WLAC during this meeting at the Central Church of Christ facility. The meeting was well supported both financially and in attendance by area churches. Plus, having the additional lessons broadcasted allowed for many others to hear the preaching of N.B. Hardeman. Lessons delivered in the War Memorial Building and in the Central Church of Christ building are both included in the book. Some suggest that this last book of sermons is the best of the five; however, I cannot see any one of these books being superior to any of the others.

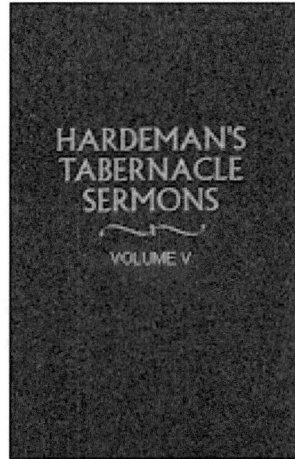

The following is a list of topics from this volume of sermons:

- Is the Bible True?
- Apostasy
- The Identity of the Church
- Paul's Charge to Timothy
- The Mission and Work of the Church
- The Commission as Given by Mark
- The Church
- The Commission as Given by Matthew

- Christianity—A New Religion; Fellowship
- Can a Man Be Saved Outside the Church?
- I Am Debtor
- Aims and Purposes of the Restoration Movement
- The Church—Its Establishment, Its History, and Its Falling Away
- Church Organization
- The All Sufficiency of the Scriptures
- Lecture on European Countries
- Lecture on Italy and Egypt
- Lecture on Palestine

In brother Hardeman's sermon "The All Sufficiency of the Scriptures," he asks a question that all people should ask when they seek to join a church which has a creed, confession of faith, articles of faith, et. al.:

> If your creed contains more than this Bible, won't you admit that it might contain too much? Let me reverse it. If the creed you have adopted, and to which you have sworn allegiance, contains less than the Bible, won't you admit that it might contain too little?

> If, therefore, any creed adopted by any organization contains neither more nor less than does the Bible, then it is exactly like God's book, and, since we have no need of two precisely alike, I am urging that you leave off that which is of human origin and simply take the Bible as your sole creed.

> People misunderstand the church of Christ many times. They ask: "Don't you folks have a creed?" We answer: "Yes." "Don't you have a discipline?" "Sure." "Have you not a confession of faith?" "Certainly so." They next ask to see it and we gladly hand them the New Testament. To it I have subscribed one hundred percent. I have pledged myself to be nothing, to accept nothing, nor do nothing other than what my creed has authorized. (Pages 136-137).

Preaching on the all sufficiency of the Scriptures and the restoration plea will generate both heat and light. Heat will be generated by those who become angry by light of the irrefutable
logic of the restoration plea and the all-sufficient scriptures.
Hopefully those who may become angry at first will be challenged to think more seriously and critically on these vital matters. Such a light will guide them along the straight and narrow
way. While we must be kind hearted to those who are lost, we
must expose the creeds of men without mercy. We must do so
in such a way to minimize the possibility of hurting others who
consider an attack on a creed as an attack on them (or their family). But the creeds of men must be laid bare by the all-sufficient
word of God.

As stated in prior reviews, the Gospel Advocate has reprinted the Hardeman Tabernacle Sermons in paperback and
these are currently available. I recommend the entire set be purchased for the church library as well as your personal library.
One of my favorite stories I heard as a student at Freed-Hardeman University was of a young student who had memorized a
bit too much of one of N.B. Hardeman's sermons to preach at
an area congregation. N.B. Hardeman trained several young
men to preach the gospel. Brother Hardeman was so esteemed
that his students reflected the impact of his instruction to the
point that his preaching students were affectionately referred
to as the "Hardeman Boys." Another one of the "Hardeman
Boys," Hugo McCord, relates the story:

> As the days passed, I became more and more indebted to
> FHC. From N.B. Hardeman I learned that preaching should
> be plain and simple. In my first gospel meeting (at Holland,
> Missouri, three Sundays, June 15-30, 1930), I virtually re-
> cited from memory brother Hardernan's sermons in Vol-
> ume I of his Tabernacle Sermons. I trust I did not say in one
> of them, that "we are thankful tonight to have in the bal-
> cony a company of the Nashville firemen." (Hugo McCord,
> "Sixty-five Years as a Preacher," Spiritual Sword, January

1995, pp. 3-4)

If you know of a young man looking to prepare a lesson, refer him to these sermons. If these were profitable to Hugo McCord in learning to preach, they certainly will be profitable by all.

Attention to Worship:
Exhortations for the Faithful Worship of God
(Sam E. Hester)

For the past two years I have had the privilege of editing our church bulletin. It is a great responsibility and conveyance of trust by the elders. We live in an age of technology unimaginable even within our lifetimes. We have been able to expand the use of our bulletin by emailing a PDF version of it for whoever would like to receive it. The ease with which it can be distributed electronically has made it feasible to utilize our church bulletins in evangelism once again where postage and material costs made it no longer feasible. Even though this has made the bulletin production much easier today than before, sometimes putting your finger on an article for a bulletin can become a challenge when it is complicated by space restrictions. So, when I came across this collection of exhortations assembled by Sam E. Hester, I purchased it with using in the church bulletin primarily in mind although it contains information that can be used in other mediums as well.

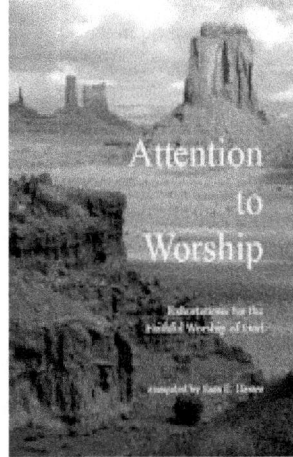

The book contains many various aspects or themes relating to worship including gospel meetings, appropriate attire, attendance, tardiness, congregational singing, study, etc. The book includes a Table of Contents to help locate the particular aspect one is looking to read. There are several pointed reminders of which we need to be reminded. One that has come to my attention is tardiness. We need to remind and be reminded of the impression we leave (whether intentional or not) when we fail to show up for services at the designated time. One wonders if some have failed to realize this is one of the clear principles involved in the Parable of the Virgins in Matthew 25!

As I scan through this collection of exhortations, I found one that I often need to remind myself of:

I Have Never Known

1. A farmer who failed in life because he quit early to attend Wednesday Bible lessons.

2. A businessman who ever lost his business because he closed on Sunday.

3. Anyone who was too tired to go to worship on Sunday & also too tired to go to work on Monday.

4. Anyone ever being made better by staying away from worship because they do not like someone who is there.

5. A farmer who became poverty-stricken because he refused to plow on Sunday but chose to go to worship.

6. A strong spiritual Christian who neglected the assemblies of the church. (pp. 108-109).

This is not the only book that brother Hester has compiled and one would do well to look at his other compilations as well. Brother Sam Hester is Professor of Bible and Director of the Christian Training Series at Freed-Hardeman University. He is also the owner of Hester Publications, which specializes in the short-run production of books that are kept in print because of his dedication. He is also one of the founding members of the "Friends of the Restoration Movement" group, which has been hosting special speakers along this line during the Freed-Hardeman University Bible Lectureship. If you have not visited the website of Hester Publications at hesterpublications.com, I encourage you to do so. You will find many books of interest for your church library. Special pricing is made available for larger purchases. Thanks to brother Hester's love of the church and her history, I have been blessed to add to my library many works that may otherwise have been unavailable.

When the Prodigal is Your Prodigal
(Steve and Kim Higginbotham)

The Higginbotham and Kenney families have known each other for years. The nature of ministry is such that times in each other's presence is limited, but there is still a bond formed. I remember my parents making a special effort to attend Frank's funeral (Steve's father) because they were preaching brothers. Like many others, we were dismayed about Steve's cancer prognosis the Higginbotham family shared with the brotherhood. We join many others who are praying for him and the family. I had heard they were working on this book, *When the Prodigal Is Your Prodigal*, and I was hoping they would be able to release the book despite the medical treatments that are so demanding on their time and energy.

The book is one that every parent and Christian ought to read. The book does detail the particulars of their family's circumstances and despair. I have witnessed from a distance the loss of Steve's father, and the threat to his health, but I was unfamiliar with the torment he and his wife, Kim, were suffering due to one of their children becoming prodigal. While some will find details curious, which will be freely and painfully given, they will better understand the magnitude of their experience and benefit from the efficacy of their writing on this subject. The reason I would encourage others to read this book is to be more aware of the silent pain and suffering some go through and be more sympathetic and compassionate. I have witnessed parents go through emotions akin to what Jacob felt when he cried out when his sons were pressing him to give them care of his

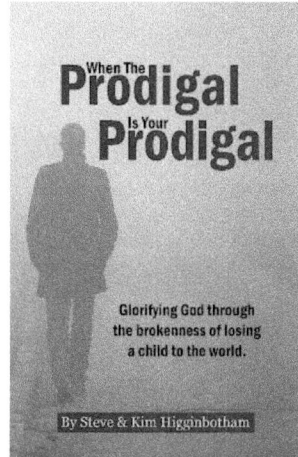

youngest son Benjamin: "My son shall not go down with you, for his brother is dead, and he is left alone. If any calamity should befall him along the way in which you go, then you would bring down my gray hair with sorrow to the grave" (Genesis 42:38 NKJV). Sadly, many suffer in silence and deprive themselves of Christians who are supposed to be burden bearers (cf. Galatians 6:2). Worse, some Christians fail to bear burdens!

The book is an excellent treatment of the subject of church discipline. It deals forthrightly with cop-outs people make to avoid administering discipline to the erring and rebelling. The book deals with the resistance, rather than support, of other Christians who were puzzled how they could withdraw from their prodigal that has gone into the far country of sin. The Higginbotham's have not only "talked the talk" but have "walked the talk" too. Anyone who reads the book will have their eyes opened on how the world can hold faithful Christians who are suffering because of their child's sin in disdain. Kim recounts the nightmare she was made to suffer on a national scale from those who have no regard for God's Word, biblical morality, and faithfulness. The lack of compassion from the so-called tolerant crowd is one that Christians need to be aware of and not naive about even if it is unpleasant. One wonders why anyone would invite more anguish by writing such a book, but after you read the book you will understand better. The book discusses the process by which the Higginbothams turned their private shame into a ministry for those broken by the loss of a child to the far country of sin. It deals forthrightly with those who twist scripture to suit their own agendas. It is an open presentation of the lessons they learned and even the blessings they have received. People who are not Christians will be shocked by this statement: "I would rather attend my son's funeral than to watch him turn his back on God and walk away to never return." The world may recoil at such words, but godly parents fully understand and will pray even more fervently to preserve their family from Satan and the world after reading this book (if they are not living such a nightmare).

Originally printed in the *West Virginia Christian*, Vol. 28, No. 2, February 2021, p. 8. *Reprinted by permission.*

Rightly Dividing The Word: Volume 1 General Hermeneutics (Terry Hightower, Editor)

This book contains some of the most important information needed by every elder, preacher, and Christian: how to rightly divide the word of God and ascertain Bible authority. The study of Hermeneutics is the study of interpreting the Scriptures and their applications to us.

There are all types of unsound voices out there saying such things as "The Bible is not a pattern for us to follow," "We cannot understand the Bible," "There are no absolutes, we cannot know anything for certain," "Drawing logical conclusions based on Scriptures is not right," and "The Scriptures do not say we cannot do such and such." Each of these views is false. This volume will help a Christian to answer all these false concepts and many more criticisms of proof-text preaching and teaching (citing Scriptures for application). In my opinion, a preacher that does not preach book, chapter, verse is not a preacher but an entertainer. The role of a preacher is to be a herald of the gospel. One cannot proclaim the gospel without using the Bible.

This book addresses such themes as: insufficient standards of authority, knowledge of the Truth can be obtained, logic and the Bible are complimentary not contradictory, how to determine Bible authority, how to choose a good translation, pattern theology, the importance of studying a verse in its immediate context, how cults and denominations mishandle the Scriptures, and the silence of the Scriptures is NOT permissive. The book

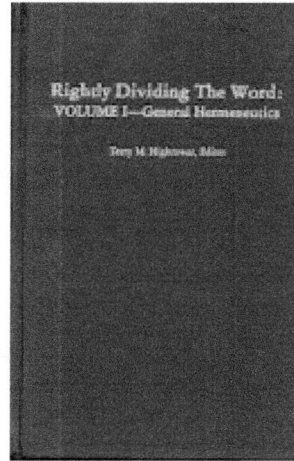

consists of a series of lectures given at the Shenandoah church of Christ and supplemental articles written by some of the most knowledgeable men among us today including Thomas Warren, Perry Cotham, Dave Miller, Wayne Jackson, Alan Highers, Goebel Music, Roy Deaver, and Garland Elkins.

Studying this book will be very profitable to all whether you have small amount of knowledge in the field of Hermeneutics or a mature knowledge of the subject matter. Please take the time and study this book!

Originally printed in *West Virginia Christian*, Vol. 8, No. 2, February 2001, p. 6. Reprinted by permission.

Rightly Dividing The Word: Volume 2
Special Hermeneutics
(Terry Hightower, Editor)

This book is the companion volume to General Hermeneutics previously reviewed. As stressed before, learning to rightly divide the word and ascertain Bible authority is essential for every elder, preacher, and Christian. This is the study of Hermeneutics.

As stated in the Foreword of volume two, the first volume:

> ...primarily involved those matters which apply to all interpreters of literature and to all portions of the Bible, whereas this present volume (II) deals mainly with Special Hermeneutics: definitions and principles which make it easier to interpret literary forms or to convey the meaning found in specific topical areas treated in Biblical materials. Since these forms or themes occur frequently in Scripture, the Bible student often can use such exegetical help. God's divine word is composed of a wide range of writings of different styles and variety of backgrounds. There are poems, songs, prayers, parables, letters, biographical accounts, victory hymns, lamentations, historical catalogs, prophecies, apocalypses, typological writings, statements involving numerology, wisdom writings like proverbs, and on and on and on.

The second volume touches on many of these forms of language and more including personification, allegories, synecdoche, metonymy, irony, sarcasm, satire, similes, and a host of

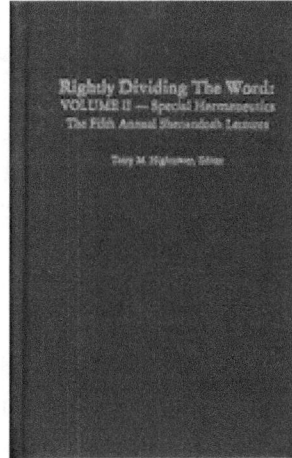

other figures of speech in the Bible. It also deals with examples and culture as it relates to Bible authority.

This book also deals with the "New" Hermeneutic, which is a re-packaging of many false concepts of times past. The recycling of these "houses on sand" is a testament to the importance of continually teaching the fundamentals of God's word. It is tragic that we are losing Christians who have become entangled with the cares of this world or are beaten down with the challenges of life and give up. It is equally tragic if we lose Christians to the "New" Hermeneutic due to it being given an opportunity to survive because of the lack of continual teaching on the fundamentals. Remember one of the lessons from Judges, "When all that generation [of Joshua's day, DRK] had been gathered to their fathers, another generation arose after them who did not know the Lord nor the work which He had done for Israel. Then the children of Israel did evil in the sight of the Lord, and served the Baals; and they forsook the Lord God of their fathers, who had brought them out of the land of Egypt; and they followed other gods from among the gods of the people who were all around them, and they bowed down to them; and they provoked the Lord to anger." (Judges 7:10-12). It is the present generation's responsibility to teach the next generation. I can recall one person lamenting a series of lessons by a preacher on why churches of Christ do not use the mechanical instrument in worship. A few years later in a gospel meeting this same person was grateful for a lesson on the same subject (by the same preacher years later). What was the difference? The person had seen the fruit of not teaching on the fundamentals of rightly dividing God's word. I suspect that this is typical of many congregations which is why the "New" Hermeneutic has achieved the success it has. Hopefully, the leadership of congregations will return to the teaching of the old paths and teach the next generation to walk therein.

The book contains a series of lectures given at the Shenandoah church of Christ and includes supplemental articles supplied by the editor, Terry Hightower, which increase the value of the work. Of particular value is the index of both volumes by author, topic, and scripture reference.

Studying this book will be very profitable to all whether you have small or great amount of knowledge in the field of Hermeneutics.

Originally printed in *West Virginia Christian*, Vol. 9, No. 5, May 2002, p. 8. Reprinted by permission.

The Bible in 3D: God's Word Revealed Through Bible Geography
(Sean Hochdorf, Lectureship Director)

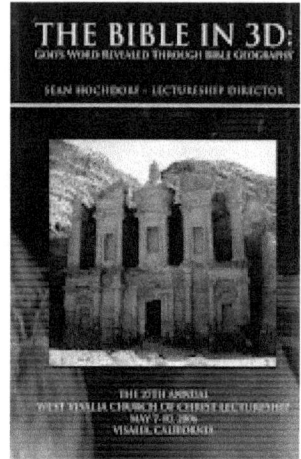

Polycarp (69 – AD 156) was a member of the church who was reported to be a disciple of the apostle John. According to his account, he appears to have been at least 86 years old when he was arrested and put to death. What was his great crime? He refused to burn incense and thus acknowledge that Caesar was Lord. When they pressed him to do so to spare his life, his response is reported to have been "Eighty and six years have I now served Christ, and he has never done me the least wrong: How then can I blaspheme my King and my Savior?" When they threatened to burn him at the stake he stood firm and replied ""Thou threatenest me with Fire which burns for an hour, and so is extinguished; but knowest not the Fire of the Future Judgment of that Eternal Punishment which is reserved for the Ungodly. But why tarriest thou? Bring forth what thou wilt!" Because he was a Christian, meaning he knew that Jesus alone is Lord, he was burned at the stake.

These events occurred in the city of Smyrna. The city of Smyrna was chosen, over other competing Asian cities, by the Roman Empire with the honor of having a temple built to Emperor Tiberius. This was not good news for the church there. As one writer noted:

> Evidently then the cult of Empire and Emperor, of Rome and Rome's Caesar, was a matter of great pride in Smyrna.

Did the Christians refuse to sprinkle incense on the fire which burned before the emperor's bust? Of course they did. To do so would be idolatry. They could not call Caesar Lord when Jesus was their Lord. But their unwillingness to conform was interpreted by the common people as a disgraceful and even treacherous lack of patriotism. — John R.W. Stott, "What Christ Thinks of the Church," Preaching for Today, Grand Rapids, MI: Wm. B. Eerdmans Publishing Company, 1958, p. 37.

Many Christians suffered at Smyrna including Polycarp, who was among many who died here for their allegiance to the Lord Jesus Christ. I find it very interesting that Smyrna is one of the churches of Asia Minor that were written to in Revelation by the apostle John. Again, Polycarp is believed to have been one of John's disciples and the letter to Smyrna dealt with pending persecution that was to fall upon Christians. The events surrounding Polycarp's death bring what John revealed to this church over fifty years prior—*"Do not fear any of those things which you are about to suffer. Indeed, the devil is about to throw some of you into prison, that you may be tested, and you will have tribulation ten days. Be faithful until death, and I will give you the crown of life"* (Revelation 2:10, NKJV). Polycarp is just one recorded example of fulfilling what Jesus rightfully expects—be faithful to Him up to and including your death.

I became more interested in learning about the city of Smyrna and *The Bible in 3D: God's Word Revealed Through Bible Geography* was a treasure of information. This lectureship book deals with several key biblical places from three vantage points—lectures on key places and corresponding events, an index to the Bible based on places of the Bible and a very informative and attractive set of maps. I found myself really captivated by much of the material in this book. Since it was published in 2006, it contains a wealth of information from past scholars and recent discoveries as well. This would be an excellent addition to the church library dealing with a subject that some may have not given as much detail to as in times past.

Originally printed in *West Virginia Christian*, Vol. 17, No. 12, December 2010, p. 8. Reprinted by permission.

From God's Mind to Man's Pen, Volume 1 (Sean Hochdorf, Editor)

This is a lectureship book from the 28th Annual West Visalia church of Christ Lectureship in West Visalia, CA conducted in 2007. This is actually a two-volume set, but this review will focus on the first volume which deals with matters relating to the text of the Bible in four different, but interconnected, areas: inspiration, canonization, transcription and translation. Knowledge in each of these four areas is critical to effectively answer questions such as "How can we know the Bible is from God?," "How do we know we have all the books of the Bible and that the ones we do have actually belong there?" "How can we know that the Bible has been faithfully copied and transmitted to us over the centuries?" and "Can I rely on my English translation of the ancient languages of the Bible?" All of these are highly relevant questions and ones which deserve serious attention. This lectureship book does a fine job of explaining these matters in a straightforward manner that is not overly technical but does not sacrifice scholarship for simplicity.

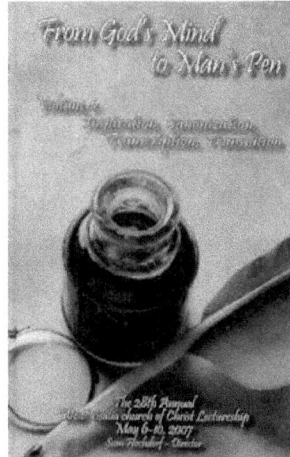

It appears the West Visalia congregation sought to conduct a very informative lectureship and if certain subjects were unable to fit the schedule, then the leadership sought qualified writers to write lectures for the book. This makes the lectureship book even more informative than merely attending the lectures alone. It is readily apparent that a lot of planning and detail work went into the making of this book.

There are excellent articles relating to evidences for the inspiration of the Scriptures, whether inspiration was at the "thought" or "word" level, and the impact of archaeology on the accuracy and inspiration of the Scriptures. There are also excellent articles on whether or not the Catholic Church gave us the Bible and about other books by Gnostic writers. Included are chapters dealing with matters such as the Received Text compared with the Critical Text, the difference between Higher and Lower Criticism and an excellent discussion about the full picture of those "copyists' errors" that all would do well to read. Included is a chapter by B.J. Clarke on whether or not Mark 16:9-20 belongs in the Bible or not that one will find informative. These is also a review of some of the more reputable translations accepted among conservative scholars such as the KJV, NKJV, ASV, NASV, NIV, ESV and others.

The articles are well written with extensive citations to follow-up with additional research for the dedicated student. Some of the subjects dealt with in this series of lectures are complex. One may not agree with every point in any book on this scale of subject matter; however, *From God's Mind to Man's Pen* is a valuable research tool from a conservative viewpoint of the Scriptures for one's study of the One who guided man's hand in the writing of His word!

Originally printed in *West Virginia Christian*, Vol. 20, No. 1, January 2013, p. 8. Reprinted by permission.

Christ or the Qur'an?
(Evertt L. Huffard)

While a student at Freed-Hardeman University, I had the opportunity to take a course entitled Leviticus, Numbers & Deuteronomy under the instruction of Evertt Huffard. There were several fascinating things that I learned from this class and was blessed by brother Huffard's extensive knowledge from touring Bible Lands. One of the subjects he taught was "The Pillars of Islam" which was requested by the Henderson Church of Christ as well.

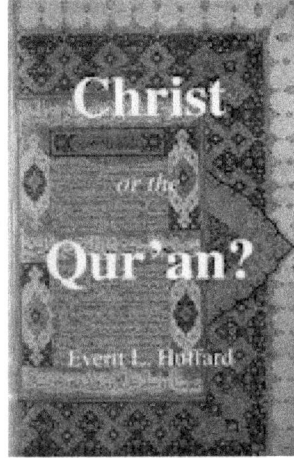

That Islam is one of the fastest growing religions in the world and is a threat to Christianity is fact. Sadly, many have only a very limited knowledge of the Muslim religion. Knowing the backgrounds and claims of Judaism, Christianity & Islam will increase one's understanding of the turmoil in the Middle East. All three religions trace their roots to Abraham. Both Judaism and Islam look at Jerusalem as a holy place in their religion. (Some in Christianity still look to Jerusalem as a religious place while NT Christians realize there is no longer any connection between Jerusalem and Christian worship today.) Since these three religions are incompatible with each other and each has ties with Jerusalem, we should not be surprised about the conflict around this city and surrounding areas.

One may be surprised to learn that Islam traces its roots to Mohammed who was born in Mecca in AD 570. Mohammed professed he had a series of revelations which were recorded to make the Muslim's Qur'an, which they consider to be the word of God.

Islam's view of Jesus is intriguing. Muslims deny that Jesus was crucified and raised from the dead. They believe Jesus was a great teacher and prophet; however, Mohammed was a greater prophet. In addition to deny historical facts surrounding Jesus' live, they discredit the teachings of the apostles and other New Testament writers claiming that Jesus did not say some of the things they claimed that he said. While outside of the Bible there is evidence testifying to his crucifixion and resurrection, there is little to no evidence demonstrating and proving Jesus was a great teacher and prophet outside of the New Testament. Indeed Jesus Christ is the most controversial figure the world has ever seen! Indeed Jesus' divinity, goodness, teaching, and New Testament witnesses stand together with the Old Testament.

One of the admirable traits of the Islam religion is their emphasis on living a lifestyle according to their doctrine (even though the doctrine is false). Muslims have five pillars: Shahada (confession of one God and Mohammed as His prophet), Salat (pray five times a day), Zakat (giving of alms), Saum (fasting), and Hajj (pilgrimage to Mecca during one's life).

These and other interesting facts about Islam are presented in this book. The book is recommended as a good early reference to lead to further research if one desires to dig a bit deeper into this major world religion. The book should provide a good perspective of this religion and will provide a framework to guide for further study.

Evertt Huffard graduated from Abilene Christian University in 1946 with a Bachelor's Degree in Bible. He received his Master's Degree in Bible from Eastern New Mexico State University. He did local church work in New Mexico, Arizona, and Texas for 15 years before entering mission fields abroad in Jerusalem from 1963 to 1970, Beirut, Lebanon from 1971 to 1974, and Amman, Jordan from 1975 to 1979. He has led several missionary trips and conducted tours of the Holy Land for several years. Evertt Huffard was a minister for the churches of Christ at

Independence, Finger, Milan, and Rutherford during his life in Henderson. He retired from Freed-Hardeman as a teacher in 1992, but continued to work with student recruitment for the Bible Department. For his many years of service in various capacities in the kingdom, he was awarded an Honorary Doctorate Degree from Freed-Hardeman University in 1997. He was an able teacher, evangelist, Christian gentleman, and good friend. Brother Huffard passed away March 7, 2004.

Originally printed in the *West Virginia Christian*, Vol. 12, No. 10, October 2005, p. 8. Reprinted by permission.

Stronger Than Ever
(Jason Jackson)

"Life is filled with swift transition…" goes the popular hymn and indeed it is. Life is filled with transitions, changes—joys and challenges; but also adversities, sickness, setbacks, uncertainties, temptations and trials. Sometimes we may seem plagued with various difficulties to the point we think we are overwhelmed, but often can look around and find someone we would not want to change places with. Even though we can find someone in worse shape than ourselves, the "misery loves company" policy is not always comforting. How can we get through this life, but live it to the fullest? The only life that is truly fulfilling is the Christian life, and the only book to show us the Christian life is God's Book, the Bible. Brother Jason Jackson's work, *Stronger than Ever: Heavenly Advice for Earthly Life and the True Stories of Real People Who Overcame Adversity and Are Strong Because of the Power of Christ*, is an important resource for those who both need to prepare for difficult times that will come (cf. Ecclesiastes 12:1f) or weather the storms that have risen in our lives. Do we really trust God and His word? Really trust? In whom do we place our trust? These are important questions we should reflect on seriously and re-examine our lives accordingly.

For example, Robert Plant wrote these lyrics in tribute to his wife: *"If the sun refused to shine, I would still be loving you. When mountains crumble to the sea, there will still be you and me."* It is a wonderful thought in regards to marital love (although not original with Robert Plant); however, marital love is

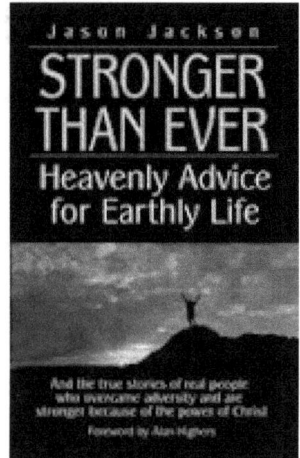

far short in comparison to God's love for us individually—both quantitatively and qualitatively. A Christian married couple is enveloped by God's love for both of them—before, during and after their marriage and respective lives. The Psalmist wrote these words showing God's love for us and how much we can depend and rely upon Him: *"God is our refuge and strength, a very present help in trouble. Therefore we will not fear, even though the earth be removed, and though the mountains be carried into the midst of the sea; though its waters roar and be troubled, though the mountains shake with its swelling"* (Psalm 46:1-3, NKJV). Drawing from this Psalm, Jason Jackson writes:

> How bad can things get in life? This psalm envisions the worst. How crucial it is that we teach our children, "No matter what happens to us in this life, we must never doubt God's love for us. No matter what, always trust in God." Look at the history of God's reliability, this psalm implores. Even if he should permit suffering in our lives, it is a divine complement to his glory (cf. 2 Thess. 1:3-5). (Page 178).

This book offers straightforward teaching from the Scriptures and advice from the experiences of others on how to live a life in spite of setbacks and adversity. It discuses adversities created by our own sins but also adversities created by the sins of others or events that appear to have no explanation whatsoever. Jason Jackson makes the excellent point that God is always the solution, not the cause of the problem. Some tend to dismiss the fortification of one's faith from the word of God (Rom. 10:17) and that is a grave error. We fail oftentimes because we do not believe, we do not believe oftentimes because we have not studied, we have not studied because....

Some fail to fully understand that a victorious life is not one that ends at the grave. There is a popular motto that states "Success is a Journey, Not a Destination." While there is truth in that, the Christian life is both the journey and the destination. This book will provide sound counsel from the Scriptures on how to prepare ourselves and our children so we can be as Jeremiah described: *"Blessed is the man who trusts in the LORD, and whose hope is the LORD. For he shall be like a tree planted by the waters, which spreads out its roots by the river, and will not fear when heat comes; but its leaf will be green, and will not be anxious in the year of drought, nor will cease from yielding fruit"* (Jeremiah 17:8-9, NKJV).

Originally printed in the *West Virginia Christian*, Vol. 17, No. 11, November 2010, p. 8. Reprinted by permission.

The Acts of the Apostles from Jerusalem to Rome (Wayne Jackson)

The establishment and growth of the New Testament church is very accurately written by the physician Luke in the book of the New Testament known as "Acts." The church grew from a relatively small group on the Pentecost following Jesus' crucifixion to over 20,000 by the death of Stephen. It would continue to grow, reaching huge numbers to the point that the city of Rome even had more than 100,000 Christians. Indeed, the history of the establishment and growth of the church is exciting to read and study.

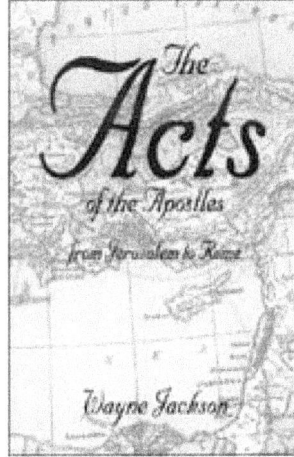

Wayne Jackson has written an excellent commentary on the book of Acts that is exciting to read as one studies Acts. I have had a copy of the book and have also secured copies of the book for my children to read as they grow older. I suggested a congregation use this book for their study in the adult class since they were beginning a study on Acts. At the time, a special price was offered for a case of Jackson's book. They decided to go ahead and use the book. They were very pleased with the book. In fact, the only complaint they had about the book was the text from Acts at the beginning of a new section was too small. (The writing done by Wayne Jackson was large enough to read; however the text for Acts is in smaller print and hard to read for some.) The book is written in such a way that it makes sitting down and reading it from start to finish a very rewarding and enjoyable experience. Sometimes commentaries are not known for the easy reading, but brother Jackson has written a very profitable book for all to be able to read, understand, and learn more about events during the growth of the early church.

The book is around 450 pages and is filled with historical background, supplemental information from historical sources, and archaeological finds that have silenced some of the charges of critics against the writing of Luke as inaccurate. Indeed, Luke was an accurate historian and archaeology has always confirmed this to be true.

In the Appendix are articles on themes that relate to the book of Acts and are very profitable reading. The Appendix includes the following subjects: Miracles, Demons, The Historicity of Jesus, The Trial of Jesus, The Use of "Believe" in Acts, The Epistles of Paul Arranged Chronologically With Pertinent Data, and Outline of the Book of Acts.

Wayne Jackson preaches for the church of Christ in Stockton, CA and has done so for many years. He has also written and published the Christian Courier, which is a monthly periodical on Biblical Studies that I highly recommend. He has also written several other commentaries and books on various religious subjects. Occasionally there will be a special bargain pack of all of his books currently in print. I encourage all congregations to seek to add all of his works to the church library. He is a widely respected writer among us. I have known Wayne Jackson now for several years and went to school with his sons, Jared and Jason, and one of his daughters-in-law, Sandy. If you have not visited ChristianCourier.com and read the wealth of material available for free, then you need to do so. His wife also has a website called "Women of Hope." His son, Jared, also writes material for children called "Christian Courier for Kids" that is excellent.

Originally printed in the *West Virginia Christian*, Vol. 11, No. 11, January 2004, p. 8. Reprinted by permission.

The Bible and Science
(Wayne Jackson)

Does science contradict or confirm the Bible? An interesting question! The answer often depends on what one accepts as "science." The Bible does not contradict scientific facts; however, there have been contradictions between the Bible and scientific *theories* or *hypotheses*. Some would claim there is no difference in the statement just written; however, they would be mistaken. Scientific theories come and go; however, facts remain. One should keep this distinction in mind when examining the subject of the Bible and Science. Some atheists attempt to blur the lines between scientific facts and scientific theories; e.g., evolution is a scientific theory, but one must remain focused on facts when looking at a comparison between the Bible and science.

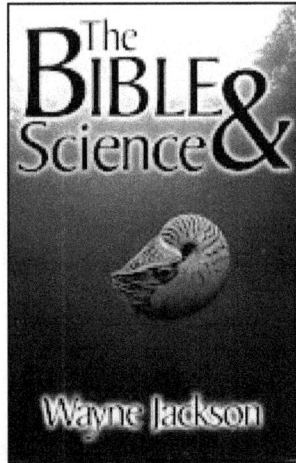

An excellent book showing the scientific accuracy of the Bible is Wayne Jackson's *The Bible and Science*. This book examines several areas of science and shows that when the Bible touches on these areas of science it does so accurately. Fields of science the book examines include astronomy, oceanography, geology, biology, anthropology, and others.

Brother Jackson does an excellent work of pointing out that there are limitations of science, despite the claims of some modern fanatical evolutionary scientists. He also cites examples of where scientists have missed the mark on more than one occasion. He also discusses alleged inaccuracies of the Bible in relation to science. It should be noted that scientific theories are not the only sources of perceived conflict between Science and the

Bible. Some have either mistranslated or misinterpreted the Bible resulting in perceived contradictions; however, further analysis of the Biblical text revealed no actual contradiction.

The Bible & Science also discusses well known scientists who believed the Bible and went on to make incredible discoveries. Men such as Johann Kepler, Blaise Paschal, Robert Boyle, Isaac Newton, Michael Faraday, Louis Pasteur, George Washington Carver, and Wernher von Braun. Quite an impressive group of scientists who did not see a conflict between science and the Bible, and the list could be expanded. We truly live in a time of impressive scientific discovery. The more scientists explore, the far more complex matters appear than they originally thought. One wonders if some of these scientists have not given consideration to the principle that a greater degree of complex design points to a greater, more complex mind which created these designs! Wernher von Braun is an example of a scientist who saw no conflict between modern scientific inquiry and the existence of God:

> "It is difficult for me to understand a scientist who does not acknowledge the presence of a superior rationality behind the existence of the universe as it is to comprehend a theologian who would deny the advance of science. Far from being independent or opposing forces, science and religion are sisters...There is certainly no scientific reason why God cannot retain the same position in our modern world that He held before we began probing His creation with the telescope and cyclotron" (As quoted by Wayne Jackson, The Bible & Science, p. 126).

Perhaps it would be well to remind ourselves that the issue is not just the harmonization of the Bible with Science. The critical issue is the explanation of Bible writers who wrote thousands of years ago. These ancient writers not only wrote correctly about scientific matters but also avoided some of the superstitious nonsense long refuted by scientists years ago which one finds in other ancient writings. How were these writers of the Bible able to reveal scientific matters beyond their ability to prove? They were guided by the mind that created them all including the book that tell us so—God.

Originally printed in *West Virginia Christian*, Vol. 19, No. 8, August 2012, p. 8. Reprinted by permission.

The Bible On Trial
(Wayne Jackson)

In the earlier days of the Restoration Movement, J.W. McGarvey wrote extensively to combat modernists who were attacking the integrity of the Bible. For example, McGarvey's book *Jesus & Jonah* is a direct response to the modernistic attack to deny the miraculous intervention of God with Jonah. The modernist seeks to treat the text of Jonah as an allegory in order to claim it was more a work of fiction rather than fact. McGarvey pointed out that Jesus quoted the events as literal and even applied the encasement in the sea creature of Jonah with the encasement of His own body in the tomb (Matthew 12:38-41). Who will you believe—Jesus or the radical critic?

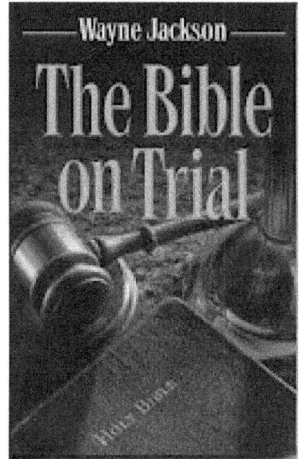

Sadly, there are those of among our brotherhood who have been influenced by such modernists. In October 2008 issue of The Christian Chronicle, there were two reviews of the soon to be released liberal/modernist "hit piece" on the Bible from ACU Press, *The Transforming Word*, by Editor-in-Chief, Mark Hamilton, Ph.D. In his review, Cecil May made the following observation about its treatment of Isaiah, "So the commentary says at least three authors over the course of three centuries wrote this long, prophetic book, though Jesus and the apostles quote from all parts of it and invariably ascribe its words to Isaiah." Again, who knows best, Jesus or these radical critics? Make no mistake! This product from ACU is a direct attack on the integrity of the Scriptures. Here is a recommendation—do not buy this product from ACU! An even better recommendation—purchase Wayne

Jackson's book *The Bible on Trial* in order to protect yourself and the congregation from these assaults on the Bible. I had the pleasure of discussing his book with brother Jackson. He mentioned that the book is partly in response to this one volume commentary from ACU Press. However, there are few direct references to the ACU product in the book since it is broader in scope to include these attacks and others from an array of critics. By the time I finished reading brother Jackson's book, I had the same feeling as when I have read J.W. McGarvey's defense against the radical critics of his day—if the matter were not so serious it would be funny how they have twisted themselves into such a ridiculous state! I stand amazed at the Bible, woven-by-God, and its ability to withstand criticisms of its integrity from assaults unknown by its writers when directed by the Holy Spirit.

The Bible on Trial draws on brother Jackson's excellent material in the *Christian Courier* plus it is supplemented by additional material he has recently written to make a stalwart defense of the Bible. The material is very enjoyable reading and includes quotations from luminaries of the past who served as presidents, judges, scientists, et al., who recognized the integrity of the Scriptures. Brother Jackson cites conservative writers outside of the brotherhood who have made similar investigations into the Bible. Also, brother Jackson cites the more prevalent works of radical critics so one can know their works as to guard against them. Brother Jackson states the purpose of *The Bible on Trial* as:

> The biblical documents are characterized by an amazing variety of evidences that authenticate the Book's claim of divine origin. In this volume some of these proofs will be discussed. Too, theories and arguments of the Bible's hostile critics will be addressed. Let infidelity put the Scriptures on trial. Let the prosecution attempt to make the case that the Old Book is a mere fraud. The defense will respond. The reader will be the jury, and the verdict will be reflected in the lives of those who judge the case. Ultimately, all will

stand before the Great Judge and give account for their verdict! (p. xv.)

Do not miss this vital book, *The Bible on Trial*. Purchase copies for your personal & church libraries, for your children & grandchildren, and begin a signup list for members of the congregation to purchase the book. Possibly the congregation may pay the freight expense as an extra incentive for members to purchase this book for themselves. Encourage lessons from this material to be preached from the pulpit and taught in classrooms. Do not miss this significant contribution by Wayne Jackson to fortify our faith from attacks without, and now sadly within, upon the Christian faith.

Originally printed in the *West Virginia Christian*, Vol. 16, No. 2, February 2009, p. 2. Reprinted by permission.

Bible Words & Theological Terms Made Easy
(Wayne Jackson)

Those who know me well realize I am an admirer of religious books and an avid student of Biblical Hebrew and Greek words and their usage. Some may not realize that, while I am a graduate of Freed-Hardeman University, I do not have a degree in Bible or Biblical Languages. I must rely more heavily on the research of others who have dedicated their lives to study one of the many areas relating to the Bible—language, geography, archaeology, apologetics, etc. As a consequence, I am always looking for materials that range in degree of difficulty with an eye for materials that will help someone new to an area of study whether they are a mature Christian not as familiar in a particular disciple or a new convert beginning their journey to a greater knowledge of God's word. I have often admired radio commentator Rush Limbaugh's use of the expression "making the complex understandable." Indeed there are things that are either complex because the subject is deep and weighty or are complex because some desire to make things appear to be more complex than may actually be. Wayne Jackson usually writes at the level for the beginning to medium-level student but does so from a scholar standpoint that truly makes the "complex understandable." He founded and edited the Christian Courier for over 40 years. If you are not reading the Christian Courier, then it is highly recommended you begin doing so. Wayne Jackson's writings can also be found on the Internet at christiancourier.com.

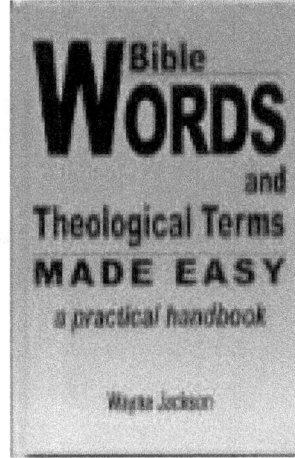

This practical handbook is just that—practical. As Jackson writes on the back cover:

> This volume has not been designed for scholars who have the ability, the time, and the resources to consult compositions that are much more erudite than this abbreviated effort. This book is intended for the average Christian student, the new convert, the Bible class teacher, or even the busy minister, who, on occasion, may need to utilize a quick reference source.

Wayne's introduction to the work is excellent and should be read first. I particularly enjoyed his discussion about whether the words or thoughts are inspired. He drives the point home when he wrote *"Jesus once declared that man must direct his life by the "words" that proceed from God (Mt. 4:4). If those "words" are not to be found in the Bible, where, pray tell, are they?"* (Page v).

This reference work is more than a discussion of words found in the Bible. It also includes entries for each book of the Bible with a concise overview of the book. Plus, terms that are used in reference to Bible study are found; e.g., exegesis. Plus, there are terms that are used in religious discussion among various groups that are defined (and corrected when necessary) such as the rapture, extreme unction, universalism, etc. There are an estimated 8,600 Hebrew and Aramaic words and 5,600 Greek words in the Bible. (The number of English words exceeds 6,000.) One can literally spend their entire lives in study of these words and be enriched by doing so. This book, which is approximately 200 pages, is far from comprehensive but it is not meant to be. This book is intended as a starting point for those who want to begin their journey of learning more about the words of the Bible and related words used in theological circles. It is a valuable reference work to begin this journey on the right step.

Biblical Figures of Speech
(Wayne Jackson)

How many can remember arguing with our siblings and use an expression that our parents heard and we were in trouble. Some of us may have been tempted to use the line "It is just a figure of speech!" as if that helped the matter any. Figures of speech can get us in a lot of trouble if we are not careful to understand what exactly they mean.

The same is true with figures of speech in the Bible—we better recognize figures of speech or it can get us in trouble as well. Wayne Jackson does an excellent job of dealing with two serious mistakes that have led many to serious misinterpretation of the Scriptures—Mistaking the Literal for the Figurative and Mistaking the Figurative for the Literal. He gives very good tools one should use to identify figurative language; e.g., when the sense of the expression contradicts other plain nonfigurative passages.

One may not realize just how large the subject of figures of speech in the Bible can be. E.W. Bullinger's Figures of Speech Used in the Bible is over 1100 pages. Bullinger catalogs some 200 distinctive figures of speech in the Bible, but estimates there are over 500 instances of figures in the Bible. That makes the study quite daunting. One should have a good working knowledge of this field, and Wayne Jackson's byline of the book "a practical guide to understanding the figurative language of the Bible" is quite accurate.

Wayne Jackson has chapters dealing with specific types of figures of speech including similes, similitudes, allegories,

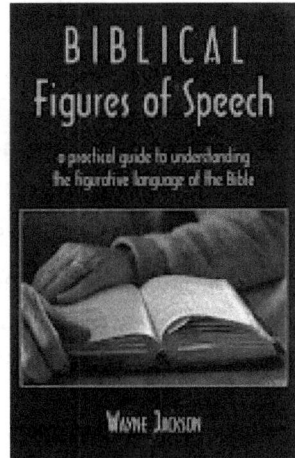

metaphors, metonymy, synecdoche, hyperbole, prolepsis, parables and typology. For those of us whose eyes begin to glaze over when discussing the difference between a metaphor and a simile, the book gives biblical example of these figures that are very enriching. In the chapter on Metonymy, Jackson writes:

> The English term "metonymy" derives from two Greek roots, meta (a change), and onoma (name), hence, "a change in name." The word has come to signify the process whereby the **name** of an object is **changed** to something else for the purpose of intensifying a comparison. An illustration will help clarify the nature of this figure of speech.
>
> A group of Pharisees once warned Jesus that Herod Antipas wanted to kill him. The Lord responded, "Go and tell that fox, 'Behold, I cast out demons and perform cures today, and tomorrow, and the third day I finish my course'" (Lk. 13:32 ESV). Christ might have said, "Herod is **like** a fox." Had he expressed it in that way, he would have employed a simile. Or, he could have suggested, "Herod is a fox." That would have been a metaphor. Instead, he dramatized the matter even more when he said, "Go tell that fox!" The ruler's name is changed to the animal of comparison; Herod **becomes** the fox! The Lord may have been capitalizing upon the tendency of the fox toward malicious destructiveness; hence, the expression may be roughly equivalent to our term "varmint." Such would surely harmonize with the ruler's character—this weakling who beheaded God's prophet (John the Baptizer) at behest of an evil woman. (Jackson, pp. 91-92).

Biblical Figures of Speech is very practical and informative. It is a work to introduce one to the field of hermeneutics—the interpretation of the Scriptures. If one does not know where to begin in this area of study, this is an excellent book to start with.

Fortify Your Faith
(Wayne Jackson)

On the title page is a fuller title for this continually relevant work by Wayne Jackson, "Fortify Your Faith...In an age of doubt." In the days when Jesus walked the earth, there were at least three responses to Him. First, there were believers who recognized with absolute certainty based on the Scriptures and accompanying signs/proofs performed by Jesus and His disciples that Jesus is the Son of God. Second, were the unbelievers, the ones who in spite of ample evidence refused to accept Jesus truly came from His Father in Heaven. Third was the sort who did not really care to investigate the actual evidence. This is like Pontius Pilate when he pejoratively asked Jesus at his trial "What is truth?" Sadly, today we have too many who ought to be believers but are more like Pilate in that they are not true seekers of the Truth. It is not that there is no evidence. It is not that the evidence is all that difficult to find. It is not that the evidence is inconvenient to weight. No, the primary reason that more are becoming like Pilate is refusal to "...prove all things, hold fast to that which is good." Notice that this is the challenge the Bible makes...search, prove & know that it is indeed the revelation of God to mankind! Too few are forfeit the challenge and are like Esau selling their birthright for a bowl of pleasures that last for a season. Do not let this happen to you or your loved ones. There are many excellent sources of evidence for Christianity. Wayne Jackson's book, *Fortify Your Faith*, is a brief but powerful presentation of the evidence dealing with the existence of God, the fallacy of

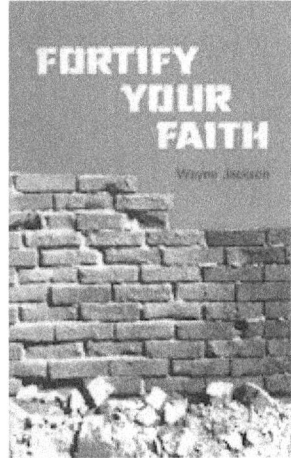

evolution, the unholy alliance of forcing evolution into creation-ism, the meaning of inspiration, and the evidence for the inspi-ration hence authority of the Scriptures. The material is truly ex-cellent even though the edition I have is 1974. But do not let a book that is over 30 years old cause you to pass it by. It illus-trates just how long the evolutionists' game has been lost by failing to not only prove their case, and their inability to answer how creationism fits more in harmony with true science then their untenable theory. The perpetuation of Darwinian Evolu-tion survives more from ignorance than an objective pursuit of truth. Here is a question that is found in *Fortify Your Faith* to consider with your friends. Brother Jackson writes:

> Time is measured in various ways. The earth revolves around the sun every 365 days, the year. It is inclined 23.5 degrees on its axis, determining the seasons. The moon re-volves around the earth each 30 days, the month. The day is determined by the rotation of the earth on its axis each 24 hours. Thus, the natural movements of the solar system mark the years, seasons, months and days; but what deter-mines the week? (Page 35.)

That sure is a good question for those who seek to force evo-lution into the Bible via the Day-Age Theory is it not? Brother Jackson proceeds to quote Alexander Campbell who recognized the significance of this fact back in 1859 when Campbell noted in *Familiar Lectures on the Pentateuch*,

> This is a question of great importance [where did the week come from?]—a question that staggers the boldest of infi-dels, and the most expert of theorists. The subject has de-veloped much ingenious thought, and profound reasoning, but we affirm that nothing on earth or in heaven can be assigned as an argument for the week, aside from the fact that the heavens and the earth were created in six days of twenty-four hours each. (Page 35.)

If you know a person struggling with their faith and want to provide them evidence to help strengthen their faith, then provide them with a copy of Wayne Jackson's book, *Fortify Your Faith*. If you can afford to do so, purchase a copy and read it in public places. If someone asks about the content, give him or her the book to read. Who knows what will come of that! (Be sure to include the church address & phone.) It is brief but powerful reading.

Originally printed in the *West Virginia Christian*, Vol. 23, No. 11, November 2016, p. 8. *Reprinted by permission.*

The Mythology of Modern Geology
(Wayne Jackson)

What an excellent title for such an important topic! Indeed the Evolutionary Uniformitarianism dogma is just that—a myth! One finds it ironic that evolutionists slander Christians with charge that our faith is based on a book of myths when a clearer example of evolutionary myths would be hard to find.

This booklet contains important information; which is devastating to one of the main pieces of "evidence" for an ancient earth. Uniformitarianism argues the layers of the earth have been laid over great spans of time. As brother Jackson points out the number of years it took to complete this layering depend on how much time the evolutionists need for their theory. A point that Wayne Jackson makes that should not be overlooked is that the amount of time estimated for the creation of these layers and the age of the earth tends to double roughly every 20 years for the last century! Jackson cites various estimates ranging from 4.3 billion years to 70 billion years, to a trillion years, and another estimate where probably all evolutionists will end up—"infinitely old."

The book points out several impasses for evolutionary uniformitarianism—missing layers, shuffled layers, layers "millions of years" old on top of layers much younger with several layers between the two, fossils in the wrong layers, and one of the more damaging pieces of evidence—polystrate fossils (fossils that intersect multiple layers of strata). How does one explain a fossilized tree trunk that bisects multiple layers of strata when

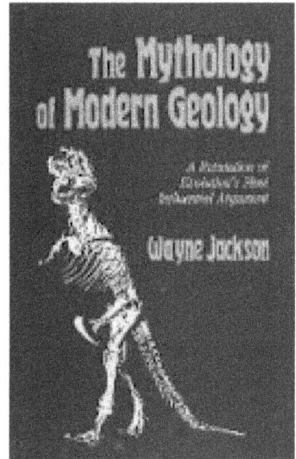

the layers are millions (or billions) of years old? Of course evolutionists have a response, but is their response convincing? Some evolutionists point to excavations that have polystrate fossils in layers that have been recently been laid in place. A follow-up question—if a person can find a polystrate tree fossil in multiple layers that have recently been laid down, then how does one differentiate some layers as "recent" and other layers as "millions of years" old when they are of similar depths? Plus, keep in mind that if all the strata layers were intact "uniformly"; i.e., no missing layers, the depth would be 130 miles deep. However the actual depth of the layers of Earth strata is 25-30 miles. How can layers claimed to be laid down over "millions of years" when trying to date the earth as "infinitely old" on one hand can then be claimed to be laid down in "few years" in an attempt to explain away the polystrate fossil argument but keep the earth strata layer still around 30 miles deep?

Of course, the evolutionists are going to continue their assaults against Christianity and the Bible. Wayne Jackson quotes Alexander Campbell whose statement in 1859 illustrates that attacks against the Genesis account of a young earth being created in six 24-hour days have been going on for some time. It illustrates that evolutionists have been trying to prove their case for nearly 150 years yet many scientist continue to not believe the evolutionary propaganda. Guess the evolutionists need more time, again! The full statement by Alexander Campbell reads:

> We are aware that some writers of modern, as well as of ancient, time, think the Mosaic account of creation should be discarded as erroneous, because the various strata of earth, according to Geology, evince a higher antiquity than five or six thousand years. The geological theory differs in some respects, from the record given by Moses. Nevertheless, we affirm his statement to be true, and shall stand or fall by it; because it does not conflict with the scope and meaning of the six days labor, as we understand them. We place the inspired record, as given by Moses, under a divine

commission, against all the theories founded upon nature or science, as interpreted by man; and we believe the Mosaic account will grow brighter and brighter, as the geological theory fades and recedes into comparative oblivion. (Alexander Campbell, Familiar Lectures on the Pentateuch, p. 69.)

This booklet is informative reading that every adult, parent, student should read. It is affordable so multiple copies could be purchased to share with others who need to know this vital information.

New Testament Commentary
(Wayne Jackson)

Perhaps one of the more antici-pated volumes among preachers is a commentary on the whole New Testa-ment; however, there are many com-mentaries on the whole Bible, Old Tes-tament, New Testament, or individual books of the Bible. What makes this particular commentary so anticipated by several preachers is the scholar do-ing the commenting!

Some have a negative view of com-mentaries regardless of who has writ-ten it. They tend to think that somehow commentaries are on the same level as a creed; however, such is not the case at all. Some creeds certainly provide commentary on the Bible; how-ever, creeds include a level of imposing authority that is missing from a commentary. No, commentaries are not Creeds, Confes-sions of Faith, Articles of Faith, etc.

I often explain that a commentary is only as good as the one doing the commenting! If I have a really difficult question relat-ing to the Bible that I just cannot figure out from the resources I possess, then I have written to brother Jackson and asked. Sometimes he gives me a direct response, sometimes he will for-ward me an article he has written, or sometimes he refers me to a book that might help my study. If I value his studious mind from years of disciplined study, then why would I be opposed to having his thoughts pertaining to the comments in book form arranged according to verses of the Bible? Generally, a commen-tary is a person's (or group's) thoughts on a given passage ar-ranged in order of book, chapter, and verse. Is there a difference

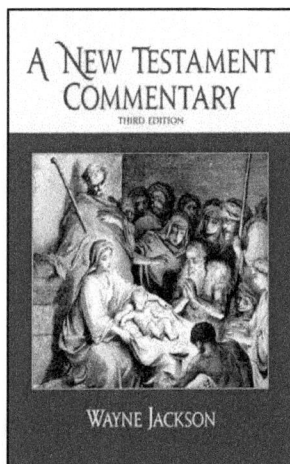

between asking a question and getting an answer from a preacher or reading his answer in written form? No. Again, it depends on who is doing the answering/writing.

Of course, writing a commentary on any book of the Bible is an ambitious task, but to write a commentary on the entire New Testament is quite a formidable project. It is why I laughed out loud when I read brother Wayne's statement in the Preface: "After chastising myself more than once for embarking upon such a daunting project, I threw myself into the delightful enterprise, laboring for long days, week after week, until I finished with the draft a few days under a year." Brother Wayne plans to continue writing his commentary series on the Old Testament. We pray that the Lord extends his life to where he can enjoy the satisfaction of completing this project!

As Editor of the *Christian Courier* since 1964, brother Wayne has published it monthly, plus books, which have benefited many in our brotherhood. The website ChristianCourier.com has been a blessing to many looking for solid and balanced answers to a host of religious questions whether for personal study or to share with others. Brother Wayne has freely shared with us the fruits of his scholarly study for years. Of course, books cost money, so we need to be willing to support sound writing if we want to have such for the future. I hesitate to use the word "brief" in describing this commentary. I prefer to use the word "concise" instead. It is arranged by the books of the New Testament and verses are organized around major points in outline format. Each book of the New Testament has an introduction including authorship, date, purpose, etc.

Be sure to obtain a copy of this volume for the church library and for your personal study before it goes out of print!

Originally printed in the *West Virginia Christian*, Vol. 24, No. 8, August 2017, p. 8. *Reprinted by permission.*

Notes From the Margin of My Bible
(Wayne Jackson)

A good friend of mine (unfortunately not a Christian) has a list of principles of sound Bible study in her Bible from when she was young. These principles were so valid that I copied them into my own Bible. These principles of sound Bible study include:

1) Praying for guidance.
2) Being able to accept correction.
3) Proving all things.
4) Realizing the Scriptures never contradict themselves.
5) Not changing the Scriptures to suit yourself.
6) Checking the contents (and contexts) carefully.
7) Gathering all relating Scriptures.
8) Accepting the Bible as its own best interpreter.
9) Not organizing poorly chosen scriptures to support an argument.
10) Using several translations.
11) Not trying to establish doctrine with Bible helps.
12) Marking your Bible.

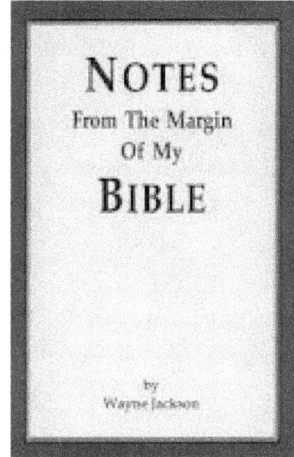

All of these principles have merit. Marking your Bible is one practice which can help you learn more about the Bible, increase your retention, and teach the Bible more effectively. I used to consider my copy of the Bible as rather holy and writing on it as a form of desecration; however, it is not holy and sacred in that sense. I began making notes in my Bible which has increased my retention and made my copy of the Scriptures more precious to me.

Perhaps you are a novice as to what to write in your Bible. An excellent place to begin is with the two above books by Wayne Jackson which are now combined into a single volume. He deals with 191 difficult passages of the Old Testament and 187 of the New Testament. Suggested methods of markings are sometimes provided. Each book is indexed by the passages it deals with for easier reference to difficult texts you want more information on. I have finished with Volume One on the Old Testament myself and the notes are rich in material. For example, a difficult passage is Zechariah 11:12-13. Men with no regard for the inspiration of the Bible such as William Barclay claim Matthew made a mistake when attributing this passage to Jeremiah (Matthew 27:9). Brother Jackson points out that Matthew states this was spoken by Jeremiah and that Zechariah states part of his writings were the words of God "proclaimed by the former prophets" (Zechariah 7:7). So one can easily tell the inspiration of the Bible is valid and Mr. Barclay is the one who made the mistake, not Matthew. Additional "Notes From The Margin of My Bible" appear in the Christian Courier which he publishes, and in the Restorer, which are beneficial. You can find Wayne Jackson's materials on the Internet at christiancourier.com.

The best pen I have found for writing in my Bible is called a Pigma Pen made by Micron. The pens are slightly difficult to find but are well worth the search. The ink does not bleed through to the other side of the page, interfering with the backside, and the ink is permanent so it prevents smudges. The pens also come in a variety of colors and tip sizes. Please be sure to test the pen to make sure it performs to your satisfaction prior to marking in your Bible.

Originally printed in *West Virginia Christian*, Vol. 9, No. 7, July 2002, p. 8. Reprinted by permission.

The Parables in Profile
(Wayne Jackson)

There are several books available on the parables of Jesus. One of my personal favorites is a small volume published in 1978 by Wayne Jackson entitled The Parables in Profile: Exegetical Outlines of the Parables of Christ. I totally agree with Wayne Jackson's assessment of the parables of Christ:

> In that marvelous galaxy of teaching that came from the lips of Christ, a solar system of parables has instructed and thrilled multiplied thousands for nearly twenty centuries. The Lord's parables contain some of the most preachable and teachable material in the New Testament and no good teacher can afford to ignore this depository [the parables, DRK] of divine information. (Jackson, Back Cover)

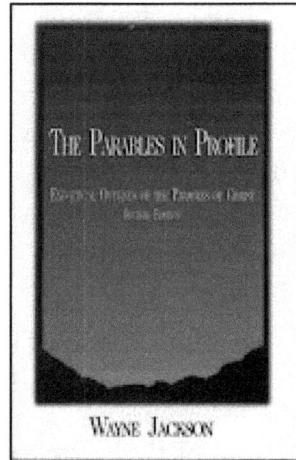

This volume contains outlines, word studies, and background information of the parables that are very profitable for study and teaching. The material is concise but contains multiple references that can easily be expanded to further enrich one's study of the material. I particularly appreciate Wayne Jackson's guidelines for studying the parables. One guideline he suggests is not to press a parable beyond its intended design to teach something that contradicts plain teaching in other passages. The book also contains several applications to our lives today that many need to be taught or even reminded of (Hebrews 5:12-14).

Wayne Jackson has published a monthly periodical of biblical studies entitled the Christian Courier for over 36 years now. He has published several volumes on various topics. He also publishes an electronic version of the Christian Courier on the Internet at christiancourier.com. I have known brother Wayne and his family for several years. In fact, I went to school with both of his sons, Jared and Jason, at Freed-Hardeman University. If you are looking for some stimulating reading, then subscribe to the Christian Courier and review other materials he has available from the website. The congregation where I attend purchases two bundles of the paper for distribution. We also have all of his books in the church library as well. I have recommended his works consistently and have always had positive feedback from those seeking more information on a given topic he has researched.

In 1998, this book on the parables was revised and reprinted with a new typeset that is more attractive and easier to read. The information is basically the same so if one has the earlier edition of the book it would make a nice gift to pass on if you purchase the new revision for yourself.

Originally printed in the *West Virginia Christian*, Vol. 8, No. 12, December 2001, p. 5. Reprinted by permission.

A Study Guide to Greater Bible Knowledge
(Wayne Jackson)

Some of us have been richly blessed with godly parents who have made it a priority to take us to Bible classes, worship services, gospel meetings, etc. They taught us the Bible at home and made sure we had excellent reading materials to instruct us in the way of the Lord. They lovingly and patiently answered our questions and followed up to make sure we had a sound understanding of God's word (Prov. 22:6; Eph. 6:1-4). If you have been blessed with godly parents, possibly this article will be an occasion to thank your parents (and God) again. (If they are no longer with you, you can still thank God for them.) However, not all of us have had this blessing. Some of us may be new Christians striving to get a grasp of the Bible, ideas on how to study it effectively, and tools that can assist. Learning God's Word is critical for not only the church but the survival of our nation. In Amos 8:10-12 there is mention of a famine of the word of God in the land, and the problems it created. In the United States, there is such a famine—not in the lack of Bibles but in the lack of reading, respect and serious study of it. But where do we begin trying to remedy the situation for someone who may not have the foundation of instruction we often take for granted? How can we help new Christians begin the life journey of drinking more and more deeply from the living fountain found in God's Word?

This is where Wayne Jackson's book *A Study Guide to Greater Bible Knowledge* can be of assistance. In chapter 8 on

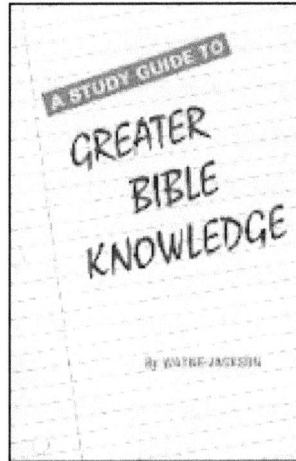

"Tools for Bible Study," brother Jackson opens the chapter with one of my favorite quotes by T.W. Brents:

> "If you will show us a man who reads nothing but the Bible, we will show you one who reads and understands very little of it."

There are reference materials available that can help others learn more about the Bible. Of course some books are better than others, but one should not ignore many of the great aids available by those who have devoted much of their lives to just one facet of Bible study. In hours we can learn what others have spent years investigating. This book helps provide not only foundation information but also guidance on how to dig deeper.

The book provides an overview of Bible History and an analysis of the books in the Bible. It discusses principles in sound interpretation of the Scriptures and various approaches one can use in study the Scriptures. It includes a chapter on the study of Bible words (etymology), grammar or syntax, and the equally important topic of context. Some do not like to study vocabulary...and it shows. Jesus used the very tense of verbs in the Old Testament to refute the critics of His day. Surely if Jesus focused on the very tense of the verb and criticized the Sadducees for not doing so, our scholarship should be no less precise.

All these subjects and more are covered in this volume in a concise manner and written on a level that new Christians can read and begin their journey to greater Bible knowledge. It would be an excellent guide for the new Christian to read and then come back with follow-up questions. Each chapter includes discussion questions that would be of assistance for a new converts class. Brother Jackson is a first rate scholar who recognizes that scholarship veiled in unnecessary complexity is of little value. In fact, words that do not teach are in direct contradiction to the meaning of "scholarship." This is not to exempt one from working at their study. Brother Jackson is an excellent researcher who writes to be understood. I have profited from his writings in the *Christian Courier* and his books for several years. I have always appreciated his commitment to write to be under-stood by new or average Bible students seeking to advance and grow. In Hebrews 5:12-14, the writer admonishes his audience that their lack of study has inhibited his ability to communicate to them fully. Brother Jackson's work provides an effective guide to transition from the milk of the Word to its meat. Jesus said *"Blessed our those who hunger and thirst after righteousness for they shall be filled."* (Matthew 5:6, NKJV) Use this book to help yourself and others gain access to the eternal food and drink of God's Word.

Treasures from the Greek New Testament
for the English Reader
(Wayne Jackson)

Treasures from the Greek New Testament for the English Reader, Wayne Jackson Archaeology is a fascinating field and offers insights that have puzzled many until it unearths the missing pieces of the puzzle to present a clearer picture of the situation. For example, it was commonly thought back in the 19th century that the language of the New Testament was so unique that it was used by the Holy Spirit exclusively. There were four basic types of Greek known at the time: Homeric, Attic, Byzantine and Modern. Archaeologists discovered that this specialized Greek was not so unique, and in fact was widely used in correspondence, legal documents and was the language of the common people. This type of Greek is referred to as koine or Hellenistic Greek. It was the predominant form of Greek after the death of Alexander the Great and was used throughout the known world approximately 300 years before and after the life of Christ. One source says the Roman Empire used this form of Greek as much as they did Latin in their writings. Wayne Jackson writes:

> "Koine Greek was the most precise instrument for the expression of human thought that the world has ever known. Little wonder then that, in the providence of God, this medium is used to convey the final revelation of heaven to humankind." (Preface).

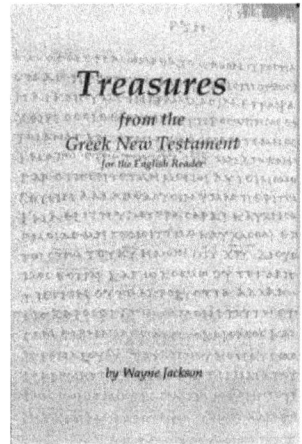

The study of a foreign language is very rewarding, but not everyone has taken the opportunity to study a language other than English. Studying Latin for a year in high school, I was fascinated to learn the history, culture and other aspects of the Roman Empire where Latin was predominantly utilized. Attempting to learn a new language is a daunting task to many, but accessing koine Greek has been made easier due to the work of religious scholars who have developed tools for those unlearned in the language so these can also explore the sacred text. The challenge is often "Where do I begin?" This makes Wayne Jackson's book so valuable. It is written for those who have not had the opportunity to study koine Greek. The book is simplistic in its approach, but weighty in its applications to the New Testament. It deals with the letters, moods, tenses, prepositions, articles and other areas of Greek grammar. The book includes an extensive bibliography referencing other works that may help one reach the next level in their study of this vital language. Plus, there is a very helpful Scripture index that will be important for those seeking to incorporate what they have learned into their study. One point that is imperative one knows: be aware of the background of a writer when reading their religious material. This is likewise true when studying writers on the Greek language and their application to doctrine. Wayne Jackson does an excellent job of pointing out the bias of some writers in relation to the Greek preposition eis. Some attempt to twist this preposition in Acts 2:38 to teach that baptism is for sins previously forgiven rather than for the purpose of removing sins. For example, "Noted grammarian A.T. Robertson, of Baptist persuasion, in a discussion concerning eis in Acts 2:38, confessed that sometimes theologian's opinion must take precedence over the grammar." (page 78). Imagine that...it does not matter what the Greek reads, what matters is what Robertson thinks it should read! It would be difficult to find a more clear confession of a theologian's bias with the sacred text. Treasures from the Greek New Testament for the English Reader indeed is a valuable introduction to a world of enriching study of the language of the New Testament.

Originally printed in the *West Virginia Christian*, Vol. 23, No. 5, May 2016, p. 8. *Reprinted by permission.*

Seeking True Unity
(Dale Jenkins, Editor)

A humorous illustration, unless you are an "over the top" cat lover, showing the difference between union and unity is tying two cats' tails together and throwing them over a clothes' line. While they are in a state of union, they are certainly not unified! There are those who claim they are pursuing "unity" but in actuality mean "union." Union does include a degree of unity; however, union includes accepting potentially many contradictory views overridden for some stated goal. Unity is a term with a greater and deeper degree of agreement, being of the same mind and action in purpose. For example, some argue they are "united" on a fundamental truth; e.g., belief in the deity of Christ, but can remain in a state of contradiction on other doctrines. This is not unity, but union. The Bible demands unity; which includes more than believing Jesus is the Son of God. Certainly the deity of Christ is fundamental for a Christian; however, it is not the only required belief in Christianity. This type of union contradicts the principle spoken of by the prophet Amos "Can two walk together unless they are agreed?"

The pursuit for unity requires effort, diligence and work. The restoration movement paints a clear picture of the fact that unity is desirable, obtainable and destructible. We learn from the restoration movement that unity can become fragile and even be broken when people allow their minds to be drawn away from the unifying body of knowledge that makes us one— the New Testament. Seeking True Unity points out a truth that,

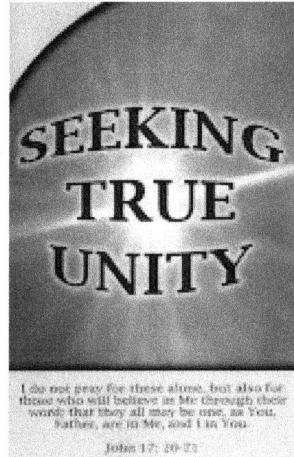

while painful, needs to be understood. When there are only two options—compromise or division over doctrine, division is better than compromise. The book includes this quote, ironically from a member of the Christian Church:

> Unity is not always correct. Division is not always wrong. What is always correct is following the Word of God and doing the will of God. Perhaps we need more division from what is not of God, in order to be more united in the things of God...True Biblical unity calls for a division or separation from that which is not of God and harmful to itself, and then it seeks what is the best of God for others. (page 54).

The book Seeking True Unity is a concise presentation on unity. Six authors, an editor and the Horse Cave Church of Christ united in their efforts to this overview of what constitutes true unity. The book explains Bible authority including one of the principles of authority that has been turned "on its head" to accommodate various innovations—the principle of silence. Those of the digression in the Restoration Movement erroneously claimed "silent" in the phrase "Let us speak where the Bible speaks and be silent where the Bible is silent" meant their objectors must be silent. This is not the meaning of the slogan as used in the days of Thomas Campbell (and a reading of the Declaration and Address clearly shows this). Being "silent where the Bible is silent" meant (and still means) refraining from the things the Bible does not authorize. If Bible authority is not found in commands, binding examples, or implications, then we should not do or teach that unauthorized practice or teaching; i.e., be silent in word and deed! The writers explain how the division over mechanical instruments in worship arose, how the division spread, and that we are facing the same threat today. It is imperative that we teach Christians this sad story of this division in order to avoid further division. This book is ideal for a newer Christian who is seeking to learn more about these issues without being overloaded with details that they may not be prepared for at their stage of development. It is ideal for classroom discussion, especially if the class has mature members who are able to contribute sage comments to help amplify the points that need to be made.

Originally printed in *West Virginia Christian*, Vol. 15, No. 9, September 2008, p. 8. Reprinted by permission.

Spiritual Patriots – Jude's Call to Arms
(Aubrey Johnson)

Make no mistake, there are wars going on across the globe, but that has always been the case and will remain to be so until Jesus returns. But as concerning as physical wars are, the greater wars are the ones of a spiritual nature. The churches of Christ are under assault from many foes from within and without. Recently I enlisted myself onto Facebook. It has been both enjoyable and a source of sadness. Sure, it is great to be reconnected with friends I have long cherished. But that joy seems to be evaporating in more in more cases as I have learned several have forsaken the faith. The faithful need to stand strong and tall! By standing firm, we will be able to hopefully save those who have lost their way. This is one of the messages of Jude:

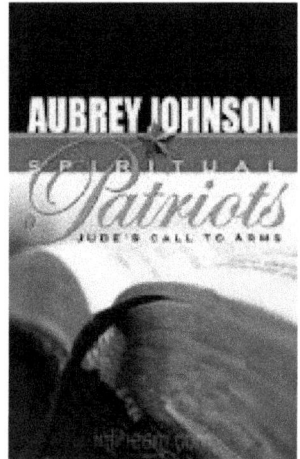

> But you, beloved, building yourselves up on your most holy faith, praying in the Holy Spirit, keep yourselves in the love of God, looking for the mercy of our Lord Jesus Christ unto eternal life. And on some have compassion, making a distinction; but others save with fear, pulling them out of the fire, hating even the garment defiled by the flesh (Jude 20-23, NKJV).

The epistle of Jude is one of the more contested books among those of the New Testament. By contested, the reference is to whether or not it belongs in the Bible. The study of the arguments opposed to and in favor of its inclusion are interesting reading. It is clear that while a few may not be as confident about Jude as, say, the Gospel of John, the resistance is rather minor. Jude is an invigorating book. Indeed, Johnson's subtitle "A Call to Arms" is right on the mark!

Recently I completed a study of the Epistle of Jude for the adult Bible class. I had actually taught on the book a few years ago, but had increased my library by this point so I decided to study the additional accumulated materials. As I was nearing the close of my study, brother Johnson's work was just being released. In fact, I obtained my copy and met the author at the Gospel Advocate Appreciation Luncheon at the Freed-Hardeman Lectureship. The week provided me the opportunity to do some night-time reading. I was able to read the book quickly due to being familiar with the subject matter, the fine organization of the work, and my abiding interest in the subject.

One of my favorite pages in the book is the Thirteen Steps to Spiritual Victory. "To know victory, I must:

1. Be willing to take a stand.
2. Adapt my plans to fulfill greater needs.
3. Never use grace as an excuse for disobedience.
4. Learn from history.
5. Fill my heart with holy aspirations.
6. Choose my path carefully.
7. Make pleasing God my highest aim.
8. Be content without becoming complacent.
9. Never underestimate the enemy.
10. Prepare daily for Jesus' return.
11. Not be easily disheartened.
12. Accept personal responsibility for my spiritual growth.
13. Trust God to sustain me through trying times." (Page 125)

If you are seeking an excellent presentation on the Epistle of Jude, which will be along the lines of waking a congregation out of its slumber, this may provide the ammunition you need.

Originally printed in the *West Virginia Christian*, Vol. 16, No. 7, July 2009, p. 8. Reprinted by permission.

Instrumental Music in The Worship
(M.C. Kurfees)

The full title of this book is *Instrumental Music in the Worship or the Greek Verb Psallo Philologically and Historically Examined*. The original copyright to this book is 1911. This gives an idea just how long the pro-manmade instrument crowd has been attempting to make the Greek word in Ephesians 5:19, *psallo*, to include or allow manmade instruments. Note that!

I recently saw a video which misrepresented the acapella position as wholly contingent on *psallo* excluding an instrument as if our whole case hinged on that one word and cited Kurfees' work as evidence. Anyone who has read this work will quickly realize the video not only misrepresents the view on Ephesians 5:19 but also this work by Kurfees. Kurfees' treatment of *psallo* was NOT to show that instruments were absolutely excluded by the term. In fact, Kurfees shows that the term was changing in meaning basically from a manmade instrument exclusively to one without a manmade instrument being required.

The Koine Greek was going through major changes due to Hellenism, and *psallo* was one such term. However, Kurfees did not advocate the position that *psallo* absolutely excludes the instrument in Ephesians 5:19. He merely proved the term had evolved to include singing without a manmade instrument being required. Or as one of the more up-to-date lexicon states "to sing songs of praise with or without instrumental accompaniment" (BDAG 1096). Incidentally, through the Byzantine Greek the narrowing would continue until in Modern Greek *psallo*

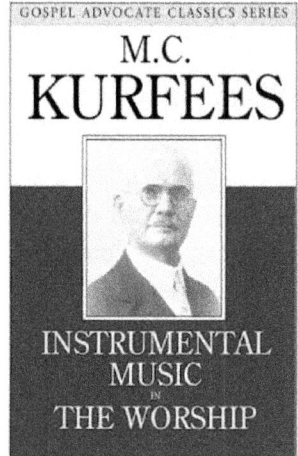

evolved to mean vocal music exclusively (BDAG, 1096). Now, why would this narrowing trend continue toward vocal only? Because the early church utilized only the human voice for centuries before the adoption of the manmade instrument intruded upon acapella music. Incidentally, acapella not only meant vocal alone but also designated the type of music—sacred versus profane.

Some claim churches of Christ are deliberately obscuring the instrument in *psallo*, but that is a false charge. Question: Why do nearly all English translations, not produced by churches of Christ, not translate *psallo* as "play"? Translators recognized that *psallo* did not require a manmade instrument but the heart as the instrument. A comparison of Colossians 3:16 also shows this to be true. The challenge to the *psallo* argument in a nutshell is this: name the manmade instrument in the verse or in the worship of the first century church. The term *psallo* is a verb which does NOT include any manmade instrument. It is modified by the God-made instrument of the heart in Ephesians 5:19. We are to make melody with our hearts in devotion to God. No manmade instruments were named or included in First Century Worship, and we should continue to abide in that pattern!

Kurfees began his research at the request of preacher students in his class on New Testament Exegesis. Why? Because preachers were looking for an answer about *psallo* as justification for manmade instruments. What started as a paper was expanded into this work for publication. Its endurance is seen in being included in the Gospel Advocate Classic Series.

If the reader would like a fuller treatment of this subject of controversy, see Dave Miller's video lessons available on Apologetics Press' YouTube Channel.

Originally printed in the *West Virginia Christian*, Vol. 30, No. 11, November 2023, p. 8. *Reprinted by permission.*

God's Amazing Grace
(Jim Laws, Editor)

The twentieth annual *Spiritual Sword Lectureship* was on the subject of "God's Amazing Grace." The lectures were delivered October 15-19, 1995 at the Getwell Church of Christ in Memphis, TN. The Getwell congregation has an exemplary legacy of producing sound conservative materials through both *The Spiritual Sword* quarterlies and lectureship books.

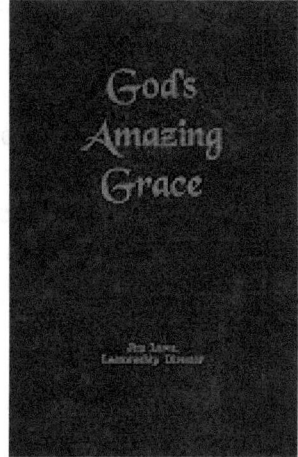

God's grace is a subject that has drawn considerable attention over the past few years. Occasionally I hear of "old preachers" being slandered because they failed to preach on "grace" as often as the *accuser* deems appropriate. Slander may seem a strong term; however, it literally means defame with false statements or malicious reports. Think for a minute about the accusation of one preacher against another preacher of "failing to teach about God's grace." How would this person be in a position to know every sermon delivered in every context by a given preacher? Sometimes when others criticize faithful teachers of failing to teach God's grace they really mean that they are not teaching *their* view of God's grace. Sadly, sometimes *their* view is the one that is actually unscriptural. Also, there is a failure to realize that when one speaks about any facet of God's Word, they are touching on the subject of God's grace. For example, some find the explanation of God's "Plan of Salvation" at the conclusion of a sermon as tiresome or trite, but they have failed to realize that attitude makes them actually guilty of what they accuse others of doing—failing to teach about God's grace. If it were not for the grace of God, there would not even be a plan for man's salvation!

It seems that much of the criticism by some stems from a desire to come as close as possible to the false teaching of denominationalism, advocating salvation is by God's grace *alone*, so as to fit in with them. While it is true that we could not be saved without God's grace, it is equally true that God's expects man to respond with faith and obedience to His offer of grace. If we were saved by God's grace alone independently of faith, obedience and works, then all would be saved (Titus 2:11); however, we know that not all will be saved. Also, this pattern of God's grace being extended with detailed instructions requiring faith and obedience in response on the part of man is seen repeatedly throughout the Bible. Those who would say that at the very end, at the Judgment, God's love will overrule His standards of righteousness, resulting in no one being sentenced to an eternal hell, are ignoring the clear patterns, teachings and precedents of the Bible. This lectureship book does a fine job of showing that grace is not just a New Testament concept and law is not just an Old Testament provision. While we are not under the old covenant; *i.e.*, law of Moses, we are under the new covenant; *i.e.*, law of Christ.

This lectureship book explores the topic of "God's Grace" in detail from a scriptural standpoint. It addresses many of these false concepts about grace. It studies the subject of grace from a topical standpoint including the source of God's grace, demands of God's grace, why it is amazing, and the requirements of accepting God's grace as a pattern throughout the Bible. The book also discusses some of the false teachings of grace and movements by those adopting these false views today. It looks at critical questions relating to God's grace such as "Are grace and law contradictory" and others. There is also analysis of some key passages relating to God's grace that are sometimes misused by advocates of "grace only" with a sound refutation of the error and exposition of the truth. There are also six book reviews worthy of study as well in the book.

The Getwell congregation has provided the brotherhood a great service by conducting these lectures and preserving them in book form for others to read and profit from. If you know of some in your congregation who may, even innocently, think we do not discuss God's grace enough, then this book will make a valuable addition to your church library for their reading.

Originally printed in *West Virginia Christian*, Vol. 20, No. 4, April 2013, p. 8. Reprinted by permission.

The Scheme of Redemption
(Jim Laws, Editor)

This book is from the 1990 Spiritual Sword Lectureship which was dedicated to Guy N. Woods. It deals with the intricate plan that God designed from before the foundation of the world to redeem man from sin and restore his relationship with God. Some have commented about the golden thread that runs through the Bible which is sometimes referred to as the scheme of redemption. When one considers the intricacies that God designed for the redemption of man, it should result in a constant state of awe of how awesome the God is that we serve. Consider Peter's words in reference to the scheme of redemption:

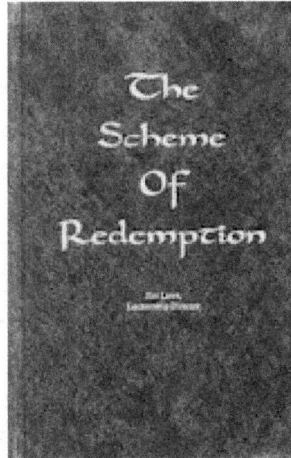

> "Of this salvation the prophets have inquired and searched carefully, who prophesied of the grace that would come to you, searching what, or what manner of time, the Spirit of Christ who was in them was indicating when He testified beforehand the sufferings of Christ and the glories that would follow. To them it was revealed that, not to themselves, but to us they were ministering the things which now have been reported to you through those who have preached the gospel to you by the Holy Spirit sent from heaven—things which angels desire to look into." (1 Peter 1:10-12)

The book is divided into five main sections. The first section is an overview of the scheme of redemption including the design of the plan by God and its design for proclamation. The second section focuses on the scheme of redemption throughout the Old Testament. It deals with the Patriarchs and the nation of

Israel and their role in the ultimate scheme of redemption for all of mankind. The third section deals with the scheme of redemption prior to the coming of Jesus. It includes comparisons of the old and new covenants in worship and other aspects relating to man's redemption. It also shows the preparation that was completed leading up to the arrival of the Messiah including the work of John the Immerser. The fourth section deals with the full unveiling of God's scheme of redemption as it was launched by Jesus and carried forth by the church. It discusses the role of the church and the Bible today in the redemptive plans of God. The fifth section deals with defenses of the scheme of redemption against errors that would blind people from the great work that God had accomplished through Christ on their behalf. It deals with the errors of Calvinism, Premillennialism, Secular Humanism, and other challenges that we must work to combat in order to show others the plan God has designed for the redemption of their souls. It shows the method with which the Holy Spirit operates today to draw mankind to the salvation of their souls—the proclamation of the gospel through the written word.

The book contains 36 manuscripts written by conservative men who respect the integrity and authority of the word of God. It would benefit students both in private and public study. I often refer to the book as I prepare lessons around this theme. The systematic structure of the book lends itself to reading straight through continuously with great enjoyment and profit. Study of this theme will prove to you that truly God is the master of the universe and is in control. We may not understand all that happens in our lives. Neither did those in the Bible. When confusing times arise that seem inexplicable, I try to remember the words of my dad—"Not all accounts are settled in this life." Indeed, God does have a wonderful plan for us in eternity that is a source of great hope for us to be able to endure whatever this life that is impacted by the sin of the world experiences.

Originally printed in the *West Virginia Christian*, Vol. 10, No. 11, November 2003, p. 8. Reprinted by permission.

Leadership Issues Confronting the Church
(Jack P. Lewis)

Leadership is vital to the success of many types of organizations including the church. Leadership can make or break an organization. There are many books on leadership. Some books are good and some are not so good. The greatest lessons in leadership for every type of good organization are to be found in the Bible. There are several good books that are in the business section of most bookstores that use themes from the Bible to teach principles of leadership; e.g., Moses On Management: 50 Leadership Lessons From The Greatest Manager of All Time.

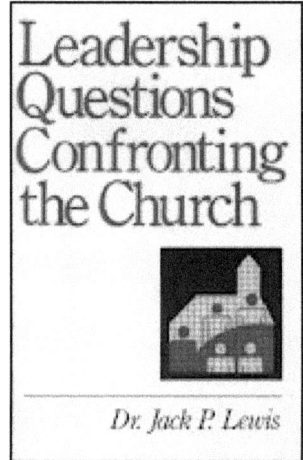

Leadership
Questions
Confronting
the Church

Dr. Jack P. Lewis

When discussing leadership issues among churches of Christ, it is imperative that terms are properly defined. Many of us know that the term "pastor" is incorrect in reference to the preacher; however, the term would be appropriate for an elder since this term is applied to this office. So it is imperative to have a clear understanding of the terms used in the Greek New Testament. As Jack Lewis explains in his chapter "Greek Words for Elders":

> The topic, "Greek Words for Elders," is of necessity tedious and technical, and all the more so for those who have not had the privilege of mastering the Greek language. Nevertheless, it is important that we examine the Greek text in studying the questions of elders. Words create the thought patterns in which men can think. There is not a one-to-one equivalence in translation from Greek into English. Since most words have more than one meaning, the English word

chosen by the translators may have some overtones quite foreign to the Greek word the original writer used; thereby to expound ideas the Bible never taught. On the opposite side of the problem, the Greek word may be richer in connotation than the English word. In such cases dependence on the English word alone robs us of concepts we need. [Lewis, p. 13.]

Jack Lewis does extensive work on defining the terms relating to elders and preachers. He does so in a scholarly fashion, but not to the point of leaving the average student of the Bible behind. The writer also deals with several aspects of leadership relating to men and the elders such as majority rule versus having an eldership. He also devotes several pages to the role of preachers and really emphasizes the importance of studying the Bible as a major role of the preacher's work. He discusses the authority of the preacher being exclusively from the word of God not their personal preferences, which is a subject many need a refresher course on.

The book is very challenging but very profitable for study. The book is just over 100 pages but it is packed with information to be meditated on. Jack Lewis is one of the most degreed Christian scholars the church has. He has doctorates from both Hebrew Union College and Harvard University. He has taught at Harding in Searcy, Arkansas and Harding Graduate School of Religion in Memphis, Tennessee since 1958. He appears regularly the Freed-Hardeman University Bible Lectureship, which I make every effort to attend.

One of the reasons I seek after Jack Lewis' writings is his reputation for scholarship. His advice to Bible students on study habits is words he has lived by:

You must apply the seat of your pants to a chair for long periods of time. Two to three hours should be spent out of class in preparation for each hour spent in class. This means that if you are taking twelve hours, then twenty-four to thirty-six hours be spent in study. That makes a total of forty-eight hours a week minimum. This time often should be even greater when you are studying at the graduate level.... There is a great difference in getting a degree and getting an education. [Lewis, p. 104.]

Take advantage of the time and energy that Jack Lewis has devoted to this volume.

Originally printed in *West Virginia Christian*, Vol. 9, No. 8, August 2002, p. 8. Reprinted by permission.

Questions You've Asked
About Bible Translations
(Jack P. Lewis)

The subject of Bible translations is very interesting and challenging. It is important for Christians to have a balanced view toward modern translations. Translating from one language to another is extremely challenging. Translating into English, a language that is ever changing, is a job that is never done. The first dictionary was published in 1928 and contained 414,800 words. By 1989, the number of words covered in the dictionary swelled to over 615,000 and it is still growing and changing! So a changing English language will require changes in Bible translations in order to effectively communicate the meaning of the Biblical text.

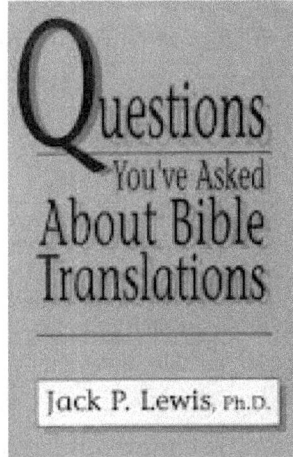

When studying about Bible translations, one must read from trusted scholars. Few there are who are considered scholars in Hebrew, Greek, and Bible Translations among the churches of Christ. One member of the church of Christ who meets these qualifications is Jack P. Lewis. Brother Lewis has two Ph.D. degrees—one from Hebrew Union and the other from Harvard. He has taught at Harding Graduate School of Religion for over 30 years and frequently appears on the program of the Freed-Hardeman Bible Lectureship to speak about various language-related themes. While not everyone will agree with anyone on this subject, it is important to read from those who have the scholarship and research to contribute beneficially to the subject.

This book is a collection of essays brother Lewis has written throughout his career in response to questions asked about

Bible translations. The book is challenging but understandable. He discusses the translation process, which is essential for one to understand the translation process to avoid misunderstanding the issues involved. Doctor Lewis writes a very effective series of articles about modern versions and attitudes relating to new translations. He also provides a valuable discussion of textual variants and their impact on translations and comparing translation to translation. There is a very good chapter entitled "Where is the Zero Milepost?" that explains the goal of translating. Jack Lewis also discusses various translations such as the RSV, NIV, KJV, ASV, and others.

Also included in this book are discussions about topics related to Bible translations. For example, what does "Fruit of the Vine" mean? Another discussion is the meaning of "Faith to Faith." Another thought provoking chapter deals with "Only Begotten." He also discusses how translations have impacted the songs that we sing in worship to God.

It is important for us to equip ourselves to effectively be able to discuss and evaluate the increasing number of Bible translations. As brother Lewis states "The task of translating is never finished, and in time those translations people depend upon may be replaced by others made by people who are interested in making God's Word available to those for whom it has been difficult."

This book will be a valuable addition to the church library and should be put into the hands of those looking for more information relating to the subject of Bible translations.

Originally printed in the *West Virginia Christian*, Vol. 11, No. 2, February 2004, p. 8. Reprinted by permission.

How We Got The Bible
(Neil R. Lightfoot)

In the age of the Internet, it is hard to fathom what writing materials must have been like during the days the original documents were written. Various writing materials were used in ancient days including stone, clay, wood, leather, papyrus, and vellum. Paper was not widely used until 800 years after the life of Christ. It is also interesting to note that document preservation was a task in and of itself. Even in our lifetime we have seen document preservation change from paper, to cassette, to floppy disk, to diskette, and now to CD. Preservation of documents back during times of the Bible was achieved by re-copying the documents on new materials that would decay and have to be constantly replaced. This is one of the reasons some works have not been preserved—they simply became no longer worth the effort to preserve over time—a strong testimony to the value of the Bible over time.

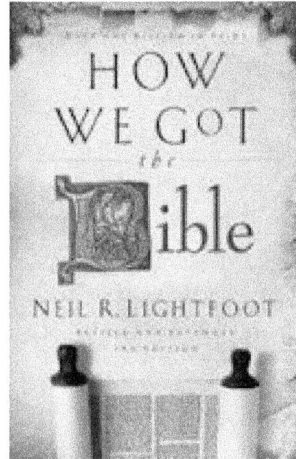

This book deals with the process used to preserve the Old Testament and New Testament manuscripts. Several important textual finds are discussed including the thrilling story of the Dead Sea Scrolls and their significance in knowing the Old Testament has been faithfully preserved by the Jews through the ages. The book also discusses the types of mistakes made by copyists, which accounts for what are called textual variants and the process used to reconcile the variants—textual criticism. The writer also discusses what books were considered part of the canon and why. He also spends time discussing the

Apocryphal books and why these are disputed and considered non-canonical.

The author then does a good job of tying all these factors together and turns to the subject of Bible translations. Having a good understanding of how the manuscripts have been preserved over the centuries is important to understand the challenges of Bible translators.

When one first discovers concepts such as textual variants, it can be rather alarming. We often talk about the Bible being inspired and without errors. That is correct when one discusses the original manuscripts. What we need to clarify is that the original manuscripts were perfect but the copies are not perfect. Today, there are no original manuscripts, only copies. But a study of this material will strengthen one's confidence that we have the word of God in our possession. Sir Frederic Kenyon, respected Biblical scholar and archaeologist, states the results of a study such as this:

> It is reassuring at the end to find that the general result of all these discoveries and all this study is to strengthen the proof of the authenticity of the Scriptures, and our conviction that we have in our hands, in substantial integrity, the veritable Word of God.

Neil Lightfoot attended Freed-Hardeman College, Florida Christian College, Baylor University, and Duke University. He has taught at Abilene Christian College and has served as evangelist for several congregations over the years. This book is a very informative and interesting work on the efforts made to preserve the word of God for all ages. This book will make a valuable introduction to the world of Biblical archaeology and its impact on the religious world today.

Originally printed in the *West Virginia Christian*, Vol. 13, No. 2, February 2006, p. 8. Reprinted by permission.

Equipping the Saints:
Fifty Years of Lectures and Articles
(David L. Lipe)

This is the first in what I hope to be in a series of books published by Stewart Publications. It would be a wonderful resource to have collected lectures and articles by certain members of our brotherhood. David Lipe has an A.A. from Freed-Hardeman University, B.A. from Harding University, M.A. from Harding School of Theology, and a Ph. D. from the University of Tennessee. He has both lectured and directed lecture-ships for several years including the Freed-Hardeman University Lectureship which he directed for 22 years. He has also worked with the South East Institute of Biblical Studies. He continues to teach and preach which he has also done for many years. I have watched him navigate the Open Forum with the Moderator and the audience. Even when frustration occurs, he makes the situation humorous and diffuses matters that may become rather tense.

My father always enjoyed hearing brother Lipe's presentations, and I quickly shared that appreciation too. I have read some of his writings, commentary, and have heard him lecture on more than one occasion. I have never been disappointed listening to brother Lipe whether it would be a funny anecdote or his analysis of a passage or topic. His humor and scholarship both come through in the pages of this work.

When I sat with him to request his signature on my copy, he asked me how he wanted me to address the book. I gave him my name tag and said, "Here is how you spell my first name."

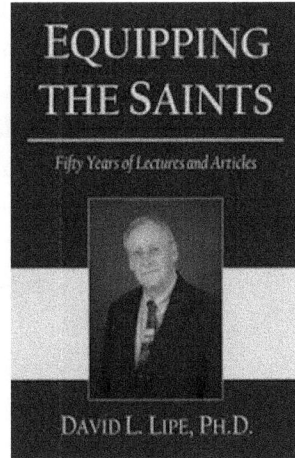

He just paused, looked at me with his trademark perplexed expression, and laughed. He is always very cordial and friendly. It is my pleasure to recommend this work to you not just because I enjoy visiting and hearing him, but the content is solid and profitable.

The book is packed with over 600 pages of articles arranged topically, but there is also a detailed bibliography with the listing chronologically too. The topics include: God, The Word of God, Jesus, Evangelism and Salvation, Faith, the Church, Worship, Christian Ethics, Eschatology, and others. When I went to the lectures at Freed-Hardeman University in 2023, this work was just becoming available and it was immediately on my list of books to purchase. It would make an excellent addition to the church library. The lectures and articles are written in such a way that everyone can profit and enjoy reading this book. He includes a final article that all would do well to read called "Take Care of Your Own Dent" that I particularly enjoyed. I salute Stewart Publications for making this available to the brotherhood, and I hope there are subsequent volumes from other scholars to come.

Originally printed in the *West Virginia Christian*, Vol. 30, No. 4, April 2023, p. 8. *Reprinted by permission.*

Proclamation and Promise:
Major Themes in the Minor Prophets
(David L. Lipe, Editor)

This writer was enriched by attending the 75th Annual Bible Lectureship at Freed-Hardeman University in February 2011. The theme was on the Minor Prophets which is an enriching study that is very much needed in our day. I found this year's lectureship especially good and commented to my father and others that I wish they would repeat the same program next year!

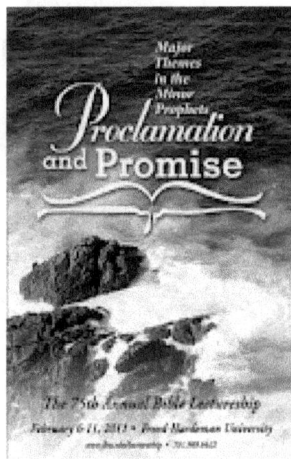

One of the nice things about this lectureship being so large is that several different approaches to the study of the theme are available. For example, I decided to attend a track (or series) that provided an overview of each of the Minor Prophets called "The-Prophets-At-A-Glance." Unfortunately I missed the lecture on the book of Jonah so I could attend a session at the Bible School Workshop on "Teaching The Minor Prophets to Adults" conducted by Clyde M. Woods.

Other tracks included "The Prophets Proclaim" which included lessons on a few of the many statements made by the prophets that we would do well to meditate upon today. For example, David L. Lipe's lecture on "Destroyed for Lack of Knowledge" is one I could not attend personally; however, the manuscript in the book is very good. Another theme of study at the lectureship I wished I had been able to attend was archaeology and the time periods of the Minor Prophets. I find it fascinating that archaeologists have found ivory panels on chairs and beds in the Kingdom of Israel which the prophet of Amos had condemned them for—abusing the poor as they pampered themselves (Amos 3:15; 6:4). There were also discussions about difficult texts and hard sayings relating to the Minor Prophets. Another nice feature of the lectureship is the variety of subject matter. For example, I was able to attend a Writer's Workshop hosted by Gospel Advocate. There were also classes on counseling and other matters. One literally cannot attend every lecture because each hour had as many as seven different lectures available.

This year's lectureship book is likewise outstanding. I wonder when E. Claude Gardner wrote the Foreword for the 1953 Lectureship Book if he had any idea just how widely known these lectureships would become. I am certain he would not realize that all volumes of these lectures are available in PDF format on a single CD at a price five dollars less than the hardbound book for 2011. I imagine he believed having the lectures on tape would be wonderful, but unfathomable that these are now on CD and available on iTunes. He certainly realized how important it would be to have printed copies that people could read, but could not have even imagined these would be on Kindle and readable on iPhones and iPads. I am sure he is thrilled to know that some of the lectures were streamed live on the Internet so that others could watch these sessions from anywhere in the world. We have so many resources available to us today than ever. How are we utilizing these?

Originally printed in *West Virginia Christian*, Vol. 18, No. 3, March 2011, p. 8. Reprinted by permission.

Questions Answered by Lipscomb & Sewell
(M.C. Kurfees, Editor)

This book is a compilation of questions and answers during the editorial tenure of David Lipscomb and E.G. Sewell for the Gospel Advocate. The book was edited in 1920 by M.C. Kurfees who was described by Guy N. Woods as "one of the most scholarly men ever to write for the Advocate." As mentioned in reference to Guy N. Woods' two volumes of Questions & Answers, effort was made not to overlap the work completed in Questions Answered that makes this volume a complementary addition for the church library.

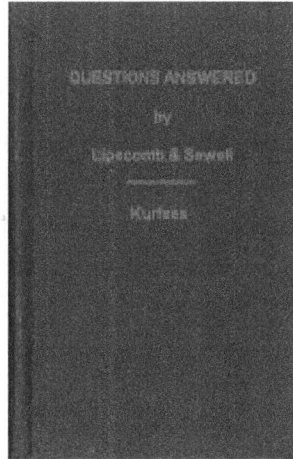

This book covers an estimated 600 subjects which are indexed in the back of the book; however, it does not have a scriptural index which makes referencing the work a little more challenging. Some subjects are dealt with twice, which appears on the surface to be redundant; however, the editor actually gives us the answers from both writers since these men wrote answers to the same question on more than one occasion. So, the research may have the answer on a subject from both David Lipscomb and E.G. Sewell rather than just one of the men.

Some of the questions asked and answered include:

- If God sees the end from the beginning and knows all that will come to pass, how can men change that order or be responsible?

- Were the men who gave us the Authorized (or King James) translation of the Scriptures immersionists—all or any great number of them?
- Is there any authority for Sunday School in the Bible?
- Are there witches, magicians, and such like, who can call up familiar spirits and talk with them?
- When was the Sabbath changed to the first day of the week?

David Lipscomb (1831-1917) served as editor for the Gospel Advocate for more than fifty years. Speaking of David Lipscomb in the 125th anniversary issue of the Gospel Advocate, Guy N. Woods stated *"...he did more than any other person of his day to preserve primitive New Testament Christianity in Tennessee and the southland. Wherever the Gospel Advocate was read in those days the church was sound and true to the Book."* In 1891, James A. Harding and David Lipscomb founded Nashville Bible School, which evolved into David Lipscomb University.

In 1870, E.G. Sewell (1830-1924) became the co-editor of the Gospel Advocate (also known as "Old Reliable") with David Lipscomb. They worked together for fifty years (in which the questions were originally answered). It is reported that the relationship between Lipscomb and Sewell was that of David and Jonathan. What a great example for fellow gospel preachers!

Some of the questions asked involve controversies that have been largely forgotten about today. These questions and answers are interesting to students of church history; however, these answers should be interesting to all of us. Just because an issue has "died down" for now does not mean it will not "heat up" in the future. When this occurs, it makes the writings of those who experienced the controversy in its "heyday" all the more valuable. This volume is over 750 pages and is a great storehouse of information that will enrich our study of the Bible.

Originally printed in the *West Virginia Christian*, Vol. 13, No. 9, September 2006, p. 8. Reprinted by permission.

The Kingdom of the Cults
(Walter Martin)

This work is a classic reference work on cults, having been first printed in 1965. The book has gone through at least thirty-six printings and the latest edition has been revised and expanded. Walter Martin is a recognized expert on the cults. He is a Baptist, founder and director of the Christian Research Institute.

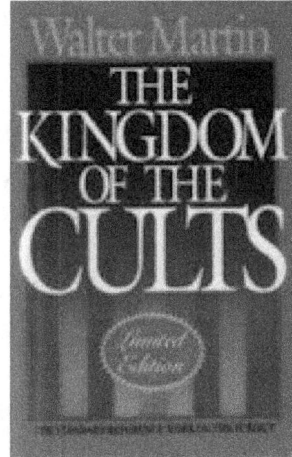

The book defines a cult as the following:

> A cult...is any religious group which differs significantly in some one or more respects as to belief or practice from those religious groups which are regarded as the normative expressions of religion in our total culture...a group of people gathered about a specific person or person's mis-interpretation of the Bible.

The author discusses the psychological patterns impacting the cults. It is important to understand the conditioning that some religious groups exercise over their disciples. The writer also discusses the importance of understanding the language among the cults. Often groups re-define terms beyond the original meanings in order to build support for their doctrine.

This work addresses the following religious groups: Jehovah's Witnesses, Christian Science, Mormonism, Spiritism, Zen Buddhism, Baha'i, Anglo–Israelism, Scientology, Eastern Religions, Islam, Seventh-Day Adventism, Unitarianism, and other cults.

Walter Martin attempts to approach each cult with a historical analysis of the rise of the cult. He then completes an evaluation of the particular teachings relating to the cult and provides a reply against the errors of the cult using the Bible.

The study of cults can be very interesting and intriguing. This writer spent several years studying Mormonism from many reference works within and without the Mormon Church. He has visited special Mormon sites such as Johnson Farm in Hiram, OH where Joseph Smith claimed to have a vision. He has also been to the Mormon Temple around Washington D.C. The sincerity of the people in Mormonism has never been questioned at any time; however, they have been misguided into a maze of circular reasoned contradictions. Their religion is a progressive one, which is a classic sign of a cult. When one becomes a Christian, they have the opportunity of learning all the teachings of the Bible prior to becoming a member. With Mormonism, small incremental doses of the poisonous doctrine of Joseph Smith and other Mormon leaders are interjected along the way. The material in The Kingdom of the Cults is an excellent beginning point in studying the various religious groups we may come across. It is important we have an understanding of these groups, their teachings, their vocabularies, and the weaknesses that can be used to try and reach and pull some of them from the abyss.

I highly recommend adding this book to the church library. One important suggestion: do not buy an older edition of this book. Purchase the latest edition of this book available. Unlike the teachings of the Bible that change not, the cults' teachings change over time which make revisions necessary.

Originally printed in the *West Virginia Christian*, Vol. 11, No. 10, October 2004, p. 8. Reprinted by permission.

The Eternal Kingdom
(F.W. Mattox)

F.W. Mattox was the founder and first president of Lubbock Christian University. He received his B.A. degree from Central State Teacher's College in Edmund, OK in 1934; his M.A. degree from the University of Oklahoma in 1940; and his Ph.D. degree from George Peabody College in Nashville, TN in 1947. Brother Mattox made several valuable contributions to Christian Education, especially a very beneficial book on church history. That book was The Eternal Kingdom which was used as a textbook for church history at Harding. The book began as a mimeographed manuscript that became so popular that the demand for the material made the publishing of the book a given.

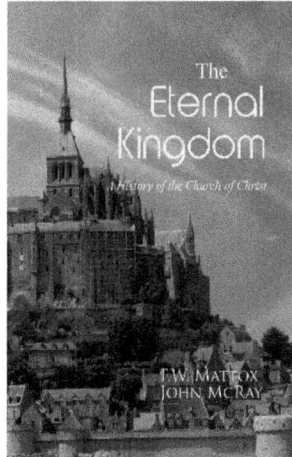

Church history is a fascinating subject to study. It is a very large field that provides many hours of profitable research for those who seek to understand where we have come from and how we got here. The Eternal Kingdom provides a very useful layout of church history that can be expanded with further research. This is a great work from the perspective of one who understands the aim of churches of Christ—to practice undenominational Christianity of the New Testament.

The layout of the book is in blocks of centuries so the chronology is kept in focus beginning with the church in prophecy and fulfillment. It discusses the progression and digression in the early centuries following the first century. The writer discusses uninspired works from those shortly after the close of the first century such as the Epistle of Barnabas. It also discusses the controversy and departures from New Testament Christianity, which eventually climaxed in the rise of the Roman Catholic Church. The book provides an overview of the various councils and false doctrines that arose as the apostles had foretold by the power of the Holy Spirit; e.g., 1 Timothy 4:1-4.

The work then deals with those who began to see the Roman Catholic Church as a great evil and sought to reform the organization during the Protestant Reformation. Men like John Wycliffe, Martin Luther, Hurldreich Zwingli, and John Calvin are discussed. The book deals with the Protestant Reformation in Germany, Switzerland, England, and the reaction of the Roman Catholic Church toward these efforts to reform the Catholic Church. It is very shocking to see the methods with which religious matters were resolved during this time. Men from this time were put to death solely for wanting to put the Scriptures in the language that people could read. During this day the Bible was kept in Latin, but this was no longer the language of the common people so they had to rely on what the Catholic clergy told them what the Bible said and meant. Men like Wycliffe, Tyndale, and Luther believed the power of the word of God was all that was needed to show the falsehoods of Catholicism. A study of this period is very beneficial in understanding attitudes that are still very prevalent today.

The history then turns to the United States and the various religious bodies that left Europe for the New World. One of the reasons these religious groups left was to escape religious persecution; e.g., the Puritans. In America, freedom of religion was protected by the Bill of Rights in the U.S. Constitution. This provided an opportunity for free religious thought to flourish. Men arose and spoke out about the errors of not only the Roman Catholic Church but also the multiplicity of denominations and parties. Men would arise and call people back to the Bible and would make great sacrifices for the plea to restore worship to the pattern of the New Testament. Men like James O'Kelley, Barton W. Stone, Thomas Campbell, Alexander Campbell, and

Walter Scott were a part of this movement. The book chronicles some of their significant contributions to the movement. It also deals with the unification of these movements based solely on the Scriptures. Indeed this is the surest ground that can unify us. Anything more or less than the word of God is a foundation of sand.

Indeed, the past mistakes of history can be repeated unless we learn from the past. Also, the great accomplishments of history can likewise be repeated if we follow the pattern of the first century and those who would seek to walk in the same paths. This book will provide a student a good reference to put the events of church history in perspective and provide a framework for future study. It will renew a person's love for the freedoms of this country, freedoms that are being challenged every moment. F.W. Mattox passed away this year on March 16, 2002.

Originally printed in the *West Virginia Christian*, Vol. 10, No. 3, March 2003, p. 8. Reprinted by permission.

Bible Questions and Answers
(Cecil R. May, Jr.)

I have been a reader of *The Magnolia Messenger* for several years. I have enjoyed the paper while it was edited by the late Al Franks, and I continue to enjoy it under the editorship of Dennis Doughty. I was blessed to know both of these men. Through the pages of *The Magnolia Messenger*, I came to know and respect Cecil May, Jr. I cut out and saved some of his columns of "Bible Questions Answered" until I could save them in PDF format. Now, these have been collected in a single volume published by Faulkner University. Since that time, I have been blessed to attend Faulkner's Bible Lectureship and meet brother May and hear him lecture. He and his wife were a delight to meet, and I am confident if you had the same opportunity your experience would be similar.

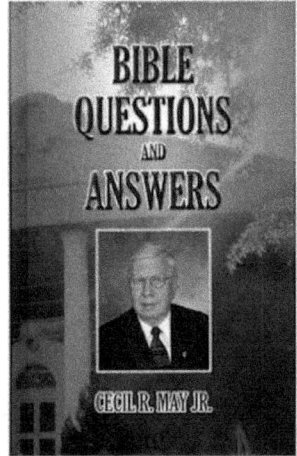

Some preachers have been using a Q&A format for some of their services. Some lectureships have Q & A formats as well. I have seen some men do this extemporaneously with questions from the floor, such as Alan Highers. Having been on an Q&A program, I can attest that the stress level for prepared questions before an audience is daunting enough. I also appreciate Robert Veil, Jr.'s column in *The West Virginia Christian* on Bible questions too. Columns and books like these can be a great reference for querists and answerers. Brother May does not shy away from questions that the answers may make some uncomfortable in their seats. For example, here is a statement he makes about proms:

I have known of too many high school girls and boys from

good families, active in church, youth groups, seemingly dedicated to the Lord, who unexpectedly became unwed mothers or fathers after attending their high school proms. (320).

As with any answer to a Bible question, the knowledge of the one providing the answer is important. May served as the Dean of the V.P. Black College of Biblical Studies at Faulkner University earlier as President of Magnolia Bible College. He holds a B.A., M.A., and M. Div. from Harding University, and was awarded the L.L.D. from Freed-Hardeman University. He has spent many years in the classroom both as student and teacher, so Bible questions and Bible answers is an arena in which he is well qualified to operate. Some questions deal with controversial subjects, so the answers may seem controversial to some readers. I am confident brother May would encourage you to "Fact Check" his remarks in accordance with the Scriptures. The book is organized by questions around a given subject, e.g., salvation, role of women, church leadership, Bible passages, etc. The book also provides a helpful Scripture Index, so the material is more accessible. Brother May provides answer to over 160 Bible questions. Brother May has been writing this column since 1980, and he continues to do so. Perhaps there will be a follow-up volume, but until then I recommend getting on the mailing list of *The Magnolia Messenger* and adding this book to the church library.

Originally printed in the *West Virginia Christian*, Vol. 30, No. 7, July 2023, p. 8. Reprinted by permission.

Thomas Campbell: Man of the Book
(Lester G. McAllister)

While reading various works in Restoration History I have notices that sometimes writings on Thomas and Alexander Campbell often end up focusing more on Alexander than Thomas. Due to the vast accomplishments and amount of influence Alexander Campbell, this is partly natural. However, one should not lose sight of Thomas Campbell and his contributions to the Restoration Movement. Thomas Campbell is a "bridge" figure from the Old World's religion to the New World's religion. Thomas Campbell was born on February 1, 1763 in County Down, Ireland, but he migrated to the area of Bethany, Virginia (now West Virginia) in 1807. Lester G. McAllister explains the significance of Thomas Campbell's place in Restoration History:

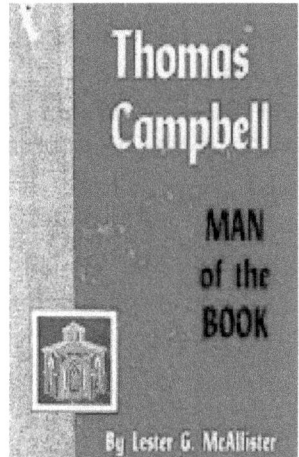

> Historians, when they have mentioned him at all, have spoken of him along with Barton W. Stone and Walter Scott as one of the founders of the movement known today as "Disciples of Christ," and as the father of Alexander Campbell. But Thomas Campbell was more than that. He was a transitional figure, forming a link between the religious traditionalism of the Old World and the spirit and zeal of the New—a man who, like so many in America, at that time, lived the first half of his life in Ireland and the last half on the American frontier. [McAllister, p. 12.]

Thomas Campbell was an exemplary educator for the time and was able to use this gift to complement the efforts he made to the restoring of New Testament Christianity in America. He was trained at the prestigious University of Glasgow and completed significant training in addition to this time at the University.

There are several contributions that Thomas Campbell made to the Restoration Movement. His writing of the *Declaration & Address of the Christian Association of Washington* in 1809 is one of the classical watershed documents of the Restoration Movement in comparison to the much earlier *Last Will & Testament of the Springfield Presbytery* from Barton W. Stone and others at Cane Ridge, KY. In the meetings leading up to the printing of the *Declaration & Address*, the slogan *Where the Scriptures speak, we speak; and where the Scriptures are silent, we are silent."* was coined. Thomas Campbell also established the first school in Cambridge, OH but also worked in schools in Pennsylvania and Kentucky as well. Due to his work in education, some such as Robert Richardson, were actually brought into the New Testament Church. Probably the greatest contribution he made was the preparation he did in rearing Alexander Campbell. Thomas was his father, teacher, counselor, and often filled in for him as editor and writer for the *Christian Baptist* and the *Millennial Harbinger*. Thomas was first and foremost an evangelist of the one church founded Christ and governed by his constitution, the New Testament.

Lester G. McAllister's biography of Thomas Campbell is an excellent work for reading and researching this period of history. At the time of publication, he was both Dean of Students and Associate Professor of the Department of Religion at Bethany College. He has done much research in Restoration History and this book is just one example of the fruits of his labor. His work is aptly cited and indexed for future study which is important because there are writings that have conflicting dates and details. If you are interested in serious study of the Campbells, then this is one work you will want to seek out.

On January 4, 1854 Thomas Campbell died at Bethany one month prior to his 91st birthday. He was buried in the family cemetery, God's Acre, in Bethany, VA (now West Virginia).

The Disciples' Prayer
(Hugo McCord)

Recently, I was requested to present a series on prayer. As I assembled reference materials, I shopped at a local used bookstore and came across a popular book that stated it was the 10th anniversary edition, and I learned it has over 1 million copies sold. I purchased the volume to see if it had any insights or approaches that I might find of use. While the book had several positive points, it also had some negative ones too. I went to my shelf and started reading Hugo McCord's The Disciples' Prayer and thought "Now this is a book on the subject that should be in new and used bookstores in a celebrated 10th anniversary edition!" Sadly, many of the works published among churches of Christ do not have the marketing support as some of large publishing houses. I believe brother McCord's book far exceeds the value of the one I purchased that day.

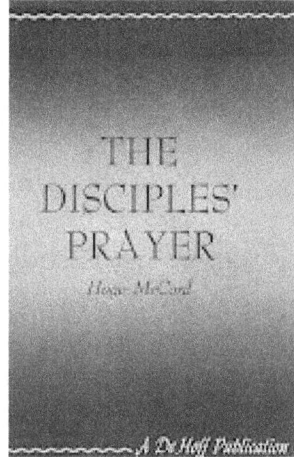

The late brother McCord wrote this book in 1954 as Vice President of Central Christian College (now Oklahoma Christian University). McCord's scholarship was well known. He received degrees from Freed-Hardeman College (now University), University of Illinois, and a doctorate from Southern Baptist Seminary. Brother McCord's dissertation was on the supposed "Synoptic Problem" which I find of interest since it is a theory of many modernists who attack the Bible. The "Synoptic Problem" claims there are discrepancies, even contradictions between Matthew, Mark and Luke. They even go so far as to suggest an imaginary author called "Q" that the gospel writers had to borrow from. Some suggest that Mark's gospel was written first and Matthew had to borrow from it. Imagine that! Matthew, an apostle who was with Jesus during His ministry, had to borrow from Mark who was not an apostle. Difficult to believe? Indeed. Occasionally McCord writings point out how these critics overlook certain realities that contradict their theories. For example, McCord's chapter on "Give Us This Day Our Daily Bread" discusses the word "daily" and how modernists have far missed the mark:

> Many scholars have doubted that the word "daily," epiousion, in this petition is a faithful translation. Actually, some great scholars have been unfamiliar with epiousion. Origen (c. 185-254) was bold to say that Matthew and Luke just made up the word. But Chrysostom, Gregory Nyssen, and Basil of Caesarea—all eminent Greek-speaking scholars—thought that epiousion really means "daily"... Centuries elapsed, and modern scholars, still unfamiliar with epiousion, refused to accept the translation "daily" (needful). However, thanks to penetrating scholarship (?), the stigma of coining the word was taken off Matthew and Luke, and laid on the broad shoulders of imaginary author "Q," from whom Matthew and Luke copied (?). So said modernists Moulton and Milligan as late as 1919. But in 1925 Q was exonerated from coining the word, for lo it was found in an old Greek housekeeping book. (Page 62)

The Disciples' Prayer discusses the model of prayer Jesus gave in the "Sermon on the Mount" in Matthew and later to a smaller group in Luke. These two accounts are not parallel in the chronological but topical sense since the Sermon on the Mount is five chapters before the model prayer of Luke 11. Also, the wording is not identical in these models which indicate it was never intended to be recited repetitively as some do—a practice Jesus warned about just prior in Matthew's account. And churches of Christ are not the only ones to point this matter out!

I found the words of Martin Luther of interest on this and more pungent:

> Thus, as we see, it was carried on in monasteries, nunneries and the whole ecclesiastical crowd, that seem to have had nothing else to do in their calling than to weary themselves daily so many hours, and at night besides, with singing and reading their Horas; and the more of this they could do, the holier and greater worship they called it. And yet among them all there was not one that uttered a real prayer from his heart: but they were all filled with the heathenish notion that one must tire God and one's self with crying and muttering, as if he neither could nor would otherwise hear; and they have thereby accomplished nothing else than to waste their time and punish themselves...with their praying.— Martin Luther, Commentary on the Sermon On The Mount, Philadelphia, PA: Lutheran Publication Society, 1892, pp. 240-269.

Brother McCord does a thoughtful and insightful analysis of what some commonly refer to as "The Lord's Prayer" or "The Model Prayer." McCord points out that it was never a prayer that the Lord actually prayed so to call it "The Lord's Prayer" would be incorrect unless one is speaking of a pattern of prayer taught by the Lord. The study of prayer has been enriching and this small volume spoke volumes compared to other works I have examined of longer length.

Originally printed in the *West Virginia Christian*, Vol. 18, No. 1, January 2011, p. 8. Reprinted by permission.

The Four-Fold Gospel
(J.W. McGarvey & Philip Y. Pendleton)

J.W. McGarvey is one of the more highly respected scholars among churches of Christ to this day. His father emigrated from Ireland to America to settle in Hopkinsville, KY where John William was born in 1829. J.W. McGarvey's exposure to the church began when he entered Bethany College which was under the control of Alexander Campbell. He had the privilege of hearing Alexander preach in the church at Bethany on multiple occasions. In April 1848 he was immersed at Buffalo Creek by one of his professors, W.K. Pendleton. Pendleton was a man McGarvey admired greatly for his knowledge and teaching ability. Buffalo Creek was the same body of water where Alexander and Thomas Campbell were immersed. McGarvey then decided to dedicate his life to preaching of the gospel. He graduated from Bethany in 1850 at the top of the class and delivered his commencement speech in Greek.

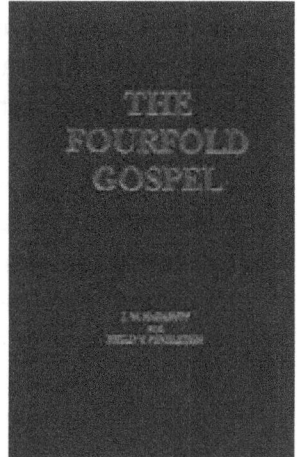

McGarvey would go on to write many valuable works which are still highly prized today including: Lands of the Bible, Original Commentary on Acts, New Commentary on Acts, Commentary on Matthew & Mark, Evidences of Christianity, Jesus & Jonah and The Authorship of Deuteronomy.

McGarvey worked with W.K. Pendelton's son, Philip, in the production of *The Fourfold Gospel*. There have been some criticisms of portions of the book that some believe to be more the work of Pendleton deserving the criticism than McGarvey. (One needs to keep in mind that this work and the commentary

Thessalonians, Corinthians, Galatians and Romans were published after McGarvey's death.) While it is intriguing to sort out this matter, one needs to keep in mind that McGarvey is not the authority *per se*. As with all the works of men—verify them with the Book of Books! The *Four-Fold Gospel* was my textbook for the class *Life of Christ* at Freed-Hardeman University. Unlike some gospel harmonies which seek to combine just the synoptics (Matthew, Mark & Luke), this work is a harmony of all four gospels. Sadly, many harmonies of the gospels are filled with a modernistic bias. Looking for a work written by a trusted member of the church who helped fight against modernism among the churches? Here it is! The work is not designed for the scholars but by a scholar for all to read and understand. It was reported that McGarvey's preaching was so easy to understand that a child could follow the lesson but would challenge any man to be able to deliver such an address themselves. This book was written for Bible Class teachers and more advanced students. While the work is easy to understand, it is not exactly a book that is easy to read from cover-to-cover so it will take time to become comfortable with the layout of material. Be sure to read the introductory material that explains the structure of the marking system prior to reading the work or you will miss some of the benefit that the writers have provided. The book is more than a chart showing the order of events of the gospels and including the Biblical text. It includes commentary from the research and a lifetime of study of McGarvey near the end of his life. There is a valuable index to all four gospels at the back of the book showing what page number the material can be found on.

John William McGarvey died on October 6, 1911 and is buried in Lexington, KY. The Four-Fold Gospel was released three years after McGarvey's death. I have had honor of standing at his grave and taking my children there as well. My hope is that they will cherish the eternal truths that McGarvey championed in his life as well.

Originally printed in the *West Virginia Christian*, Vol. 16, No. 10, October 2009, p. 8. Reprinted by permission.

Handbook of Denominations in the United States
(Frank S. Mead & Samuel S. Hill)

The number of religious bodies out-side of the body of Christ is staggering. This book details 200 different denominations in the United States during the 1990s. Denominationalism is a direct contradiction to the prayer for unity made by Jesus. There was no denomination until hundreds of years after the establishment of the one true church during the first century. A fundamental question we must always ask our misled friends in denominations—"Is the name of your denomination in the New Testament?" Indeed there is something in a name!

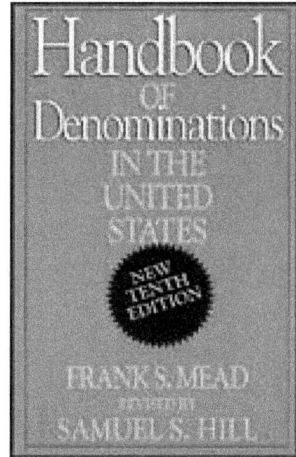

A member of the church of Christ did not publish this book; however, there is a wealth of information about denominational bodies in the United States. The writers group some denominations under broad categories (which further illustrated the divisive nature of denominationalism) including: Adventist, Baptist, Brethren, The Christian Church (The Stone-Campbell Movement), Church of God, Episcopal/Anglican, Friends (Quakers), Judaism, Latter-Day Saints (Mormon), Lutheran, Mennonite, Methodist, Moravian, Old Catholic, Orthodox (Eastern), Pentecostal, Presbyterian, Reformed, and a host of other religious groups that do not fall into these categories. A brief article is written about the founding of the denomination, its headquarters, population estimates, sponsored institutions, and peculiar teachings.

In the Appendix there is a wealth of valuable information including a listing of headquarter addresses for Denominations and schools associated with the organization. There is also a very informative glossary of terms in the Appendix as well.

Let me emphatically state that I do NOT believe the church of Christ is a denomination. A denomination is part of a whole of religions established by men, but the church of Christ is the whole body of Christ, not a part. With this in mind, it is interesting to read the information the writers provided about Churches of Christ. The text reads as follows:

> A distinctive plea for unity—a unity that is Bible-based—lies at the heart of Churches of Christ. It is believed that the Bible is "the beginning place," in and through which God-fearing people can achieve spiritual oneness—to "speak where the Bible speaks and to be silent where the Bible is silent" in all matter pertaining to faith and morals. Consequently, members recognize no other written creed or confession of faith. In all religious matters, there must be a "thus said the Lord."

The book goes on to describe churches of Christ as follows:

> Stressing strict adherence to the New Testament pattern of worship and church organization, they refused to join any intercongregational organization such as a missionary society. Worship was simple, and they opposed the addition of instrumental music on the grounds that the New Testament did not authorize it and the early church did not use it.

Is it not amazing how accurate the plea of churches of Christ is stated in this book? It is tragic that some read this book and do not see the confusion of denominations versus the simplicity of the New Testament pattern! This reference book is a valuable tool to learn about various religious groups from a denominational source. It illustrates how denominations are like the grains of sand of an unstable foundation while the church of Christ is found upon the rock of Jesus Christ!

Originally printed in the *West Virginia Christian*, Vol. 11, No. 8, August 2004, p. 8. Reprinted by permission.

The Book of Genesis: Foundational Truth and the Unfolding of God's Plan for Redemption (Memphis School of Preaching Lectures, Curtis Cates, Editor)

The first book of the Bible, Genesis, is an exciting study of the beginning of the world to where the Israelites enter into Egypt thanks to the providential care of God through Joseph. As the title of the book suggests—"Foundational Truth," this is exactly what the book of Genesis is about. Having a firm understanding of Genesis is critical for understanding the Bible and the reason the world is in the state that it is. Christians do not have to wonder how the earth and man got here. All the Christian needs to do is read and marvel!

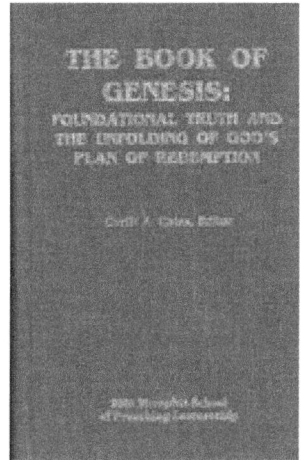

The book edited by brother Cates is the written record of the 2001 Memphis School of Preaching Lectureship. The book is dedicated to the memory of Rex A. Turner, Sr.; which sets a very high bar to be achieved. This monumental lectureship book passes the bar! Rex A. Turner, Sr. truly exemplified the phrase "a [Christian] gentleman and a [Christian] scholar." Anyone who has read Turner's works should agree.

The book contains a series of textual lectures that are arranged in the order of the text. There are also excellent articles on why we should study the Old Testament. Also included are articles which address false concepts such as Theistic Evolution, Gap Theory, and Documentary Hypothesis and false attacks on Genesis in order to prop up such false concepts such as Genesis being mythological or poetical. Included are lectures on some of the men and women in Genesis. One lesson that we often lose sight of is that our actions have consequences. Sometimes these consequences have effects that can outlive us. Studying the right and wrong decisions of the people in Genesis should remind us that what may be a bad situation for us may be a great blessing for others; e.g., Joseph. There are many consequences (good and bad) that the origins of are recorded in the book of Genesis.

The lectureship book is over 1,000 pages and is in larger print type for easier reading. Contributors are faithful men and women who have written articles that are enjoyable to read. This book is a very valuable addition to the library of the church. One mistake that some make is thinking a study of Genesis for adults would be worn out from teaching in the school years. Do not make that mistake. There are many who have never studied the book, have not studied it for years, or have never studied it on an adult class level. It was my distinct pleasure to have the late Professor James Tollerson for Genesis & Exodus at Freed-Hardeman University. The class was as thrilling as I remembered studying it growing up. Of course, Dr. Tollerson was prepared to teach. This book will assist in one's preparation.

Originally printed in the *West Virginia Christian*, Vol. 14, No. 3, March 2007, p. 8. Reprinted by permission.

God & Government
(Dave Miller)

Polybius (ca. 200–118 BCE) was born in Arcadia of Greece, and through his father's influence, he had over 40 years of experience in politics, diplomacy, and war. He witnessed the growth of Rome from a city to a republic. He wrote 40 books of history, but only five are extant (along with several fragments of the other works). He took the study of history very seriously:

> What man is so indifferent or so idle that he would not wish to know how and under what form of government almost all the inhabited world came under the single rule of the Romans in less than fifty-three years (220–168 BC)? (Polybius, Histories I.1).

The twin enemies of ignorance and apathy are a serious threat to any republic including our own. Polybius argued that the best type of constitution was one that blended the three main types of government identified at the time: kingship, aristocracy, and democracy:

> For it is evident that we must regard as the best constitution a combination of all three these varieties since we have had proof of this not only theoretically but by actual experience. (Polybius, Histories, IV.3).

Some erroneously think our national government is a democracy when it is actually a republic. Polybius was among the first to speak of what has been called anacyclosis (circulation) which is the view that a nation may go through various types of

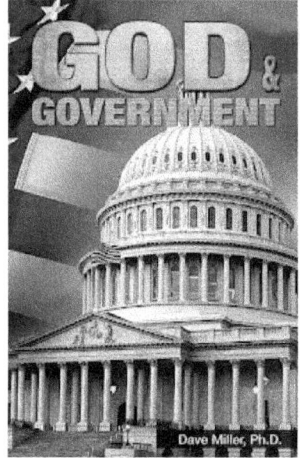

government in a cycle from monarchy to democracy with stages in between. He argued the best way to break this cycle and provide true stability was to have elements of each. Our constitution blends these three varieties: kingship (executive branch), democracy (legislative branch), and aristocracy (the judicial branch).

The Founding Fathers were knowledgeable of these types of theories, plus they clearly were influenced by the OT model of the civic nation of Israel. It is no accident that the expression that we are a nation of Judeo-Christian ethics is used to describe the United States. These themes are touched on in Dave Miller's excellent work, God & Government in a series of eight essays. Several important subjects are discussed including: the origin/purpose of government, unalienable rights, the nature of law, how the government operates, capital punishment, care of the poor, welfare, entitlements, qualifications of rulers, taxation, and illegal immigration. Each of these essays is supported by materials from the Founding Fathers and/or the Scriptures. The essays will challenge one's thinking, and some will not agree with every point made, possibly because of teaching we have not received in public school. For example, there are some who think socialism rather than capitalism is more suited to Christianity; however, that is a misconception of both systems. Acts 2:44–45 and 4:32–35 are often cited as support for socialism; however, Miller shows that the context of these passages does not support the way socialism operates. Depending on one's view of the purpose of government, the response to these essays may not only challenge one's thinking but likewise challenge their views or feelings. Dave Miller does an excellent work of interweaving passages and principles from the Bible that will be beneficial to all regardless of where they may be on the political spectrum. Each essay is very well documented with endnotes for further study and verification. There are indices of subjects, names, and scriptures included which facilitate easier reference to the material.

Thomas Jefferson once wrote, "wherever the people are well informed they can be trusted with their own government." How well are we educating our children on the foundation of our republic and the philosophies undergirding our constitution? Have we become so far removed from the issue that we would surrender our freedoms (including religion) without making a single argument or defense? This book will help shore up the foundation in what has been reported lacking in the education of our young people. It should be read by every concerned citizen of the United States, even those who claim dual citizenship in Heaven.

Originally printed in the *West Virginia Christian*, Vol. 27, No. 7, July 2020, p. 8. *Reprinted by permission.*

Hidden Meanings Buried in the Bible
(Dave Miller)

The subtitle of this book is *Achieving a Better Understanding of the Bible via Its Cultures and Languages*. This is a newer work from the pen of Dave Miller who serves as the Executive Director at Apologetics Press. The vast range of history covered in the pages of our Bibles presents a thrilling challenge to study and contextualize.

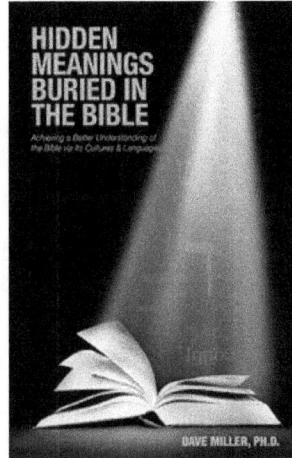

The book is designed for class study or personal study. There are about 450 review or discussion questions in the book and an answer key is provided. The book is indexed by Scripture references and over 300 endnotes. Dr. Miller has presented a study that will help all who may not be as familiar with what some may classify as "oddities" of the Bible; although these are not really "oddities" but matters that some are just not familiar with. I have not sat down and read those book cover to cover, but instead I have found portions of it interesting to sit and read at various intervals.

For example, what is the meaning of the term tetragrammaton (four letters), and why is it rendered Jehovah or Yahweh in various translations or commentaries? How did these two names come from the same four letters (YHWH)? Or why do some translations use the word "hell" but other translations sometimes use the word "hades"? There are other matters that may escape one's notice. For example, why do some translations italicize certain words in our printed Bibles? There are cultural matters that brother Miller explains, such as why did Boaz received a sandal from his relative in relation to marrying Ruth?

Or why did people tear their clothes in the Bible? There are several questions answered in this book that I am sometimes asked by those curious about the Bible but are sometimes reluctant to ask. Occasionally I am asked about foot washing as a religious ritual today, and why we do not practice that in our services. The book addresses this matter too. There are important matters pointed out that some often overlook. For example, some claim that the food provided during the exodus was a natural substance in the wilderness; however, the word manna means "what," as in "What is this?" Obviously, if the Israelites did not recognize the substance in their natural world, then the modernist's attempt to deny the miraculous provision of God falls as flat as a pancake. Words such as "messenger" and "angel" which come from the same Greek word (*angelos*) are explained so readers can recognize that such words have different meanings and the context of the passage helps determine the better English word to convey the original meaning.

Several of these matters I have learned over the years from Apologetics Press, the Christian Courier, or other writings. Still, there are those who are not familiar with these resources, and this book may serve as their introduction to further study.

Originally printed in the *West Virginia Christian*, Vol. 30, No. 8, August 2023, p. 8. *Reprinted by permission.*

Is Christianity Logical?
(Dave Miller)

Perhaps you have heard others re-
mark, as I have, that common sense has
become rather uncommon these days.
Some seem to think that Christianity
does not make any common sense. Or
put another way, Christianity does not
make any logical sense. Some claim that
logic and religion are mutually exclusive, meaning these disciplines never intersect. Dave Miller's latest book is a direct challenge to such an illogical or irrational viewpoint—rational meaning
logical, and irrational meaning illogical. The Bible mandates that
we are to think about walking with God from a rational or logical
standpoint, *"Come now, and let us reason together"* (Isaiah 1:18
NKJV). The transliterated Hebrew word for "reason" is yâkach
which means "to prove, decide, judge, rebuke, reprove, correct,
be right" (*Brown-Driver-Briggs*). So, God challenges our mental
faculties as well as our emotions. Miller correctly points out
that:

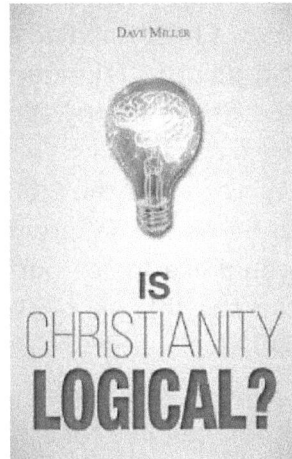

> Many well-meaning, religious people take the foolish posi-
> tion that truth is elusive and unattainable, and that doctri-
> nal correctness is unimportant and unnecessary. Only in
> the task of interpreting the Bible do such people take the
> position that truth is relative, always changing, and some-
> thing of which they can never be sure (4).

The book deals with several relevant questions:

- Is Christianity irreconcilable with logic and reason?
- Is "faith" accepting what you cannot know or prove?

- Did Jesus expect people to believe Him without proof?
- Does Christianity require evidence and proof before being accepted?
- Is the religion of Christ "better-felt-than-told"?

I first met Dave Miller in 1993 when he was lecturing on "How Christ Handled Controversy." Since that time, I have made it a point to take our family to his seminars, gospel meetings, and other events. We taught together at Alkire Road's Future Preacher Training Camp, but I was also his student for his class on "Logic and the Bible." When he was in our area, I invited him to be on my TV program, "Light From Above." For those who would like to see our discussion on some of this material, you can see this on YouTube by searching for "Light From Above #299."

I was very pleased to see this material published in a format that is suitable for class or personal study. The work is less than 100 pages, so it would be easy to share with someone without a substantial hit to the wallet. Included are 130 study questions to help generate discussion and the answers are provided for those who stand before an audience to teach.

Dave Miller has a B.A. degree in Speech & Bible from Lubbock Christian University, M.A. degree in Speech Communication from Texas Tech University, M.Div. and M.A.R. from Harding School of Theology, and Ph.D. in Rhetoric and Public Address from Southern Illinois University. Dr. Miller has been the Executive Director of Apologetics Press since 2005.

Piloting the Strait
(Dave Miller)

On one occasion the congregation where this writer attends needed me to fill in due to the absence of the regular minister. They had a special request— "please deliver a lesson on the New Hermeneutic so we know what this issue is about." What a huge topic for such a little amount of time! At that time, Piloting the Strait had not been written; however, I had recently acquired Dave Miller's articles related to the subject which were invaluable for the lesson. The material was excellent and I wished that it would be preserved in a longer lasting medium. This wish was granted with the publication of Piloting The Strait: A Guidebook for Assessing Change in Churches of Christ.

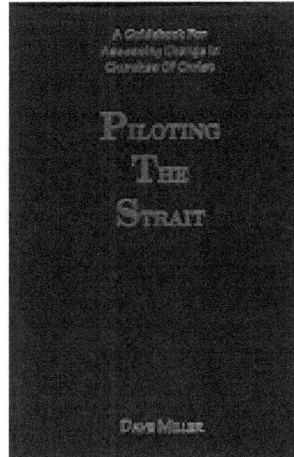

This book is a primer on the changes that some are trying to push on churches of Christ. The New Hermeneutic is only "new" in that it is new packaging of old liberal attacks on the authority of the Bible and how we ascertain Bible authority. Part III: The Mechanism For Change: The "New Hermeneutic" is a very effective discussion of the intentions and consequences of the New Hermeneutic. It is critical that all understand the philosophy of this movement (which will probably resurface again under a different packaging).

I first remember hearing Dave Miller lecture at the 1993 FHU Bible Lectureship and was very impressed with his effective defense of the Scriptures. He was speaking on the subject of "How Christ Handled Controversy." Everyone should read that lecture and fully understand the methods that the Master used to deal with His opponents. I remember vividly the point Dave Miller made in that lecture in regards to our need for "book, chapter, and verse" preaching in our pulpits. He stated, "Note that Jesus' persistent allusion to scripture is all the more remarkable when one considers the fact that Jesus was God and therefore was originating scripture with his own utterance. Yet He quoted scripture over and over again." If Jesus quoted the Old Testament to sustain his logical arguments against His critics, then we should do and demand no less than book, chapter, and verse preaching and teaching.

Piloting the Strait begins with a discussion of the roots and catalyst for change. These factors need to be studied and reflected upon. It shows how pop culture and modern society has impacted views some have regarding religion. It then discusses the goal of the change agents in regards to music, preaching, prayer, leadership, worship styles, and other areas where those who trouble the church are seeking to spread their teaching. It also discusses the motivation for those seeking to change. Some say we cannot know others motives so we should not judge them; however, Jesus said in Matthew 7:20 "By their fruits you shall know them." We need to realize that while there are false teachers who are misguided, there are others who would make profit for themselves at the expense of those who seek the truth. 2 Peter 2:1-3 is very plain about the sinister motives of some false teachers—"But there were false prophets also among the people, even as there shall be false teachers among you, who privily shall bring in damnable heresies, even denying the Lord that bought them, and bring upon themselves swift destruction. And many shall follow their pernicious ways; by reason of whom the way of truth shall be evil spoken of. And through covetousness shall they with feigned words make merchandise of you: whose judgment now of a long time lingereth not, and their damnation slumbereth not." We should do all that we can to protect ourselves and others from the efforts of those who would change the church into something that is not the church of the New Testament.

The work also has a critical section on the antidote for this change movement. It discusses Bible truth and authority. It discusses the priority that must be given to God and His word.

This book is very valuable for all congregational leaders and members to read and understand. Hardeman Nichols' recommendation is right on the mark in reference to Piloting the Strait: "...penetrating insight into the very critical problem in which change agents are attempting to turn the church of our Lord into just another one of the many sects. This book is a 'must' for every leader in the church."

Dave Miller has three Masters degrees from Texas Tech University and Harding Graduate School of Religion. He holds a Ph.D. from Southern Illinois University. He has served as the Director of the Brown Trail School of Preaching and has now begun working with Apologetics Press. There are several books written about the issues that confront us in the church today. This is one book that should be in every religious library and encouraged to be read.

Originally printed in the *West Virginia Christian*, Vol. 10, No. 2, February 2003, p. 8. Reprinted by permission.

Richland Hills & Instrumental Music
(Dave Miller)

The subtitle of this book is "A Plea to Reconsider." Perhaps you have not heard that Richland Hills, which has over 6,400 members, has decided to utilize mechanical instruments in their worship to God.

One topic we often discuss is how to build up area churches without violating their autonomy. Some argue that things would be easier if the church's organization was more humanly centralized and hierarchical. However, one of the pitfalls of a human hierarchical arrangement is that if a hierarchy digresses, so often do the majority of churches under it. A decentralized autonomous organization is less impacted by digression by local congregations. To say that churches are autonomous does not mean they are without government. All churches of Chris are centralized under one head—Jesus Christ, have appointed leadership—elders, and are under one constitution—the New Testament.

Apologetics Press and Sain Publications have attempted to prevent the spread of the digression into instrumental music. Dr. Dave Miller, Executive Director of Apologetics Press, has written a 150-page response to the adoption of the instrument by Richland Hills. The plan is to distribute these books to as many churches as they possibly can. They are seeking financial support to postage and the printing of additional volumes as needed. Perhaps this is an opportunity for the leadership of your congregation to send materials to area churches in an effort to shore up their teaching on this subject as well? A website is set

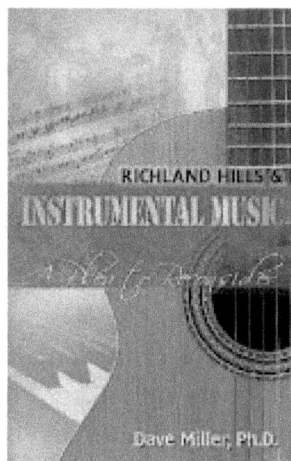

up for this book at *RichlandHillsAndInstrumentalMusic.com*. Copies of the book may be ordered at the site, or an electronic PDF copy of the book can be downloaded for free.

One of the items I sometimes see by those advocating digression is an assertion that they have already studied/know/answered all the arguments of a given issue. For example, Richland Hills' preacher stated he spent three days at Abilene Christian University studying all the debates and materials printed by those opposed to the instruments over the past 100 years. On the surface that may seem impressive, but Dave Miller lists a few books (the list is not exhaustive) totaling easily over 3,000 pages not including journals, tracts, and other materials. That is a lot of reading for three days! This type of assertion is meant to impress those who are willing to put their trust in a man rather than investigating themselves. Christians need to heed the words of John— *"Beloved, do not believe every spirit, but test the spirits, whether they are of God; because many false prophets have gone out into the world."* (1 John 4:1)

Please resist the temptation of thinking this is not an issue where you worship. A couple of years ago I was disappointed to hear a young person who was born and reared attending the congregation where I attend state "I don't know what the big deal is about instrumental music. The Bible does not say you cannot use the instrument." I pointed out that the question of authority is two-fold. The issue is both what the Bible says you cannot do, but also what it says you can do. Indeed the proverb is true—"an ounce of prevention is worth a pound of cure." If your congregation has not studied this matter in some time, then I highly recommend Dave Miller's book as greater than an ounce of prevention.

Originally printed in *West Virginia Christian*, Vol. 15, No. 8, August 2008, p. 8. Reprinted by permission.

The Silencing of God:
The Dismantling of America's Christian Heritage
(Dave Miller)

I have heard of Dave Miller's DVD "The Silencing of God" but have only recently viewed it. I was able to get a preview at a Bible Reading Marathon conducted by the Toledo Road Church of Christ of Lorain, Ohio at the Black River Amphitheatre with the Scriptures being read by teenagers over a 24-hour period where Brother Miller was able to speak at this event. While he and I were discussing our concern about the direction our country is being pushed, I asked brother Miller if he thought about putting this material in book form so people could communicate these vital facts documenting our nation's Christian heritage with others as they are able more easily. I was delighted to hear that a coffee table full-color edition of the book had just been published. As the adult class where we attend began viewing the DVD, I ordered a copy of this book for the church library. It is an excellent product both from content and the attractive quality of printing.

Those who know me personally know I attempt to keep up on national politics and the forces that are attempting to take us further away from God. So, the material in the DVD was not a total shock to me. What was surprising to me is the voluminous efforts early leaders made to ensure all knew our county was established to be a Christian nation—monuments, money, manuscripts, correspondence, speeches, mottos, oaths, songs, constitutions—Federal and States, etc. I often hear people say the United States is not a Christian nation and was never designed to be one. That the Founding Fathers desired to establish a secular government that merely tolerates various religions. I knew before watching the DVD that was absurdly FALSE. The Founding Fathers wrote the First Amendment to protect religious freedom as opposed to the sinister twisting of the phrase, "a wall of separation between church and state," in a letter by Thomas Jefferson to a Baptist association to reassure them that the Federal Government would not interfere with religion to restrict the exercise of religion. I am alarmed that some fail to realize the Bill of Rights, the first ten amendments, were written to preserve individual freedom from government interference. Particularly alarming is that few seem to realize that the freedom of the Press and Religion go together—these two are both in the First Amendment. Ask yourselves, "If the Press was being treated by the Federal Government the same way Christianity is, would they tolerate it?" It is a highly relevant question!

What I learned from the DVD is just how overtly the Founding Fathers and early leaders were in favor of New Testament Christianity. Sometimes people like to refer to our "Judeo-Christian Heritage"; however, the Founding Fathers were more specific to our Christian Heritage. They pointed out that we are a tolerant Nation because of, not in spite of, New Testament Christianity. The degree to which they expressed this was rather eye-opening to me. One of the quotes I vividly remember was by John Jay, the first Chief Justice of the first U.S. Supreme Court. The early founders of our Nation were not shy about affirming the importance of Christianity to the preservation of the Nation. John Jay wrote about supporting infidel (non-Christians) leaders:

> Providence has given to our people the choice of their rulers. It is the duty, as well as the privilege and interest, of **our Christian nation** to select and prefer **Christians for their rulers.**—Page 89.

268 | GIVE ATTENTION TO READING

Some refuse to be involved in politics in any way and prefer to avoid all discussion on this subject; however, political and societal forces are pushing churches into areas that we cannot support; e.g., accepting the homosexual lifestyle and using our tax dollars to fund abortions. If we do not use our rights to make Christ's views, which must be our views, on these two subjects clear to our leaders, then we will lose these two battles. And these two highly activist lobbies will not be interested in letting the church exempt herself. I wish we could continue in the luxury on relying on others to shoulder the political fight so we can focus solely on spreading the gospel, but we cannot. We must devote resources in this struggle too, or our ability to spread the gospel may be severely hindered. If we do not bow to our knees in prayer to God, we may find our knees forced to the ground against our wills and then we will be willing to pray to God but it will be a cry out to God in despair.

I found the words of President James A. Garfield, a member of the Christian Church, to be worthy of adoption:

> Now, more than ever before, **the people are responsible for the character of their Congress**. If that body be ignorant, reckless, and corrupt, it is because the people tolerate ignorance, recklessness, and corruption. If it be intelligent, brave, and pure, it is because the people demand these high qualities to present them in national legislature.... If the next centennial does not find us a great nation...it will be because **those who represent the enterprise, the culture, and the morality of the nation do not aid in controlling the political forces.**—Page 89.

It is time for Christians to be "strong in the strength which God supplies thru His beloved Son."

Denominational Doctrines
(Jerry Moffitt)

I have been honored to teach a class at the West Virginia School of Preaching called "Denominational Doctrines." I posted on a Facebook page reported to be of preachers asking for input on a textbook for this class. I was a bit disappointed that there were questions about why there would be such a class. Really? This is a class to train preachers on denominations, their respective doctrines, and how to answer error with Scripture. Now, I will grant that there are other relevant subjects for a man training to be a gospel preacher, but I would not say those other subjects are more important. Paul instructed Timothy as an evangelist: *"All Scripture is given by inspiration of God, and is profitable for doctrine, for reproof, for correction, for instruction in righteousness, that the man of God may be complete, thoroughly equipped for every good work"* (2 Timothy 3:16–17 NKJV). A sound gospel preacher does not have the authorization to pick and choose whether he is to reprove or correct.

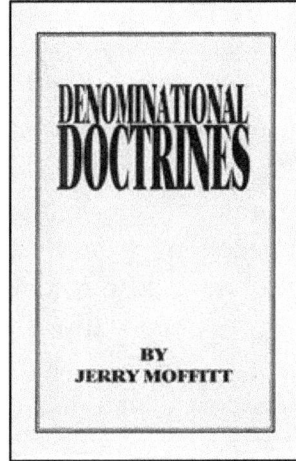

Jerry Moffitt has written and debated for several years. He has spent most of his life in pursuit and defense of divine truth. As I have been going through my late father's library, I have come across several books, workbooks and other materials published to answer the errors advocated in denominations and cults. I am concerned in our offensive "non-offensive culture," that we may have become too timid in our defense of the truth. I try to impress on my students that there is no room for being caustic, full of rancor, or have a tongue dripping with malice in defending the gospel because the truth is offensive enough. Be kind, considerate, friendly, and compassionate with people in error. Expose the error, save the sinner! This work is over 650 pages and full of great teaching material.

This work deals with a host of pertinent issues including the authority of the Bible, the nature of faith, baptism, Calvinism, premillennialism, and various religious bodies in our nation today. Moffitt provides solid refutation to many of the doctrinal errors that are advocated in manmade creeds, disciplines, and other sources. He also provides an overview of some of the prominent cults and the major tenets of their religion. I caution my students to verify a doctrine is still being taught by an organization because sometimes they change their doctrines. But be sure to point out to whom you study with that man's doctrines change but God word never changes. There are several solid books on this subject that have been published that have points that are now out of date. Not because the writer made a mistake, but the doctrine was in error. Whether the newly adopted doctrine is correct or not still must pass the same truth test as the Bereans administered: *"they received the word with all readiness, and searched the Scriptures daily to find out whether these things were so"* (Acts 17:11 NKJV).

Originally printed in the *West Virginia Christian*, Vol. 30, No. 6, June 2023, p. 8. *Reprinted by permission.*

Nichol's Pocket Bible Encyclopedia
(C.R. Nichol)

One of the earliest religious books my parents gave to me was a 200+ page little black book small enough to fit into my shirt pocket entitled Nichol's Pocket Bible Encyclopedia. From this invaluable book I drew material for my first attempt at delivering a lesson at the Weirton Heights Church of Christ that was supposed to be 10 minutes. Being so nervous I think I finished my material in less than 7 minutes. My father stated that this little book is full of excellent material that one could preach from their entire career. While I have not put this to the test, I am confident that many lesson that need to be taught in our pulpits could be organized from the material in this book.

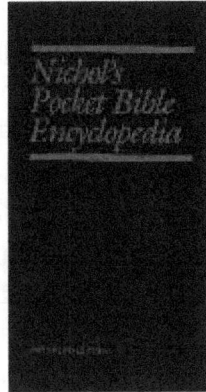

Some time ago, I read a review in *The Messenger* about this encyclopedia which I enjoyed so much I saved the article for reference in preparation of this article. Charles Ready Nichol was an effective evangelist, debater, and writer. Every Christian should pursue his debates and books. I recently saw where all his published works are now available on CD. Based on what I have seen of his writings, I am confident this CD would be a wise investment for those who are able to use electronic books on the computer. The Gospel Advocate has recently reprinted his series of books entitled Sound Doctrine that would be another fine edition to a church library.

C.R. Nichol lived from 1876 to 1971. He was a fellow debate student with another famous debater among us, Joe Warlick. He attended Nashville Bible School under David Lipscomb and James Harding. His sermons were described as so filled with information that the audience was captivated by the sheer volume of material presented in such a short amount of time. By the time he was 28 he had already been in sixty debates, but before his career would be over the number would climb to 300. He was also president of Thorp Spring Christian College in 1916. He also worked closely with both the *Gospel Advocate* and the *Firm Foundation*. It is estimated that he baptized over 30,000 people by the time he reached his prime. He has had a tremendous impact on many other preachers that would contribute greatly to the cause of Christ as well; e.g., Foy E. Wallace.

The book has a table of contents of nearly 60 topics that provide for quick access to material on various subjects. Relevant scriptures are quoted in the manuscript for quick review. One of the practices that C.R. Nichol incorporates is to use multiple passages from differing angles to more illuminate the truth on the topic. For example, on the subject of the Holy Spirit, C.R. Nichol stated:

> If the Spirit comes directly from God to convert sinners, the Bible is not true—unless the Spirit comes to the sinner to bring the 'law of the Lord,' the converting power. If it is necessary for the Spirit to bring the 'law of the Lord,' then the Bible does not contain the 'law of the Lord,' and if the Spirit must come directly from God to convert, then the Bible is not true, for it says: 'The law of the Lord is perfect, converting the soul.'

> One must 'see, hear and understand' to be converted. Jesus says the one 'having heard the word, keep it, and bring forth fruit with patience.' Lk. 8:15. If man is converted by the Spirit, independent of the word of God, and saved when converted, then he is saved without faith. 'For faith comes by hearing the word of God.' Rom. 10:17. But if the Spirit converts him and enables him to believe, then he had to be converted before he could believe, and as God saves the converted, it follows that he was saved before he could believe. If it is said that the Spirit in his power is necessary

to enable man to believe that he might be saved, then the law, the converting power, can have no effect on the sinner to convert him till the Spirit operates on the sinner. If this position be true, the Spirit itself does not convert the sinner, but operates on the sinner to enable him to believe. If this be true, then a sinner cannot believe without this operation, and as he cannot be saved till he believes, then he cannot be saved till the Spirit operates on him. The matter stands thus: The Spirit operates on the sinner to enable him to believe. All the Spirit operates on will believe (if this is denied, then the Spirit failed in its work), and all who believe will be saved. Then if man is lost, it is because God withholds the power which would enable him to believe and be saved, and then sends him to hell for not believing. Per the theory: Man can't believe till God sends him the enabling power of the Spirit; but God does not send the power to all men by which they are enable to believe, and then sends them to hell for not believing. Reader, do you believe that God is so unjust? I beg you, accept the truth; the Spirit has given the word—the law of God. You are to believe his word, obey him, God saves you. (pp. 138-139)

This is only a fraction of what he writes on this topic. He goes onto list passages that show works of the Holy Spirit and the works of the word of God being joined together. For example,

the Holy Spirit sanctifies (1 Cor. 6:11) but the word also sanctifies (John 17:17).

The encyclopedia, which was copyrighted in 1949, is still available for purchase—another testimony to its enduring value. Its size makes the book fairly inexpensive to purchase and share with others. It makes a great reference work for new converts who need further instruction in the word of God. I highly recommend it for young men working to develop material for sermons.

Works Cited:

Mel Futrell, "Nichol's Pocket Bible Encyclopedia," The Messenger, Knoxville, TN: East Tennessee School of Preaching, July 2001.

Nobel Patterson, "Restoration Leaders—C.R. Nichol," Opening Our Eyes to Jesus from Darkness to Light in Acts, Henderson, TN: Freed-Hardeman University, 2004, pp. 341-345.

Earl Irvin West, The Search for the Ancient Order, Germantown, TN: Religious Book Service, Vol. 4, 1987.

Originally printed in the *West Virginia Christian*, Vol. 13, No. 3, March 2006, p. 8. Reprinted by permission.

Balance:
A Tried and Tested Formula for Church Growth
(Ira North)

I recall *Balance* by Ira North coming out back in 1984. My father had purchased two copies of it to share with the leadership and membership of the congregation. He wanted everyone to read what was a new work in 1983 but is now reprinted in the Gospel Advocate's Classics Series. I have both copies of that work from my father's preaching days. It is among my treasured books and includes signatures of several saints that have since gone onto their reward. My father requested that everyone who read one of the copies sign their names to it.

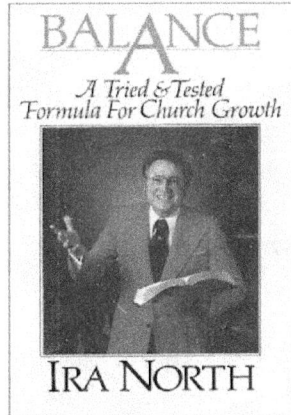

I recently had the blessing of taking "Education Program in the Church" taught by Dr. David Powell at the FHU School of Theology and this was one of the several works we were assigned to read. Part of the assignment of reading this work was writing a book review of it including some background information on brother North. Some called him "Fiery Irey" and he work a bright red sport jacket to match. Dad and I were able to see it on display at the Gospel Advocate Bookstore several years ago now.

Ira North conducted the *Amazing Grace Bible Hour* which was aired on television originating from Madison, Tennessee. It was formatted more like a Bible Class; however, it did have congregational singing from the Madison Church of Christ. I recall my parents watching it when it was available in our viewing area. The congregation in Madison grew from 400 to 4,000 membership. While circumstances vary from congregation to

275

congregation, I believe all can profit from reading (or re-reading) this book.

North uses Acts 2:40–47 as his text and model for this work. In it, he stresses the importance in balance in three major areas of work: teaching, evangelism, and benevolence. North suggested this model led to church growth then and will do so today. He emphasizes ten principles of church growth that were successful where he labored for several years. Ira North stated that the key to church growth is found in Ephesians 4:3, "endeavoring to keep the unity of the Spirit in the bond of peace" (NKJV). Of this passage, North noted the "number one problem in the local congregation today is keeping the unity of the spirit in the bond of peace." The point needs to be made from our pulpits continually. Bickering and backbiting have ruined many congregations, and we must be on guard to squash such from our conduct. The apostle Paul wrote "But if you bite and devour one another, beware lest you be consumed by one another!" (Galatians 5:15) Leadership needs to be vigilant that the truth of God's word is taught, but they also need to be on guard to make sure it is presented in love and free of rancor, malice or a caustic attitude. The truth will be offensive enough; we cannot allow our imbalance to be a stumbling block to the lost learning the gospel.

Originally printed in the *West Virginia Christian*, Vol. 30, No. 12, December 2023, p. 8. *Reprinted by permission*.

Conversions in Acts
(Basil Overton)

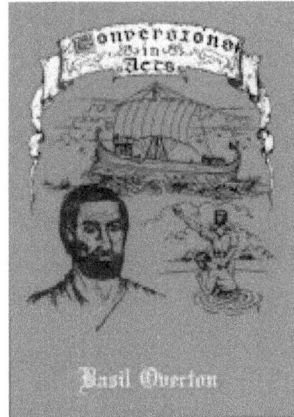

I was recently honored to participate in a gospel meeting preaching one
night on the theme of "What Must I Do
To Be Saved?—Lessons in Conversion
from the Book of Acts." My topic was
the conversion of the treasurer of Ethiopia. I had long desired to have a copy
of Brother Overton's book Conversions
in Acts, but had not found the time to
purchase the book. But, the book was
added to our family library as a congrat-
ulatory gift from brother Overton on the occasion of the birth of
our son, James. The inscription reads, "I hope that James will be
a faithful and able gospel preacher—Basil Overton." I hope his
inscription inspires our son to fulfill this high and noble position
in the kingdom.

This was the first book I pulled from my shelf to review in
preparation for this sermon. The book is very concise at just over
100 pages, but the lessons are weightier when compared to
some other books of much longer length. There are those who
complain about the faithful proclamation of the plan of salvation at the conclusion of a sermon. I had a discussion with a
friend who was of this persuasion. I asked why one would not
offer an invitation for those who wanted to respond to the message proclaimed. When he stated he had no problem with inviting people to obey the gospel, I realized his issue was not with
the invitation. The real complaint is the explanation of the gospel plan of salvation as part of the invitation. Inviting people to
obey the gospel without telling them what to do is like telling
them to take medicine without directions. In my opinion, any

preacher who refuses to explain the gospel plan of salvation at the end of a lesson is in "dereliction of duty" and should be fired. Likewise, any church leaders who would forbid the proclamation of the plan of salvation should be rebuked. I cannot fathom why some attack the instruction on the steps needed to obey the gospel other than being ashamed of the gospel.

Conversions in Acts examines several incidents of conversions in Acts. Of course, not all of the six steps to salvation are necessarily listed as: Hear, Believe, Repent, Confess, Baptism & Live Faithfully. However, one can readily see this pattern throughout these acts of conversion. For example, the man from Ethiopia heard the gospel preached to him from Philip. Based upon his query for baptism, his belief in the Son of God is implied. His repentance was already demonstrated in his willingness to travel such a distance to worship God in Jerusalem. His confession is recorded plainly in the text as well as his immersion. Although we cannot validate for certain that he remained faithful, there is historical reference that he went back and preached in Ethiopia. Why is it important to study these acts of conversions? Because the only way to become what they became is to do what they did! We cannot become a New Testament Christian unless we follow the commands, examples and implications in the New Testament.

This book also contains chapters dealing with miracles, Holy Spirit baptism, and the gift of the Holy Spirit. All are well written and readily adaptable to sermons that should be preached. The book first appeared as a series of articles in The World Evangelist. Thankfully, J.C. Choate published these articles in book form and several copies were printed.

Brother Overton is the founder of The World Evangelist and has been its sole editor since 1972 until it ceased publication in 2004—over 32 years of articles designed to take the gospel to the world. I have heard that plans are in the works to convert all the issues to a CD, which I hope comes to fruition. His work as editor has had a very positive influence among the brotherhood.

I was honored to attend an Appreciation Dinner at FHU Lecture-ship in his honor. He commented on his view of editing religious journals that should be followed by others. He is also retired Vice President and Bible Professor from Heritage Christian University (formerly International Bible College). He has been a gospel preacher since 1945.

Indeed one of the greatest questions, "What must I do to be saved?" is one to be studied and preached. This book will assist in teaching and preparing others to share the gospel plan of salvation.

Originally printed in *West Virginia Christian*, Vol. 15, No. 3, March 2008, p. 8. Reprinted by permission.

Evolution in the Light of Scripture, Science and Sense (Basil Overton)

Organic Evolution is a great evil and falsehood being passed on as truth in our schools. The impact of this godless system has contributed to the great evil mankind has inflicted on their fellow man. For example, abortion, euthanasia, and attempts at human cloning have been accepted largely because we have reduced mankind from created in God's image to that of the animals with organic evolution. Tragically, our school systems teach the theory of organic evolution as fact while they cannot teach Biblical Creationism (whether it is treated as fact or a theory). If we do not teach our young people the truth about the creation of the world and the fallacy of evolution, then who will? The evidence for Biblical creationism is abundant and actually requires less blind faith then evolution.

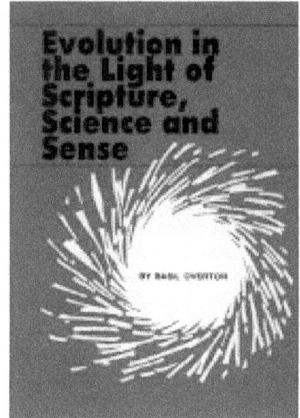

Some are intimidated to teach this subject to young people because they do not consider themselves scientists. This is sad because it discounts the fact that the best scientists in the world reject organic evolution. The silence of the churches will speak volumes to young people who will mistake our timidity on the subject as a lack of scientific evidence for creationism. Or as brother Basil stated the matter:

> Many of our young people are slipping away from us, not because we do not have the truth, but because we are allowing the enemy to do a better job of teaching them than we are doing. This is a disgrace to us, and it is a tremendous

loss to the Lord and his kingdom. So we must teach and teach and teach and ground our children and young people in facts and truths based on the scripture. (p. viii.)

Brother Basil Overton has produced a very profitable book that I wish all congregations would spend at least a quarter of Bible Study to study. It is divided into twelve chapters and includes discussion questions at the conclusion of each chapter. It discusses the fact that it is easy and reasonable to believe that God exists. There is scientific evidence that the earth is young. He cites numerous examples that demonstrate the fallacies of organic evolution. He also deals with another key point—one cannot believe both the Bible and Evolution. The term "theistic evolution" refers to the false concept that God used organic evolution to create the world. It tries to claim that both evolution and the Bible are in harmony with one another. There is no middle ground between evolution and the Bible, and true science supports the Bible.

Studying this book will equip one to teach young people that there is an abundance of evidence for Biblical creationism. It will equip our young people with the truth in front of so-called scientists who try to deny the existence of God and affirm the godless theory of evolution. This work exposes the fallacies of tenets of evolution that makes one wonder how anyone could accept the theory of evolution. Some of the fallacies of evolution are indeed humorous when one applies sense to the matter. Hopefully someday our country will silence the efforts of organizations such as the ACLU in its removal of God from our public schools. They are not only removing God from the schools, but they are removing truth (John 17:17). If we are not willing to equip ourselves to the task of eliminating organic evolution and upholding biblical creationism, then who will? It is a war for the souls of our children, and it is time for soldiers of Christ to arise and protect our children and defend the faith.

Originally printed in *West Virginia Christian*, Vol. 9, No. 6, June 2002, p. 8. Reprinted by permission.

Gems From Greek
(Basil Overton)

The term etymology means "The origin and historical development of a word, as evidenced by study of its basic elements, earliest known use, and changes in form and meaning." (American Heritage Dictionary, p. 451). At Centralia High School, I took a year of Latin that has forever impacted my view of language. The study of words—etymology, has always been intriguing to me. Another person captivated by etymology is brother Basil Overton, or as he put it during our recent visit "I am a word nut." Brother Basil has written an excellent work on the language of the New Testament—Koine Greek.

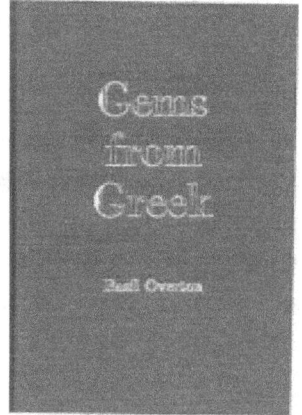

Koine Greek was the common Greek language of Jesus' day. Koine Greek was an enigma for many years. Koine Greek is different from the more popularly known classical Greek. There existed a popular theory among scholars about Koine Greek:

> Within the last hundred years scholars still thought that the language in which the New Testament was written was a special language of the Holy Ghost. They said the Holy Spirit moulded a distinctively religious mode of expression with which to write the New Testament. (Gems From Greek, p. 5.)

Imagine the embarrassment of such scholars when the efforts of biblical archaeology discovered numerous documents containing Koine Greek including receipts, grocery lists, contracts, love letters, military documents, and business letters.

Many are familiar with the World Evangelist, which Basil Overton founded and has edited for nearly 30 years. One of the featured columns of this paper is "Gems from Greek." After sixteen years, these were collected into book form and are now available through Christian bookstores and The World Evangelist.

Sadly, our culture has moved away from encouraging students to learn other languages. By learning another language, a person's view of the world is greatly enhanced. I do not know Koine Greek, but I do fully agree with Brother Overton's assessment about learning about words of the Bible:

> This book is the product of my curiosity. I believe one can become a Christian, live the Christian life, and go to heaven, if he never knows a word of Greek. But, there is personal satisfaction in gaining insights from the study of Greek.... I have never taught a class in Greek. I have studied it for personal satisfaction. The lessons in this book are designed to help everyone who reads them not just to learn a few Greek words, but to learn some great spiritual truths and lessons, and to be encouraged to serve God better. (Forward).

This book provides a good introduction to the topic including the relationship between Greek and English. It explains the difference between translation and transliteration, which is very important to understand. It includes word studies on various topics and from various books in the New Testament, which are indexed in the table of contents. Speaking from personal experience, the study of this subject is very profitable. A person who finds great satisfaction from the study of New Testament words finds it disappointing when he or she cannot convey this enthusiasm to others who have lost a thrilling method of studying God's word. If you have the resources, then purchase this book. Upon my recommendation, a Christian brother, Chris Funkhouser, purchased the book as a gift for his father-in-law. He later told me his father-in-law was thrilled with the book, and you will be too.

Originally printed in *West Virginia Christian*, Vol. 9, No. 4, April 2002, p. 8. Reprinted by permission.

Seven Score Short Sermons
(Basil Overton)

This book contains 140 sermons that are grouped in areas of: Bible, Sin, Jesus Christ, The Resurrection of Christ, Faith or Belief, The Conscience, Baptism, What is a Christian, The Church, Apostasy, Music in Worship, Catholicism and Related Matters, The Sabbath and the Law, Miscellaneous, and Strong Drink. On average, each sermon is approximately 1.5 pages in length. Brother Overton has done an excellent job in being concise in this work so as to pack a substantial amount of information relating to fundamentals of Christianity. It takes effort and determination to write on a topic in such a short format and get across the points one needs to make.

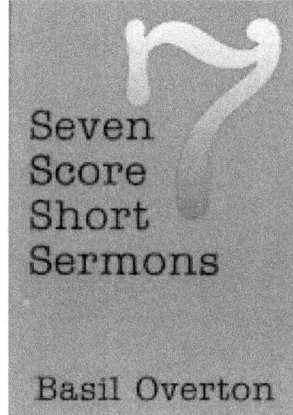

It is important for growing Christians to learn the first principles New Testament Christianity. With the fragmented/segmented schedules some have today it becomes a challenge to find blocks of time to read. This work provides an excellent format to assist with this challenge. Each sermon is self-contained so the book can be put down and picked back up over the course of reading. It contains instruction for new Christians that will educate and strengthen them. It is also good material to read as part of your family's devotional. The author's stated design for the book is to be used for bulletins, magazines, newspapers, and to be shared with those not yet Christians. If feasible, a copy should be given to each new convert along with *Why I am a Member of the Church of Christ* by Leroy Brownlow. If a copy could not be given, then placing a copy in the church library for Christian to borrow and return when done is recommended.

An example of Basil Overton's pointed lessons relates to the Catholic's Church. The Catholics sometimes claim that they had given us the Bible as we have it today. This is very important since the Mormons attempt to give the Catholics the same credit so they can accuse them of tampering with the text. Both the Catholics & the Mormons are incorrect. In AD 397 was the first council that determined what books would be in the NT; however, we have copies of manuscripts which predate AD 397 which proves there was not tampering with the text as some would have us believe. Also, Boniface III was the first official pope, a title that he claimed for himself in AD 606. So the succession of popes from Peter to John Paul II is not continuous or even true. Brother Overton's tone is not caustic and shows true concern for the truth and those in error.

Brother Overton is the founder of *The World Evangelist* and has been its sole editor since 1972. The World Evangelist has been in publication until 2004—over 32 years of articles designed to take the gospel to the world. His work as editor has had a very positive influence among the brotherhood. Brother Overton was kind enough to print my first article. He was one of my father's instructors at Nashville Bible School. He is also retired Vice President and Bible Professor from Heritage Christian University (formerly International Bible College). As a young boy, I first remember meeting him at Cane Ridge, KY as he spoke on the topic of the Restoration Movement. Whenever feasible, I seek to hear him preach or to visit with him. He once told my father that he preferred to be introduced simply as a "Gospel Preacher" rather than a recitation of his academic qualifications. He has been a gospel preacher since 1945.

Some of the sermons from this book have also been printed in tract form entitled "Truth Tracts." This provides another medium to share these lessons on the fundamentals of Christianity with those who visit our assembly or outside the assembly.

The World Evangelist 1972 – 2004 on DVD
(Basil Overton, Editor)

In 1972, Basil Overton was asked by the President of International Bible College (now Heritage Christian University) to begin a paper evangelistic in scope and international in focus. Brother Overton borrowed money to finance the launch of *The World Evangelist* which fulfilled that request for over 32 years. Many writers' first writings appeared in the paper, including my own. At the Annual Appreciation Dinner at 2000 Freed-Hardeman Lectureship the Overtons were honored for their many years of service in various capacities. I recall the words brother Overton spoke on this occasion, and several times prior, about the importance of editors of our papers to remember the audience. People will be turned off by caustic and mean-spirited material and consequently will turn a deaf ear to our plea for the gospel. Even material that may be factual and not malicious can be construed as mean-spirited and become a stumbling block to those who would otherwise obey the gospel. Brother Overton encouraged us not to forget the work of evangelism. In May 2004, the final issue of *The World Evangelist* appeared. While it contained notice and farewells, the main thrust was evangelism including articles on first principles as it always had. In fact, the final issue was 16,000 copies and was mailed all over the world. Sister Overton, or as Basil called her "My Margie," also regularly wrote for the paper in the column "Woman to Women" for nearly 27 years.

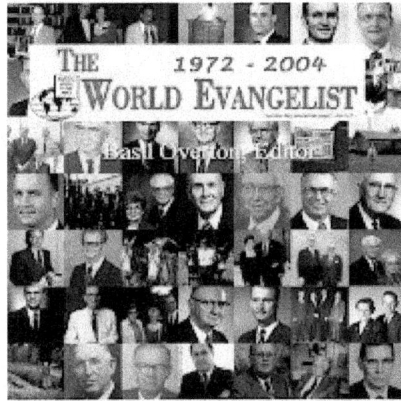

Brother Basil is a people person! He loves souls and is a soul winner. I cannot think of a single person who has said a disparaging word about the Overtons which could carry any weight with anyone that had a casual knowledge of the Overtons. They are above reproach. Brother Overton often said he preferred to be introduced simply as a "gospel preacher" rather than "Doctor Overton." One may not realize that he graduated with the highest honor conferred by Freed-Hardeman College under the esteemed N.B. Hardeman in 1949. He also obtained a Bachelor's degree from Eastern Kentucky State University, Master's degree from University of Kentucky, and Doctorate from Morehead State University. Brother Overton resisted the temptation to have these degrees interfere with his ability to relate to everyone. According to the introduction of his 2004 book, A Book About the Book, he has written nearly 2,500 articles! Many will recall his love of days gone by with his "Mule Musings" column. I always appreciated his "Out of My Memory" and "Gems from the Greek" columns and recall him stating he was a "Word Nut." He has published over 50 tracts and several books. His writing is clear, concise and convincing. If someone had an idea or a special event, Overton would encourage them to send it into the paper. If the person was reluctant to write, brother Overton would really pour on the encouragement. Because of that encouragement, the paper had pieces of information that may have otherwise gone unnoticed.

Each issue of *The World Evangelist* was a storehouse of information including restoration history, first principle lessons, Bible class lessons, Bible geography, introductory material on books of the Bible, book reviews, current events, lives of preachers, elders, teachers, lectureships, and congregational events. In fact, the book reviews in *The World Evangelist* provided me with the idea to write my own for *The West Virginia Christian* and my first blog. Accessing this information is a daunting task for any researcher, but thankfully we live in an age where computers make material more accessible. Brother Tom Childers approached the Overtons about scanning the paper for a DVD that could produce the paper exactly in the layout it was published but also searchable. The Overtons quickly agreed and also offered hundreds of photographs related to the paper. Due to the format of the paper, a special scanner was purchased to scan the paper so it could be available for others in the future. The paper is in PDF format that includes a search engine that can literally pull up every instance where a word occurred in the 32 years of the paper. Imagine the information available to researches at their fingertips! For example, I recalled many articles brother Overton wrote relating to J.D. Tant, whom he greatly admired. When I was preparing my lecture on the life of brother Tant, one of the very first tools I used was this DVD. Simply by typing in the name "Tant" in the search engine brought up every article Overton had written about him or published by J.D. Tant plus any other mention of Tant's name by other writers.

The Overtons have enriched our lives with *The World Evangelist* and thanks to the work of Tom Childers, this enrichment can continue. The cost of the DVD at the time of release (and possibly still is) was $25.

Originally printed in the *West Virginia Christian*, Vol. 16, No. 6, June 2009, p. 8. Reprinted by permission.

Foy E. Wallace, Jr. — Soldier of the Cross
(Nobel Patterson and Terry Gardner, Editors)

Foy Esco Wallace was born September 30, 1896 and died December 18, 1979. Foy's father had four sons all of who were preachers. Foy E. Wallace, Jr. was involved in the major controversies confronting the church from 1930s to the 1960s.

Soldier of the Cross chronicles the life of Foy E. Wallace, Jr. with extensive photos, essays, articles about and by brother Wallace. Terry Gardner provides an excellent series of articles that were reprinted from Faith and Facts, which covers brother Wallace's life from sunrise to sunset.

Foy Wallace will most likely always be remembered for his defense of the truth against the assault of premillennialism. The controversy was started by the speculative writings of R.H. Boll. Foy Wallace accepted a debate challenge by Charles M. Neal, an associate of Boll. Two debates were held one in Winchester, KY and the other in Chattanooga, KY. The first debate was published and Neal abandoned the second debate. Through the debates and writings of Wallace, premillennialism was stopped in its tracks.

Foy Wallace served as editor or staff writer of the *Gospel Advocate* (1930-1934), original *Gospel Guardian* (1935-1936), the *Firm Foundation* (1936-1937), *The Bible Banner* (1938-1949), and *Torch* (1950-1951). Wallace also wrote several books including: God's Prophetic Word, Bulwarks of the Faith, The Mission and Medium of the Holy Spirit, and The Instrumental Music Question.

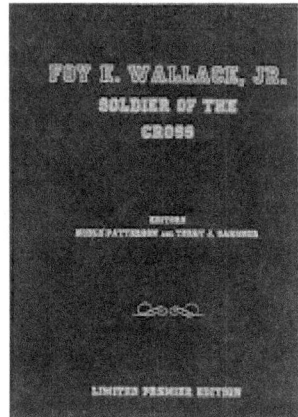

Foy Wallace was also known for long, extensive sermons. People would travel far and wide to hear brother Wallace preach for as long as 2 to 3 hours. Hugo McCord relays a story of his driving 450 miles to Washington, NC to hear brother Wallace only to have brother Wallace insist that Hugo do the preaching that night!

Foy Wallace conducted gospel meetings across the country. In fact, he had put over 300,000 miles on a 1966 Buick Skylark. A grateful set of contributors raised funds to replace the Wallace's car with a new Buick in 1974. Wallace's impact is seen in a several page birthday card for his 83rd (and last) birthday, which was signed from preachers covering 40 states and reads like a "Who's Who Among Preachers for the Churches of Christ."

One of the great examples Foy Wallace left for us was his devotion to his wife who suffered from a rare cerebral stroke in 1952. Virgie, his wife, was told she would never walk again but with the efforts of Foy, she would be able to walk with a cane and walker for a while. Foy Wallace took his wife with him on all his meetings. He would bath, dress, and care for her with great devotion. Some say the memory of an old white haired man pushing his wife in a wheel chair will be forever etched in their memories.

Foy E. Wallace, Jr. is buried in Hereford, TX. His stone reads "Soldier of the Cross." His wife is now buried along his side with the inscription "Faithful Companion." I have never met Foy E. Wallace, Jr., but I have met his son, Wilson Wallace. One can have a great appreciation of Foy E. Wallace by reading his works. He is one of my heroes and I hope someday to meet him after this life is over.

Originally printed in *West Virginia Christian*, Vol. 8, No. 10, October 2001, p. 4. Reprinted by permission.

Onward, Crispy Shoulders! An Extraordinary Life With An Extra Chromosome (Mary Haakenson Perry)

The quality of life is a hot topic in our society. Tragically, there are many who, for the sake of convenience, disregard those whose "quality of life" does not measure to their standards. One group that so many often undervalue is the one with Down syndrome. There are some whose hearts have grown so callous and calculating, that one wonders where our society is heading if more of their thinking pervades our so-

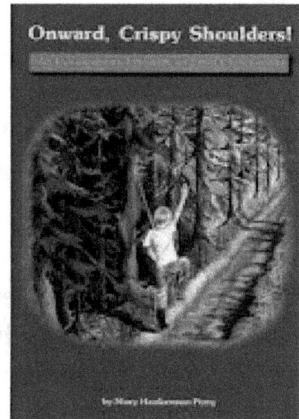

ciety. Not every decision in life is an economic decision.

How do we teach our children about the sanctity of life and that every human life is special? How to we impress on our culture that life is not something that we should treat so cheaply? What can be done to reach those who have such an "optimization" mentality to show them that what may not be optimal is not necessarily undesirable?

One of the ways we attempt to teach our children about the sanctity of life is to take them to nursing homes. Where we attend, we have a regular nursing home service each month. We make it a point not only to attend but to also be sure your children interact with the residents there. How will they know to love old people or those unable to care for themselves if they do not spend time with them? Where we attend there is a lady who has Down syndrome. She is one of the sweetest residents there. My children enjoy visiting with her. What does one think their attitude will be toward those less fortunate? For parents who say things like "Going to the Nursing Home is not for me," pray that you never have to be a resident of one yourself! What if your children grow up with such an attitude? I often wonder that if I am in a nursing home someday if anyone from the churches will even care to visit much less conduct a service there.

One of the many wonderful people I had the privilege of hearing about and eventually meeting from my wife's home congregation is James Haakenson or Jimmy. Jimmy was born with Down syndrome in 1945. In his day, people did not know much about this condition. Even diagnosing his condition was a major challenge for doctors. Imagine trying to rear a child with Down syndrome in Alaska. Jimmy had a tremendous work ethic and was able to rise above assumed limitations to astound everyone who knew him. He was able to hold a job at the local school district and serve in the worship services of the church. While he did not understand everything, he did understand the gospel and, at his insistence, was immersed for the remission of his sins. He knew that baptism was not only a serious matter, it was an imperative matter! The title of this book is Jimmy's pronunciation of one of his favorite hymns "Onward, Christian Soldiers."

Anyone whose have ever had the blessings (and yes, burdens) of caring for children with special needs will find this book a balm of encouragement. The Haakenson family's determination and steadfastness in supporting Jimmy is moving. They were determined to provide all they could for their son and to give him every opportunity to succeed. The life of Jimmy Haakenson will amaze you. For those who do not understand or have never been exposed to this type of situation, the book will give you some insight into the life of the families with children of special needs. It will show you that, while some may consider such conditions as undesirable, God's blessings and grace outshines all.

President Reagan once stated, "We cannot diminish the value of one category of human life—the unborn—without diminishing the value of all human life." This is true. One needs to

remember what happened when the world allowed a govern-
mental regime the power to begin sterilizing and killing for the
sake of society—The Holocaust. If our nation continues to allow
the slaughter of innocents on one side of the journey of life, then
what makes one believe it will stop its hand at the other side of
the journey of life? May we truly be able to wish for God's love
and mercy as we have been demonstrating it to all of our citizens.

Modern Messages From the Minor Prophets
(David Pharr)

If a preacher is looking for good sermon material to preach that a congregation really needs to hear, then the preacher should spend some time in the study of the division of the Bible we call the Minor Prophets. This reminds me of a story about Tom Butterfield (or as I have heard him affectionately referred to as "Old Tom") who wrote to his brother George asking him to send Tom some sermons he could use. George sent him a New Testament! That will preach!

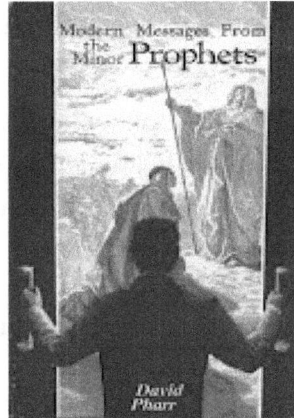

The term "minor" is not in reference to their worth or importance but to the actual length of the writings when compared to the "major" prophets. The Minor Prophets are abundant in lessons for Christians in the United States. I have several good books on the Minor Prophets, but David Pharr's book is one I wanted to add to my personal library. It is an excellent source of material that can be converted to sermons that congregations need to hear! In fact, this material was a series of lessons presented at a Preacher's Workshop, but the demand for the material led to the publishing of brother Pharr's material in book form.

Often we hear about our country being given over to materialism. Indeed this is a disease that appears to have infected some in the church. The condition today is not unlike the situation when God sent the prophets to teach and warn Israel to "consider their ways"; e.g., Haggai 1:5. Indeed, many in the church and our nation need to reflect on their priorities. In his outline, "Stealing From God But Cheating Self" from Malachi 3:8-12, brother Pharr's conclusion states:

> We have been commanded to give as we have prospered. Liberal giving is an act of faith. Covetousness and the miserly giving that proceeds from it are characteristic of criminals and heathen, not faithful servants of a beneficent God.

This book will show us what messages God gave through the prophets for the nation of Israel to reflect upon. Indeed we need to hear and heed the messages of the Minor Prophets.

David Pharr attended Freed-Hardeman College (and was classmates with Alan Highers, Editor of The Spiritual Sword), Rio Grande College, and Southern Christian University. He was the former director of the East Tennessee School of Preaching. He has published the Carolina Messenger for several years and is a frequent writer for The Spiritual Sword. Any material written by brother Pharr is worth our consideration.

Originally printed in the *West Virginia Christian*, Vol. 12, No. 2, February 2005, p. 8. Reprinted by permission.

Thy Kingdom Come — The Truth About the Rapture (David Pharr)

It is amazing to study false systems of religion that claim biblical support alongside the Bible. It is amazing in the sense that the Bible so soundly defeats error and truly is "...a light to our path." (Psalm 119:105)! A primary example of a false doctrine that twists the Scriptures "...to their own destruction," (2 Peter 3:16) is premillennialism. It is truly sad that multitudes of people believe in some version of premillennialism. There are several good books written from among our brotherhood that are worthwhile studies on this topic. A new book has been written by David Pharr and is excellent.

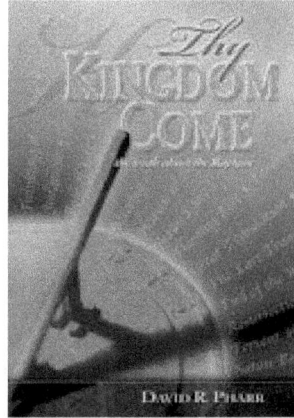

The book is perfect for classroom instruction/discussion. It is available in paperback and is approximately 150 pages in length. This book is not a direct treatment of the "Left Behind" series; rather, it is a scriptural refutation of the doctrine the "Left Behind" series clearly advocates—premillennialism. Some thought The Late Great Planet Earth was a work of fiction. Likewise, the "Left Behind" series is categorized as fiction (rightfully so) but is packaged to advocate the doctrine of premillennialism. The popularity of the "Left Behind" series is just one reason for us to be knowledgeable about what the Bible really says on this subject. Thy Kingdom Come is an excellent book to read for either private or group study.

People of Jesus' day were looking for a restoration of the physical kingdom of David's day. Even today, people are still waiting for the restoration of the physical kingdom of the Jews in Palestine to usher in a new period in world history. This is a doctrine of premillennialism. As David Pharr rightfully observes, "The whole scheme of a coming Rapture, Tribulation, or Millennium—as well as theories of different resurrections and judgments—is rooted in the mistaken concept of an earthly kingdom."

There are widespread efforts to convert multitudes to the false system of premillennialism. As Christians, we should not look to get these false teachers off of our doorsteps, but should send them on their way with some things to think about. Some are criticizing the churches of Christ as alienating the denominations by our actions. My response is that the agent of alienation is the Truth! We have a reputation of preaching and defending the truth. I pray we continue to do so with love!

David Pharr attended Freed-Hardeman College (and was classmates with Alan Highers, Editor of The Spiritual Sword), Rio Grande College, and Southern Christian University. He was the former director of the East Tennessee School of Preaching. He has published the Carolina Messenger for several years and is a frequent writer for The Spiritual Sword. Any article written by brother Pharr is worth reading and this book is very profitable as well. One of the many highlights I experience at the FHU Bible Lectureship is visiting with David Pharr. I look forward to future visits together. I have heard he plans on devoting more of his time to gospel meetings. This is indeed good news to the brotherhood who are able to secure his talents for a gospel meeting.

Originally printed in *West Virginia Christian*, Vol. 12, No. 12, December 2005, p. 8. Reprinted by permission.

Medley of the Restoration
(Dabney Phillips)

When selecting books to review, I generally refrain from referencing a location to purchase a book from unless there is a compelling reason to do so. This is one of those compelling reasons. Sam Hester, owner of Hester Publications, reprints books in paperback and makes them readily available for distribution. Brother Hester is a Bible Professor at Freed-Hardeman University and we both share similar interests—books and Restoration History. In fact, he conducts the Restoration Tour in Henderson, TN during the FHU Bible Lectureship (which I highly recommend). Feel free to visit his website at hesterpublications.com or email him at shester@fhu.edu.

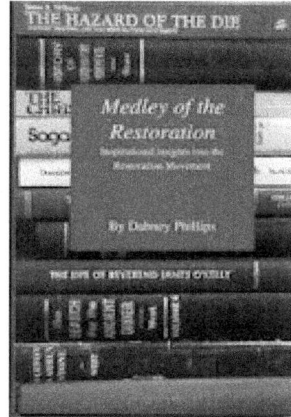

Medley of Restoration includes anecdotes of Restoration Leaders which are intriguing to read. The book includes humorous events as well as tragic ones. Some of the wives are discussed in this book. The book also provides brief stories about Blacks and the Restoration Movement. The book truly is a medley of topics relating to the Restoration Movement. The book is brief and rather inexpensive. It is a good way to introduce others to key participants of the call of people back to the Bible.

One of the preachers I always enjoy hearing on Restoration History is Basil Overton. Speaking in Martinsburg, WV on the WVC Lectureship he impressed upon the audience that the pioneers were not perfect so Restoration History is filled with mistakes made along the way. But, brother Overton would go on to say, the Restoration Plea of going back to the Bible for our sole authority is perfect. There are those among us who are using/twisting the writings of some of pioneers to take us away from the aim of that perfect plea.

Dabney Phillips taught at David Lipscomb and Restoration History at Faulkner University or several years prior to his death. He attended David Lipscomb College, Harding Graduate School, and other colleges.

Originally printed in the *West Virginia Christian*, Vol. 12, No. 3, March 2005, p. 8. Reprinted by permission.

Restoration Principles and Personalities
(Dabney Phillips)

When I recently guided a tour to Alexander Campbell's home in Bethany, WV, I was looking for some stories about some of the Restoration Pioneers to pique interest in others to read further of those who did so much to call us away from denominationalism and back to, using a Campbell term, "New Testament-ism." Restoration Principles and Personalities contains stories about Alexander Campbell, Barton W. Stone, "Raccoon" John Smith, Walter Scott, Moses Lard, J.W. McGarvey, and others. It also discusses prominent schools and periodicals of the period. The book is easy to reference and enjoyable to read.

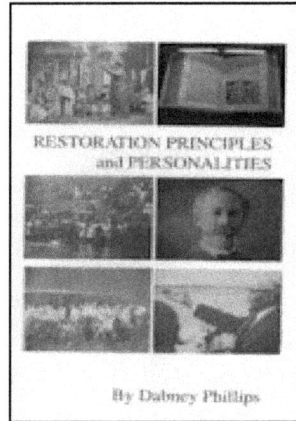

Be sure to read other works on Restoration History because historians are fallible and sometimes leave unintentional mistaken impressions. Also reading related works sometimes dispels misconceptions that are often made. One I found in this book relates to the drowning of Alexander Campbell's son. The book states he drowned in a pond on the farm; however, other sources state he drowned in Buffalo Creek that had flooded and created what is sometimes called a mill pond. Reading additional works provides other worthwhile perspectives. In fact, Medley of Restoration, also by Dabney Phillips, records the death being in Buffalo Creek.

Dabney Phillips taught at David Lipscomb and Restoration History at Faulkner University or several years prior to his death.

He attended David Lipscomb College, Harding Graduate School, and other colleges.

Originally printed in the *West Virginia Christian*, Vol. 12, No. 3, March 2005, p. 8. Reprinted by permission.

N.B. H. –
A Biography of Nicholas Brodie Hardeman
(James Marvin Powell & Mary Nelle Hardeman Powers)

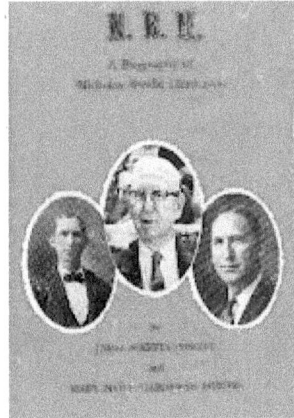

It is inspiring to read biographies of those who have fought to overcome obstacles, sacrificed their interest for noble causes, and have made significant contributions to Christianity and the world such as A.G. Freed and N.B. Hardeman. Freed-Hardeman University's impact for good has been felt abroad. When I was pursuing a full-time evangelist work, I often heard statements to the effect that since I was from Freed-Hardeman College it was assumed I was also sound in the faith.

Nicholas Brodie Hardeman (NBH) was born on May 18, 1874 in the small town of Milledgeville, TN where his father was the town medical doctor. NBH began to study the field of medicine but quickly decided this was not his field of interest. Eventually he would enroll at Georgia Robertson College in Henderson, TN (this school met in the building known as Milan-Sitka which was razed in 2004). He both taught and studied for his M.A. degree, which he obtained in 1899. On April 18, 1897, A.G. Freed was to preach at Enville, TN. He decided that he was unable to conduct a service so he sent N.B. Hardeman in his place. Brother Hardeman attempted to get out of the speaking, but ultimately agreed to go in brother Freed's place. Then about six weeks later brother Freed sent brother Hardeman to start a gospel meeting in his place at Juno, TN stating he would be along by hopefully Monday. Hardeman began the meeting preaching day and night while eagerly waiting for brother Freed to arrive. Finally, Freed arrived on Thursday and decided brother Hardeman was doing so well that Freed insisted Hardeman finish the meeting he had started. So, brother Freed is to be largely credited for grooming N.B. Hardeman as preacher as well. Brother Hardeman states he "drifted into preaching" with "fatherly propulsion" from A.G. Freed. N.B. Hardeman would go on to deliver a series of sermons known as "Hardeman's Tabernacle Sermons" , which were printed in two prominent papers in the State of Tennessee.

Nicholas Hardeman had several debates, two of which were printed—Boswell and Bogard. The story of his debates is very interesting reading. Brother Hardeman's debate with Ira Boswell over the instrument stopped the boastful offense of the Christian Church in Tennessee. Perhaps a surprising fact about N.B. Hardeman was that he once led singing while his wife played the piano in church. The Hardemans and many of the Henderson church studied themselves out of the error of using instrumental music in worship. Indeed leading people out of digression was possible then and it is still possible now.

This biography provides a thorough view of this great man's life and contributions to Freed-Hardeman University, the church, the community and abroad. It deals with the highs and lows of brother Hardeman's career until 1964. (Brother Hardeman passed away in 1965.)

E. Claude Gardner was president at Freed-Hardeman College when I was a student there. I remember brother Gardner's announcing the change of status of Freed-Hardeman College to University. He then made the following statement, which should serve as a reminder to our Christian College Presidents and Board of Directors that there are some things that should never be for sale. President Gardner stated:

> Freed-Hardeman College has not always been the name of this institution. In 1908 to 1919 it was called National Teachers Normal Business College. Predecessor colleges dating back to 1869 had these names: Henderson Male &

Female Institute, then Henderson Male & Female Masonic Institute, West Tennessee Christian College, and Georgia Robertson Christian College. The last name was given after Mr. Robertson made a gift of $5,000 to honor his daughter. The gentleman who works in acquiring funds for universities and colleges recently told me that he had three clients ready to give $50 million and one for $25 million with the understanding the name of the institution would be changed to honor the donor. In no wise would I entertain recommending to our board the change of a name away from honoring two great men, A.G. Freed and N.B. Hardeman, for any amount of money.

Originally printed in the *West Virginia Christian*, Vol. 14, No. 5, May 2007, p. 6. Reprinted by permission.

Expository Dictionary of Bible Words
(Stephen D. Renn, Editor)

The study of tracing a word's origin, meaning and usage over time is known as etymology. It has been said that words are the vehicle of thought and that one cannot know a thought without the use of words. This is a valuable point for those who believe in thought inspiration over word inspiration— without words there is no thought! The study of biblical words has one that has fascinated and enriched my study of God's word for as long as I can remember, so I am always on the look for valuable reference tools that assist with enriching my knowledge of words. This Expository Dictionary of Bible Words is a valuable resource in learning words and their meanings in Hebrew, Aramaic and Greek.

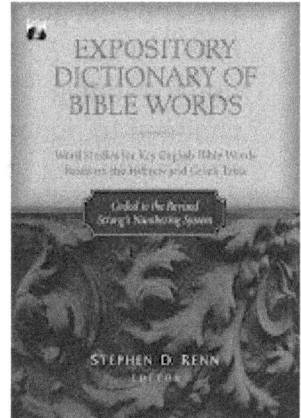

The book states it covers over 7,260 Hebrew and Greek words. It groups these words under an English word in the Bible so one can see not only how Hebrew and Greek words relate to one but how they relate to the given English word. The Hebrew word(s) and Greek words(s) is provided with an English transliteration and definition of how the term is used in the Bible. Each Hebrew and Greek term is coded to the Strong's Numbering System which makes comparative study much easier. In addition, there are valuable articles discussing various points relating to the subject at hand. There are also cross-references to other English words which may be of use. In the back of the book are indices to Hebrew and Greek words which show a listing of every English word that these words appear. These indices show how English words relate to one another and the original term itself.

Included in some editions of this work is a bonus CD that includes the entire book in PDF format that is searchable. It also contains other valuable reference materials such as *Young's Literal Translation, Matthew Henry's Concise Commentary, Smith's Bible Dictionary, Torrey's New Topical Textbook, Bible History in Old Testament, Lightning Bible Atlas* and others. The work claims to be "a feature-rich modern replacement for the classic *Vine's Expository Dictionary*." While the work is extremely valuable, I would prefer to think of this work as a strong comparative work to Vine's work rather than a replacement to it. If you enjoy *Vine's Expository Dictionary*, then you will also appreciate this dictionary as well. The structure of this book is unique as to provide further insight that is available with Vine's. *The Expository Dictionary of Bible Words* is an extremely valuable reference tool for those who wish to explore the meaning of Hebrew and Greek words more fully and how they relate to our English Bibles. For a more studious review of the work, I suggest reading Wayne Jackson's article on the material at christiancourier.com/articles/1048-new-expository-dictionary-of-Bible-words. One will want to be sure and keep brother Jackson's observations in mind when utilizing this valuable reference work.

Stephen R. Renn served as the Head of Bible Studies and Academic Dean at the Syndney Missionary and Bible College where he lectured on Old Testament and Biblical Hebrew for over 15 years. He also serves as Coordinator of Language Teaching in Australia.

Truth for Today Commentary – Exodus
(Coy D. Roper)

Many may recall the movie, "The Ten Commandments." I was under the impression it was new when I first saw it on TV; however, it was released ten years before I was born! I can recall studying with great delight the story of the Exodus as a young person in Bible Class, which was taught by my mother. The story of the enslavement and liberation of the Israelites is among the greatest stories that have ever been told. One of the greatest things about the story is that it is true! The family of Jacob (called Israel by God) goes into Egypt as a family, but they come out as a nation in fulfillment to God's promises to Abraham, Isaac and Jacob. I enjoyed watching the movie at home, but I also recall my mother challenging me to pick out inaccuracies of the film based on Bible Class. I sometimes wonder how well I would do today.

I was reading some statistical studies about society's knowledge of the Bible and found two interesting trends. First, atheists & agnostics know the Bible far more than some realize, even better than "Bible Believers." Second, one study suggested that Christians, by the survey's classification, overestimate how well they actually know the Bible. Perhaps you know where in the story Exodus begins, but do you know where in the story the Exodus ends? Do you really know what happened in the book, or has it become fuzzy now? This should be a wake-up call that we all need to learn the contents of our Bibles better. Bible classes help, so do sermons (at least these should); however, there is so much more to know which may increase our faith. Of

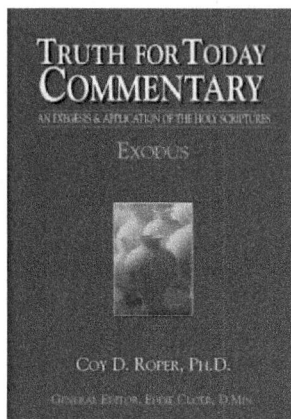

course, we need good tools to fortify and enrich our study of God's word. Some tools are better than others.

The Truth for Today Commentary series seeks to provide solid explanation of the text, plus applications of the text to our daily lives. Those familiar with the publishing work of Eddie Cloer have been appreciating his efforts along these lines for some time now. If you are looking for solid biblical research by faithful members of the church, then you do not want to let this series of commentaries escape your notice. Coy D. Roper is a highly degreed student of the Scriptures and has preached the gospel for over 50 years. He has served as Director of Graduate Studies at Heritage Christian University (formerly International Bible College). I have not had the pleasure of meeting him yet, but I hope to some day because his scholastic studies have enriched my study. I am thankful for him and others who "put themselves out there" so we can learn from them, regardless of the fact that others may scoff and criticize. I am not saying one will necessarily agree with every point in any of these books, but that does not mean you cannot learn from them. Remember, the Bible is always right!

I was blessed to have the late Dr. James Tollerson at Freed-Hardeman University for his instruction in the class of Genesis & Exodus. Recently I have just completed a series of lessons preaching through Exodus. I found my old class notes very insufficient, partially because I knew the material so well because of the diligent instruction of my mother. So, when I recently sat down to assemble a fresh study of the subject, I examined several reference works to aid me in my study. *The Truth for Today Commentary on Exodus* was one that I did not return to the church library shelf until my study was complete. I highly recommend pursing the *Truth for Today Commentary* series for your private and public study. These books are not inexpensive; however, there is a difference between the price paid and the value received. These books are of high value!

Originally printed in the *West Virginia Christian*, Vol. 22, No. 10, July 2015, p. 8. *Reprinted by permission.*

The History of the Christian Church
(Philip Schaff)

This is an extremely valuable eight-volume set for those studying church history. It contains footnotes, charts, maps and each volume has an alphabetical index. At this writing, I am working on a study of the Gospel of John; one of the books of the New Testament with the strongest external evidence supporting its canonicity and authorship. This set was invaluable in assembling this material. I bought the set on the recommendation of Dr. Clyde Woods, one of my professors at Freed-Hardeman University, over fifteen years ago. I have not once regretted my purchase. Sadly there are those uninterested in church history. But it is critical for us to keep the facts of history in our minds. I believe that one of the rises to skepticism in the form of post modernism is traceable to the ignorance of church history. For example, the fiction/nonfiction work *The DaVinci Code* generated much excitement driven by a conspiracy theorist mentality; which grows in the fertile grounds of ignorance. Dr. Schaff breaks down the periods of church history as the following:

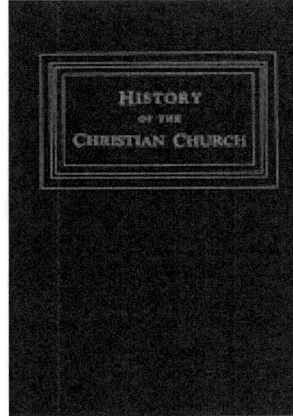

- APOSTOLIC CHRISTIANITY (AD 1 –100)
- ANTE-NICENE CHRISTIANITY (AD 100 – 325)
- NICENE & POST-NICENE CHRISTIANITY (AD 311 – 600)
- MEDIAEVAL CHRISTIANITY (AD 590 – 1073)
- THE MIDDLE AGES (AD 1049 – 1517)—in two volumes
- MODERN CHRISTIANY & THE GERMAN REFORMATION
- MODERN CHRISTIANITY & THE SWISS REFORMATION

Some unfamiliar with the periods of church history may find the following overview helpful. Generally, the Apostolic Period is recognized from the times of Christ to the death of the last apostle, John around AD 100. The Latin preposition ante means "before" so the Ante-Nicaea period is between the death of the apostle John but before the Nicaean Council. Much persecution of Christians occurred during this period. This period was brought to a close when Constantine put an end to Christian persecution and recognized Christianity as a state religion with the Edit of Milan in AD 313. Constantine convened the Nicaea Council in AD 325; which began the period of creeds and legislative decisions for Christianity. Out of this period began the rise of the papacy concluding with the rise of Pope Gregory I in AD 590. The Medieval Period is when the church continued to insert itself into the civil government. It is also when the Roman Catholic Church of the West became distinct from the Orthodox Church in the East. The Medieval Period closed with the death of Pope Boniface VIII in 1303. After the Medieval Period arose the Renaissance and Reformation Era, which would last until the Treaty of Westphalia ended the Thirty Years War in 1648. The Thirty Years War is an important event to remember since it was a bloody war between Catholics and Protestants. There were two major Reformation Movements during this period with Luther in Germany and the other under Zwingli in Switzerland. Also during this period the printing press invented by Johannes Gutenberg revolutionized the world, especially Christianity, since it placed the Bible back into the hands of the people. Subsequent movements would arise from John Calvin, Menno Simons, Henry VIII and others. This period would be the rise of Protestantism, which would continue to last into the Modern Era until the momentum of those seeking to go back before Luther, the Popes & Councils, and back to the New Testament pattern—the Restoration Movement grew. The goal of the Restorers was (and is still) simple but formidable—to call men out of Protestantism,

Catholicism, and a host of other "isms" to join in what Alexander Campbell called New Testament-ism.

Philip Schaff (1819-1893) was a German Reformed church historian. He was educated at Tubingen, Halle, and Berlin, and later took a position as Professor of Church History at Union Theological Seminary, New York. Schaff taught church history at German Reformed Seminary in Mercersburg, PA and Union Theological Seminary in New York.

The Forgotten Commandment
(Ed Smithson)

This is one of the best books on church discipline I have seen thus far. There are probably other good books on this subject, but I have yet to find one superior considering its conciseness. Perhaps the book would be more accurately titled The Ignored Commandment rather than the forgotten one. That church discipline is commanded in the New Testament is readily apparent to all who are familiar with the contents of the sacred book.

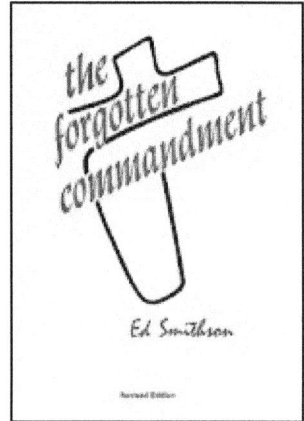

When reviewing materials on church discipline, I always search how it deals with those who forsake and abandon the assembly. To be clear, reference is not to those who occasionally have to miss due to sickness or work. Also, reference is not to those who cannot participate in every program that the church may be involved in. Who is under consideration are those who have made it a habit of missing to the point that newer members may never even realize a person was ever a member of the church. In this book, Smithson elaborates accurately some of the excuses some use to exempt themselves from disciplining those who forsake the assembly. The writer explains:

> "In recent years brethren have come up with another device to try to get away from taking action in the form of withdrawal of fellowship from those who will not attend the services. For years we have heard 'they have withdrawn from us, therefore we cannot withdraw from them.'" (Smithson, page 27).

Smithson provides many effective points that refute this dangerous notion. First, we are to withdraw from those who walk disorderly—*"But we command you, brethren, in the name of our Lord Jesus Christ, that you withdraw from every brother who walks disorderly and not according to the tradition which he received from us."* (2 Thessalonians 3:6). The word "disorderly" is a military term meaning "to be disorderly of soldiers marching out of order or quitting ranks to be neglectful of duty, to be lawless to lead a disorderly life."[1]

When one forsakes the church, there is no clearer example of walking disorderly. Second, refusing to discipline an erring Christian up to and including the point of withdrawal clearly contradicts the parable of the lost sheep. The church is supposed to go out and search/recover those who have become lost in the world. In Bible Class the other day we were discussing this verse and a military person pointed out another military principle here—"No man left behind." That the church has been somewhat negligent in this matter each will have to determine. I know of a congregation that has not withdrawn from an erring member in over 20 years. Some may not have elders and believe that gives them a pass on this command. However, while not having an eldership oversee a progressive discipline process may make the process more challenging, it does not make it impossible. In fact, if one reads Jesus' explanation of progressive discipline in Matthew 18:15-17 there is no reference to elders in the process. Of course elders should be consulted and probably best to include in phase two (not phase one) of the process. One has to ask, honestly, is it a lack of need or a lack of heed?

This book addresses several other key principles of church discipline and objections to its practice in a very effective way. One final point I want to emphasize is that administering

---

[1] Bible.crosswalk.com/Lexicons/NewTestament-Greek/grk.cgi?number=812

discipline is an act of love. The goal is always the restoration of the soul to God. When we resist practicing church discipline as God has commanded, we are either implying we do not believe in God's plan or we do not care what God has said. God's plan works and we had better give serious consideration to these matters. This book appears to be designed for class study and is an excellent resource for those who need to return to the old paths; c.f., Jeremiah 6:16.

Originally printed in *West Virginia Christian*, Vol. 18, No. 6, June 2011, p. 8. Reprinted by permission.

Tracing Our Steps – A Chronology of the Restoration Movement, Volumes 1& 2 (John T. Smithson, III)

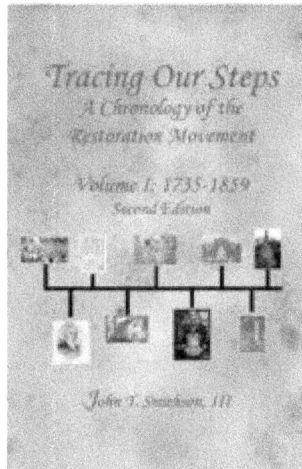

Hester Publications is reprinting some of the most treasured works of the restoration movement including recent research materials from this area of study. While attending the Freed-Hardeman Lectureship in February 2010 I was delighted to obtain an expanded and updated two-volume set of this valuable reference work. When I was preparing for presentations on some key figures of the Restoration Movement such as Thomas Campbell and Benjamin Franklin, I found the first edition of Tracing Our Steps to be of great service in organizing my material chronologically. It provided other key surrounding events to include more of a historical context surrounding these giants advocating what Alexander Campbell often called "The Ancient Order of Things." As the back cover well states,

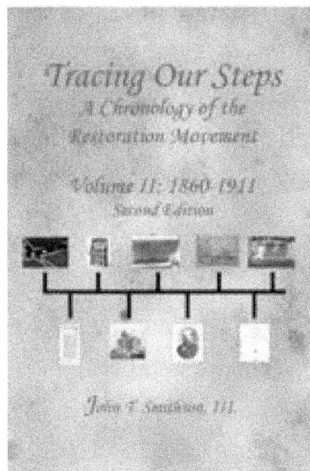

"A chronology helps one get a bigger picture of things. When a towering figure dies, for instance, one might be tempted to worry about the future of the church in a certain locale. Examination of historical facts, however, will show us that great leaders are continually being born as great leaders are dying."

The format is very straightforward. It is organized by dates in bold on the left with important events relating to the timeframe. One of the interesting and challenging facts of restoration history is conflicting dates. Some records are rather sparse and there are times when two dates are assigned to the same important event. Smithson has made it a practice to note significant events in history of churches of Christ and was able to compile this information it these two volumes.

Some may find it hard to develop an interest in history of any subject, much less Restoration History of the New Testament Church. One way to whet one's appetite for the subject matter is to tour restoration sites such as the home of Thomas & Alexander Campbell in Bethany, WV, Cane Ridge Meeting House near Lexington, KY, and several other significant sites. There are several exciting opportunities to attend guided tours by informed brethren. I would like to highlight two such opportunities. Each first Sunday in August, the North Lexington Church of Christ hosts its Restoration Workshop which includes tours of significant restoration sites in and around Lexington, KY where opportunities to learn about important figures such as Barton W. Stone, J.W. McGarvey, Raccoon John Smith and others are readily available. To learn more about this great opportunity, visit the North Lexington church of Christ website at northlexingtoncoc.org. Another tour is being conducted by a recently formed group of restoration historians known as "The Friends of the Restoration." This group is comprised of several excellent historians including the author of this two volume set, Scott Harp, who operates a restoration history website at therestorationmovement.com, Tom Childers who has made available several excellent materials on DVD, Sam Hester who owns Hester Publications and is a professor at Freed-Hardeman University, Ancil Jenkins, William Kilpatrick and others committed to learning and preserving Restoration History. The group is planning on a tour from Freed-Hardeman University in Henderson, TN and will visit places such as the Disciples of Christ Historical Society and the Gospel Advocate in Nashville, TN, the Mulkey Meeting-house in Tompkinsville, KY, Lexington Cemetery in KY, Broadway Christian Church, Transylvania College, Cane Ridge Meeting-house, Bethany in West Virginia, Hiram College and James Garfield's home and monument in northeast Ohio. The trip is scheduled from June 14-20, 2010. If interested, be sure to visit their website for additional information at friendsoftherestoration.com/. For me, I could not think of a better vacation than this trip! While I cannot attend this trip, if the Lord is willing, I plan on joining and assisting with their visit to sites relating to James Garfield.

Churches of Christ have a rich historical legacy in the United States. Certainly, mistakes have occurred in the past but that is all the more reason to study the past to avoid the tendency of repeating mistakes. The restoration movement did not begin in America nor does it end here. We need to always keep in mind the ground that has been fought and won for the preservation of New Testament Christianity *lest at any time we should let them slip.*

Fundamentals of the Faith
(David E. Sproule, II)

Fundamentals are so vital. A healthy congregation needs to have regular preaching on the fundamentals. After all, a healthy congregation is a dynamic group and will include those who may not be as knowledgeable about the fundamentals. One does not need to have a class "on the side" for these subjects. Perhaps we may have not preached or taught on these for so long that a congregation needs a refresher course too? I have adopted a phrase that I use when I am teaching something that I believe to be fundamental but am concerned may be perceived as elementary: "I know that you may know these things, but I want to make sure that you know that I know these things." A preacher that *refuses* to preach on the fundamentals is a threat to a congregation, and a preacher ignorant of the fundamentals is no better. The fundamentals should never be viewed as "out of style."

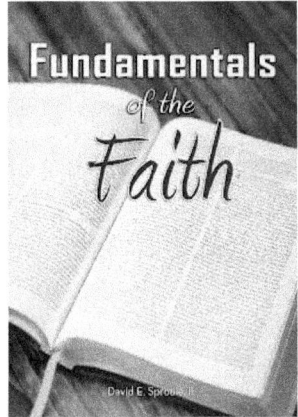

With delight I received *Fundamentals of the Faith* by David E. Sproule, II. I have known David for several years now, as we have a mutual friend, Dr. Clyde Woods (AKA "Doc"), at Freed-Hardeman University. After spending some time looking over select chapters such as "Music in the Worship of the Church," "The Role of Women in the Church," and "Marriage, Divorce and Remarriage" I wanted to make others aware of this material. There are actually two versions of this work: one is a teacher's edition and the other is a student's workbook. After looking over the book's table of contents and reading what is happening in various parts of the brotherhood, I realized that this set of books could be an invaluable study to teach these fundamental truths once again. The material could be taught in adult or teenage classes, or sermons could be developed from this material. For example, I appreciate David's emphasis on both marriage and divorce with the statement of understanding these matters in God's eyes as "The Only View That Matters!" The Student Workbook has portions of the material as "Fill-In-The-Blanks," but the basic material is present and nothing is lost by an overabundance of "Blanks." There are 20 subjects covered in this material. The material is formatted in sentence outlines, so it is highly organized and very easy to follow the flow of thought. The detail in these books is substantial, so it would be unwise to think one can just breeze through these matters.

David Sproule serves as one of the evangelists at the Palm Beach Lakes church of Christ in Florida. I always look forward to hearing David lecture at the Freed-Hardeman University Bible Lectureship. I also look forward to seeing him at Doc Woods' "Bargain Book Finders" booth where we talk books or "talk shop." On the subject of fundamentals of the faith, Sproule wrote: "New Testament Christianity, with all its doctrines and practices, finds its roots and origin in 'the faith' (i.e., the one gospel system) revealed and established within the pages of the New Testament." David Sproule's study is a great resource for lessons from the pulpit or the class lectern. Surveying the religious climate of our day, certainly a case can easily be made for the need to regularly study the fundamentals of the Christian faith! When we have congregations adding instrumental music, moving women into leadership roles or leading in worship, the time for the fundamentals is now! If you would like to order the book in bulk, I suggest you contact the Palm Beach Lakes Church of Christ. You can also find these books online at Amazon, but if you want to order in bulk you should contact the congregation directly.

Originally printed in the *West Virginia Christian*, Vol. 26, No. 12, December 2019, p. 8. *Reprinted by permission.*

The Life of Jesus Christ
(James Stalker)

If one is familiar with various treatments of the life of Jesus of Nazareth, then they know books come in various sizes, approaches and viewpoints. Some books on the life of Christ are clearly better than others. Some treatments of the life of Christ are not worthy of print. One classic treatment that is better than several others is by James Stalker entitled *The Life of Jesus Christ*. My dad first brought this work to my attention. In fact, he purchased a copy for me on one of our many bookstore expeditions insisting that I would enjoy reading it (despite some of its flaws). For several months he would occasionally ask if I had read the book yet. This prompted me that I had better get the book read! I was glad that he encouraged me to read this popular work because other people's use of the term "masterpiece" in reference to it seem to be appropriate.

It has been printed and revised in several editions since its original publication in 1880. In fact, Leroy Brownlow even reprinted an edition of the work back in 1995 with the title of *For All My Special Days: Important Dates and People to Remember*. If one is familiar with the use of the Internet, then one can obtain the entire book for free in PDF format. There are several Internet sites that have reprinted the book as well. All this provides testimony on the enduring value of the work. The book is a concise treatment averaging around 175 pages. It provides an excellent overview of Jesus' life from his arrival on earth until his ascension back to heaven. The writer provides historical settings of the period which enriches the reading as well.

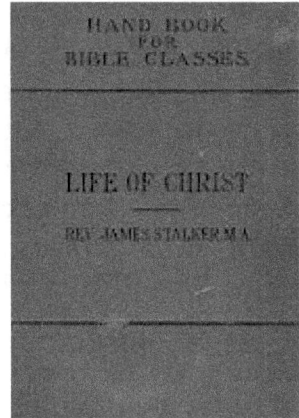

I appreciate Stalker's treatment of various subjects relating to the life of Jesus. For example, consider this statement about the years of Jesus life that are not revealed:

> It was natural that, where God was silent and curiosity was strong, the fancy of man should attempt to fill up the blank. Accordingly, in the early Church there appeared Apocryphal Gospels, pretending to give full details where the inspired Gospels were silent. They are particularly full of the sayings and doings of the childhood of Jesus. But they only show how unequal the human imagination was to such a theme, and bring out by the contrast of glitter and caricature the solidity and truthfulness of the Scripture narrative. They make Him a worker of frivolous and useless marvels, who moulded birds of clay and made them fly, changed His playmates into kids, and so forth. In short, they are compilations of worthless and often blasphemous fables. (p. 16).

I wish more modern day "scholars" were more respectful of the authority of the Scriptures and would not rush into spinning their fanciful theories for gain or notoriety!

James Stalker (1848-1927) was born in Scotland. He served as professor of church history in the United Free Church College in Aberdeen from 1902 to 1926. Of course, one will have to read with a discerning eye, but his "The Life of Jesus Christ" is highly respected for its conciseness and simplicity.

Since I first read this book, I have looked for used inexpensive copies to recommend to friends so they could enjoy reading the book as well. I have received comments about how much the person had enjoyed reading this book. Perhaps you will find a copy of this book in a used bookstore for a very reasonable price. If so, you should pick up a copy to consider for the church library.

The Case for Christ
(Lee Strobel)

One day I was visiting a Barnes & Nobel Bookstore in Lyndhurst, Ohio and
came across a book entitled The Case for
Christ. I remembered hearing about this
book from several individuals from various parts of the country. Remembering
the title (since it had come up so many
different times), I started to read the
book in the store. From the first few
pages, I was hooked on the book. I decided that I had better purchase it or I
would be in trouble for stealing the book by reading the whole
thing in the store.

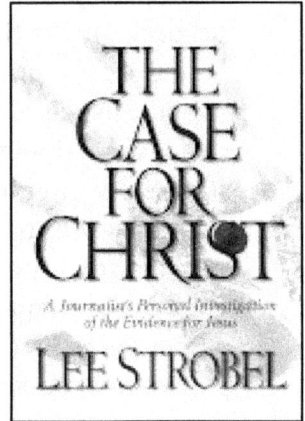

Lee Strobel has a Master of Studies in Law degree from Yale
Law School and was an award-winning journalist for the Chicago
Tribune. He began his search as an admitted atheist who was
irritated that his wife had become a follower of Christ. He became rather curious about her actions after she converted and
launched out on an investigation that convinced him that the
evidence in favor of Jesus being the Christ is overwhelming. He
interviews some of the most reputable authorities on the text of
the gospels such as Bruce Metzger. He also interviews Edwin
Yamauchi who is one of the nation's leading experts in ancient
history including the historical existence of Jesus of Nazareth.
Strobel interviews other experts and answers such fundamental
questions as: "Can the Gospels be trusted?" "How do we know
the Gospels are accurately transmitted to us?" "Is there external
evidence that there really was a man named Jesus?" "Was the
death of Christ a hoax?" "Is there any evidence for the resurrection?" and a host of other questions.

Christian Evidences is one of the most exciting fields to read and it is sad that many do not read more in this area of religious literature. God has provided us so much evidence that can be read and verified which should strengthen our faith when difficult times arise. One of my favorite passages in the Bible is Romans 10:17, "So then faith comes by hearing, and hearing by the word of God." This shows us that the word of God, not some mysterious experience or force, when studied will produce faith in honest hearts. My father often tells of a man that closed his Bible and prayed for faith, but faith did not come. One day, he came across this passage and decided that he would pray and then open his Bible and faith has come ever since. God has provided us so much evidence. Is it not tragic that some fail to even investigate it? This book is a good starting point to begin such an endeavor.

A note of caution about the book: the writer is, sadly, not a member of the church of Christ and espouses a plan of salvation that is contrary to the New Testament. There may be other points in the book that one may not agree with; however, the overall thrust of the book is excellent.

Originally printed in *West Virginia Christian*, Vol. 9, No. 9, September 2002, p. 8. Reprinted by permission.

Strong's Exhaustive Concordance of the Bible
(James Strong)

One would be hard pressed to find a tool more effective and beneficial to studying the word of God than a concordance. A concordance allows the inquirer to find that difficult to find passage he or she cannot locate.

James Strong (1822–1894) was professor of exegetical theology at Drew Theological Seminary. Strong was an American Methodist who was born in New York City and died in Round Lake, New York. He, and a team of others, spent more than thirty-five years in preparation of this concordance. It was first published in 1890 and remains a popular seller to this day.

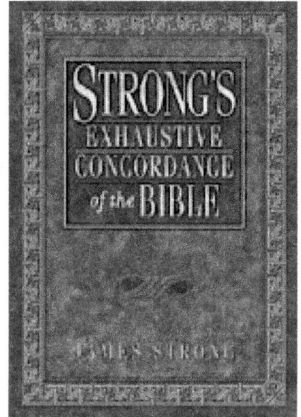

The term "exhaustive" means it contains a reference for every word in the King James Version Holy Bible. For example, if you wanted to find all the occurrences of the term "baptism" the concordance would give you a citation for each occurrence, a portion of the passage, and a number.

James Strong assigns each Greek and Hebrew term a reference number often called a "Strong's Number." There are 8,674 Hebrew and 5,624 Greek words numbered in the concordance. Many other Bible helps (Thayer's Greek Lexicon, Vine's Expository Dictionary) are keyed to Strong's numbers which helps locate and facilitate the use of other research material without having to know Greek or Hebrew.

The concordance is group by the English word in the translation, not grouped by the Hebrew and Greek terms. Another invaluable way to study the Bible is by the grouping of Hebrew and

Greek words rather than the English translation of the words. An excellent concordance that is structured by Hebrew and Greek terms is Young's Analytical Concordance of the Bible. The Strong's Concordance also provides a lexicon (or dictionary) of the Hebrew and Greek terms that are brief but very valuable. If you do not have a concordance and you can only afford one, I recommend Strong's Concordance for your home Bible study primarily because of the recognition of the Strong's Numbering System by other major reference works.

Originally printed in *West Virginia Christian*, Vol. 7, No. 12, December 2000, p. 8. Reprinted by permission.

J.D. Tant Texas Preacher
(Fanning Yater Tant)

One of the more colorful preachers to read about is J.D. Tant (1861-1941) who was born during the Civil War. He was a great proclaimer of New Testament Christianity and an example of the great sacrifices many made for the cause of Christ. Reading this biography about brother Tant will astonish a person today to see the degree of sacrifices made by those during the pioneer days.

The book is filled with stories you will want to read over and over. My favorite part of the book is to read about the various humorous encounters J.D. Tant had during his life. In fact, so many stories existed in and out of the book that one of the chapters of this book is entitled "I Never Deny Anything They Tell On Me." Basil Overton in the World Evangelist relayed one of my favorite stories about Tant. This story is a sample of others you will find in the book. You can just feel the angst from the person who shouts at Tant.

> A church that did not believe baptism was essential to salvation told him he could preach in a revival meeting for them if he would not mention baptism. Brother Tant agreed to do it, and some of the members of the church of Christ thought he had lost his mind. At the conclusion of his first sermon in the revival while brother Tant was explaining God's plan of salvation, he said, 'Jesus said go into all the world and preach the gospel to every creature. He that believes and does what I am not supposed to mention in this revival will be saved.' He did the same with several other New Testament passages on baptism and finally

some leader in the church spoke loudly to brother Tant and said, 'Go ahead and say baptism!' (World Evangelist, 12/97, p. 4).

One of the facts that impressed me is how brutal conditions were and how rough those of the denominations could be as well. It is said that brother Tant went into the pulpit and stated he brought two deacons with him to help keep the peace while he preached. He promptly laid to revolvers on top of the pulpit. The book is truly exciting reading. You will laugh and nearly cry from the laughter and tears.

One of the lessons we need to remember arises from the mistreatment brother Tant received from the hands of the brethren. Brother Tant kept on preaching despite numerous setbacks. Hopefully the book will inspire congregations to a greater attention to the care of gospel preachers. I hate to hear brethren criticize preachers unjustly. I can only imagine how God feels about it. At the conclusion of one meeting in which Tant was promised payment but the brethren reneged on it, Tant said they would pay him at the judgment. That is true, brethren. We need to be sure to treat these servants of God as such.

J.D. Tant is truly one of the exciting characters of our history to read about. The trials, tragedies, and triumphs of the Tant family will uplift you and inspire you to put forth a greater effort for the kingdom. A short review such as this is totally inadequate to convey the profit from this book. It is one of the most enjoyable books I have ever read. When you finish this book you will want to read the book of reflections by his wife, Nannie Green Yater Tant.

Originally printed in the *West Virginia Christian*, Vol. 9, No. 12, December 2002, p. 8. Reprinted by permission.

Reminiscences of a Pioneer Preacher's Wife
(Nannie Yater Tant)

"Behind ever great man is a great woman" is indeed true. My father often reminds me that a preacher's wife can be either a great asset or great hindrance to his work. Thankfully we have biographies of preachers such as Thomas & Alexander Campbell, Barton W. Stone, Benjamin Franklin, and others who have made tremendous sacrifices for the gospel. Sadly, there are not as many biographies detailing the sacrifices their wives made so their husbands could GO and preach the gospel. One preacher who made enormous sacrifices to preach was Jefferson Davis Tant (or better known as J.D. Tant). Tant would operate a farm, rear a family, and still hold protracted gospel meetings away from home for weeks at a time. How did he accomplish this? Because of the sacrifices of his wife, Nannie Yater Tant. The trials that this pioneer preacher's wife endured are difficult to fathom in our day of modern technology. To use another expression of my father, "we are standing on the shoulders of giants." Nannie Yater Tant recorded her experiences in this autobiography; which was a major source of information for her son's biography of her husband entitled J.D. Tant – Texas Preacher. Both books are excellent and both are worthwhile reading together.

J.D. Tant's parents were devastated by the Civil War as their home and eleven farms were destroyed by General Sherman. The family never recovered from this loss. Nannie Yater Buckner's family was affluent. When her family learned of Nannie's desire to marry J.D. Tant; a traveling preacher, rough Irishman,

and impoverished, there was much opposition. However, as Nannie's mother fought her Baptist family to become and marry a Christian so Nannie fought her family to marry J.D. Tant. She arrived at his home to be met by two children from J.D. Tant's first marriage. (His first wife had died of pneumonia while working the farm in J.D. Tant's absence due to preaching.) She was trained to be a schoolteacher, but she was rarely able to teach in public school. She turned down other suitors who would have provided a much easier life than the life of toil, sickness, deaths, poverty, natural disasters, crop failures, adversity, perilous relocations, and adventure the likes some of us can barely imagine. Often when we speak of pioneers we are thinking of men in the early days of the restoration movement. In this case, the term includes this but also refers to the days of the settling of the West. In fact, on a tour of Oklahoma that Nannie attended with J.D. Tant, the Army was on the hunt for the recently escaped Comanche Geronimo! She often worked the farm alone so J.D. Tant could continue to preach and debate for the cause of Christ. Both of them equally considered their work to further the gospel in Texas and beyond. With the upbringing she had, there must have been times she wondered if she was made of the material to endure such hardship.

Indeed, the wives of preachers have made great sacrifices. Sacrifices today may not reach the same degree as the days of yesteryear; however, many choose to avoid the life of a preacher or preacher's wife to this day because of the sacrifices that must be made. Thankfully, there are those who are willing to make these sacrifices that we may grow thereby. We must remember that these are the Lord's servants, cherish and treat them the best we are able. One wonders if such a life is worth it? To answer, consider these words from Mrs. J.D. Tant:

> "...I have not one moment of regret for the choice I made. It has been a life filled with incredible hardships and difficulties, but equally incredible have been the reward and the happiness. I have been richly blessed, and if the choice

were to be made over again, and I could know the kind of life I was entering, my answer now would be as unhesitating and as whole-hearted as it was then. Not every woman could be happy as a "preacher's wife," but for me it was the only life I ever wanted. (Page 19).

Originally printed in the *West Virginia Christian*, Vol. 15, No. 10, October 2008, p. 2. Reprinted by permission.

Creation Compromises
(Bert Thompson)

Sometimes compromise between two parties is viewed as a method to reach a better condition. However, compromise is not always necessary or beneficial. This book deals with the compromises many have made between evolution and creationism which some call theistic evolution. One of my favorite quotes on the authenticity of the six 24-hour days of creation is by none other than Alexander Campbell:

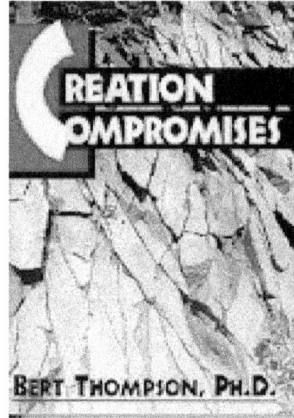

> We are aware that some writers of modern, as well as of ancient time, think the Mosaic account of creation should be discarded as erroneous, because the various strata of earth, according to Geology, evince a higher antiquity than five or six thousand years... We place the inspired record, as given by Moses, under a divine commission, against all the theories founded by nature or science, as interpreted by man, and we believe the Mosaic account will grow brighter and brighter, as the geological theory fades and recedes into comparative oblivion.[1]

This book exposes the false compromises of the creation account including, sadly, those advocated among us. Brother Thompson explains several false theories and the faults of them including: Double Revelation Theory, Day-Age Theory, Gap

---

[1] As quoted by Wayne Jackson, "The Age of the Earth," The Spiritual Sword, Memphis, TN: Getwell Church of Christ, Vol. 26, No. 3, April 1995, p. 15.

334 | GIVE ATTENTION TO READING

Theory, Progressive Creationism, Modified Gap Theory, Non-World View, Multiple Gap Theory, and the Framework Hypothesis. The author carefully explains how accepting one of these compromises is undermining the word of God.

There is no reason to deny the days of creation to be six 24-hour days. When interviewing preachers I ask if they believe the days of creation to be twenty-four hour days or many years. Any response other than twenty-four hour days reveals either a compromise made or ignorance on the subject. If your faith in creationism is weak and you want it strengthened, then all you have to do is study the ample supply of evidence supporting creation. Many will not heed to creationism because they realize, if it is true; they are accountable to God. Some reject the account of creation because they do not respect the integrity of scripture as much as scientists who assert they "know" more than a preacher. Bert Thompson has a Ph.D. in microbiology from Texas A & M University and has taught in the College of Veterinary Medicine at A & M University. For someone to go through the attempts of indoctrination and peer pressure of his colleagues and professors in science and come forth a defender of the faith is a tremendous example and encouragement to us.

Originally printed in *West Virginia Christian*, Vol. 7, No. 8, August 2000, p. 3. Reprinted by permission.

The Effective Edge – How Christians Today Can Accomplish the Lord's Work (Gregory A. Tidwell)

This is the first book by the new Editor of the *Gospel Advocate*, Gregory Alan Tidwell and is titled *The Effective Edge – How Christians Today Can Accomplish the Lord's Work*. I had the pleasure of hosting brother Tidwell at our Area Men's Meetings here in Wadsworth. (These meetings are primarily for preachers and elders but all are invited to attend.) I was excited to have the new Editor for a publication that many of us have long admired; especially since he lives in Ohio, no offense intended.

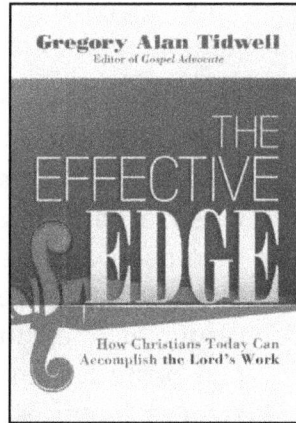

At this meeting, Greg had just received the shipment of his new book, published by Gospel Advocate Company, and I was able to obtain a signed copy from him.

Different people like different books for different reasons. Sometimes people are busy and do not have the time to read a more lengthy composition but still want a fresh reminder on the skills they need to be successful. And what is more important to be successful at than the Lord's work? That is, we should desire to be successful at the Lord's work. Could it be that many of us pay mere lip service to such a notion? It may be a painful thought but one we ought to give thought to—if we cannot find the time to do the Lord's work now, then can we honestly expect the Lord to find time for us in eternity? We may expect such, but there is such a thing as unrealistic expectations. Recall these sobering words from Jesus—*"Not everyone who says to Me, 'Lord, Lord,' shall enter the kingdom of heaven, but he who does the will of My Father in heaven. Many will say to Me in that day, 'Lord, Lord, have we not prophesied in Your name, cast out demons in Your name, and done many wonders in Your name?' And then I will declare to them, 'I never knew you; depart from Me, you who practice lawlessness!'"* (Matthew 7:21-23, NKJV).

I appreciate these words from the book and tried to reflect on them as I read through it trying to keep an open mind—

> **Effectiveness is in short supply. In the church, as in government and business, the lack of effectiveness hinders our success and limits the good we can accomplish. Often, when faced with failure, we seek an easy scapegoat rather than deal with the hard task of owning up to problems in our thoughts and actions. We imagine if only we had more resources, knew the latest methods, or were free from certain obstacles, then we would succeed. Blaming circumstances, however, misses the mark. We must look deeper. We must look at ourselves and, with honesty face our own failures. (page 11.)**

The book is concise so a person who is unable to devote large blocks of time can easily work through the excellent material in this book. Through the book, Tidwell takes on a discussion of effectiveness in various areas of our Christian vocation: leadership, example-setting, goal-setting, stewardship, planning, standards, fellowship, communication, discipleship, representation, guidance and service. Quite easily, each of these chapters could be converted into books, but effort has been made to be concise, in an effective way. As the words of Shakespeare in Hamlet state "Brevity is the soul of wit," Greg Tidwell's book is concise and in an effective way! The book is designed to be also used in Adult Bible Class format with questions for discussion. Perhaps this book will provide an excellent teacher the means by which we can all learn to be more effective in our work for the Lord.

Fundamentals of the Faith
(Rex A. Turner)

Churches of Christ seek to grow both in spirit and in number. If a congregation is growing, then it will have people in attendance at varying maturity levels. Hence, an education program and preaching ought to be careful to include regular teaching on the fundamentals of New Testament Christianity. If topics such as the design of baptism, the identifying marks of the New Testament church, the frequency of which to observe the Lord's Supper, and others along these lines have become mundane to a congregation, then most likely they are not evangelizing. True Christians never tire of hearing the fundamentals preached in a sermon. In fact, they become distressed if they do not hear these preached forcefully and frequently. Of course, there are those who indeed are prepared for the meat of the Word (Hebrews 5:12-14), but an indicator of that readiness is the realization that there are those who still seek the milk of the Word as well (1 Peter 2:2). We must always be aware that there are those who need to be reminded of the fundamentals (Jude 3), fortified with the fundamentals for their own protection (Romans 16:18), and even be rebuked with the fundamentals (Titus 1:9) to save their souls.

There are several excellent topics covered in this book in a very scholarly but readable manner. One of my personal favorites is "The Faithful Preacher Must Be Able to Run With Horses" which he delivered at the Harding Graduate School of Religion in 1969. He compares Jeremiah 12:5, "If thou hast run with the footmen, and they have wearied thee, then how canst thou

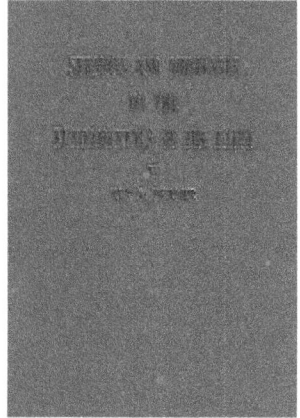

contend with horses." In this chapter he identifies several horses of spiritual darkness that the preacher must be able to run against—materialism, indifference, worldliness, liberalism, and self. It is an excellent encouragement to preachers and all of us. Turner observes:

> As was the case with Jeremiah, so is the case with the preacher—and or every Christian for that matter. The faithful preacher of today must be prepared mentally and spiritually to run with horses. This necessity has been the case in every age, but it especially the case in this age. The present spiritual climate—or rather the want of it—projects the fact that without a doubt the preacher of today faces many grave trials as well as many alluring temptations. Already certain well qualified preachers of our personal acquaintance have become so wearied by running with the footmen that they have given up the full-time ministry. At times there are young men who are commencing a study for the entering of the ministry. Jesus said: "No man having put his hand to the plow, and looking back, is fit for the kingdom of God." (Luke 9:62). – (Pages 3-4.)

Other subjects in this book include evidences for the resurrection of Jesus, NT interpretations of OT prophecy, matters of faith and opinion, the observance of the Lord's Supper is only on the first day of the week, instrumental music in worship is sinful, the plan of salvation, the identifying marks of the NT church, unity, and not conforming to worldliness. In his discussion on Christians and worldliness he makes a very salient observation— "...in this alluring, comfortable, and affluent society, Christian have no burning desire to go to heaven. They like things just as they are now here on earth." (Page 197). That was written in 1970, years before a certain politician laid claim of inventing the Internet. Can anyone doubt that these words are even more true today with conveniences we have that were not thought of nearly forty years ago?

Dr. Rex A. Turner founded and served as President of Alabama Christian College for many years. He lectured and wrote widely. As part of the college's 30th anniversary celebration, he was requested to collect in book form representative samples of his sermons, lectures and articles the school wanted to print in his honor and benefit Christian education. Due to the rapid response to advanced orders the volume was released in 1972 and is still available. The Alabama Christian College was among the first to utilize modern technology so students could study remotely for advanced degrees in ministry. The institution was known as Southern Christian University for many years and one of the early institutions to offer the doctorate. It is now known as Ambridge University. The university chartered the Turner School of Theology in 1999 in honor of Rex and Opal Turner's sacrifice and years of service to the university. Brother Turner passed away February 13, 2001.

This is an excellent book to give to someone who is looking for reading to help fortify his faith. Our hope is that there are many readers of this work for years to come. May we never grow weary of the fundamentals and be able to run with horses.

Originally printed in the *West Virginia Christian*, Vol. 16, No. 12, December 2009, p. 8. Reprinted by permission.

Systematic Theology
(Rex A. Turner, Sr.)

If I were to suggest a book that should be read by every Christian, this would be one of the first ones. The book covers a broad range of topics on theology in a scholarly manner. Concerning Systematic Theology, the Spiritual Sword gave the following review:

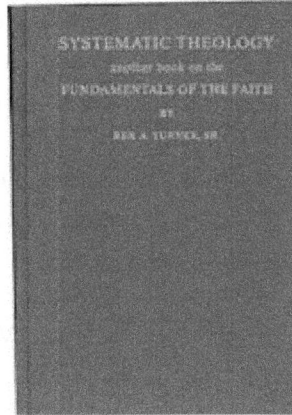

> ...this book is a survey of significant biblical themes. Beginning with a discussion of inspiration of the Bible, it proceeds through a study of authorship of the first five books of the Old Testament, the supposed priority of the gospel of Mark, the attributes of God, the doctrine of Satan, the nature of man, the virgin birth, the death and sufferings of Christ, the nature of the church, and numerous other topics of vital concern. It is one of the most valuable books available for a serious study of biblical truth.[1]

One of my concerns is that some in the church fail to understand that "educated" men make mistakes. There are numerous instances when you have two highly degreed men on the opposite sides of an issue. Some do not have an understanding of the implications of certain "facts" that they read. For example, if someone says "Scholars believe that Mark was written before the other gospels." Would we question that? Is it even important? Some may teach that Mark was written first and have

---

[1] Alan E. Highers, Editor. *Spiritual Sword*, Memphis, TN: Getwell Church of Christ, October 1993, Vol. 25, No. 1, p. 48.

no other implication in mind; however, there is a large group of religious scholars that do not respect the inspiration of the Bible and the dates of the completion of the gospel is one of their places of attack. Rex Turner explains the liberals attack on the inspiration of the gospels:

> One chief holding of the liberals of the New Testament field of study is the doctrine of the priority of Mark with respect to the synoptic [same common view] gospel records. The liberals hold that the gospel of Mark was written earlier than the gospels of Matthew and Luke; that Mark copied from a source which they labeled Marcus Q; that the gospels of Mathew and Luke were copied from Mark together with the compilation of numerous other sources; and that the two gospels [Matthew and Luke] were completed in the second half of the first century. The findings of those liberals falls under the heading styled, the "Synoptic Problem."[2]

There is strong evidence that Matthew was the first gospel written. The order in which the gospels were written is not the issue *per se*. The issue is whether Matthew had to borrow from Q and Mark to write his gospel or did he write with his own experiences guided by the Holy Spirit? This is an outright attack on the inspiration of the New Testament writers. Can you honestly believe that Matthew, an apostle of Jesus, would have to borrow from Mark (who was not an apostle) and some other documents to write his account?

The book is very well written and the author is eminently qualified to write such a work. Dr. Turner holds a B.A. in history and English from Samford University, an LL.B. from Jones Law School, M.S. degree and Ed.D. from Auburn University. He served as the first president of Faulkner University for 31 years and Southern Christian University for 15 years. He is currently

---

[2] Rex A. Turner, Sr., Systematic Theology, Montgomery, AL: Alabama Christian School of Religion, 1989, pp. 39-40.

Chancellor of Southern Christian University and Professor of Old Testament. The Gospel Advocate published an issue in honor of his 80+ years of life and service.[3] He is a great scholar and a kind Christian gentleman.

Originally printed in *West Virginia Christian*, Vol. 7, No. 6, June 2000, p. 8. Reprinted by permission.

---

[3] F. Furman Kearley, Editor, Gospel Advocate, Nashville, TN: Gospel Advocate Company, September 1993, Vol. 85, No. 9.

A Prayer from Heaven – The Model Prayer as Evidence for the Deity of Christ
(W. Terry Varner)

One of the intriguing questions I ponder, relating to the false view that God is not involved in the fate of nations or the affairs of men, is this: why did Jesus teach His disciples to pray as John had taught his disciples to pray too (Luke 11:1)?

If one of the tenets of deism is that God "wound up the world" and lets it spin on its own without further action or intervention by God, then why would we be taught about prayer and encouraged to pray by the Son of God? The fact of the matter is that many underestimate God's actions in the world. They seem to think that God only operates supernaturally rather than through His natural laws to accomplish His will. This is one of the subjects of Habakkuk—God is active among the nations even when these nations are unable to detect His actions. The founding fathers of our nation recognized that God was active in the rise and fall of nations, as seen in their reference to Him as "Divine Providence," and they sought His assistance in the formation of these United States. Sadly, the founding fathers of our nation are often misrepresented or misunderstood.

This book drives at fundamental points relating to the model prayer: God exists! God listens! God takes action! I appreciate the way Charles C. Pugh III describes this book as exegetical, devotional, and apologetic too. To some, the concept of the model prayer and apologetics may seem rather tenuous; however, if there is no God then to whom are we praying and for what

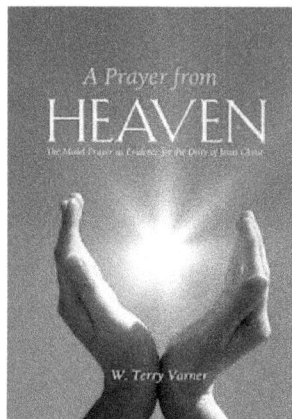

reason? Indeed prayer and apologetics go together! W. Terry Varner, as Editor of Sufficient Evidence and co-founder of the Warren Christian Apologetics Center, certainly knows his way around the apologetics field!

The book is devoted to several themes relating to the model prayer: reverence, adoration, sovereignty, obedience, dependence, forgiveness, guidance, deliverance, and praise. Each of these themes is discussed in the context of the model prayer. The material is rich and well worth the study. In addition, there is a helpful appendix relating to our model, our example, Jesus Christ and how He was a man of prayer too. The book also includes a helpful Scripture Index, plus each chapter has a detailed bibliography for those seeking to consult additional works on the subject.

One wonders how many of our problems today could be alleviated if we prayed more? Do we pray enough? Do we pray at all? We need to be people who listen to God through His word and talk to Him through the blessed avenue of prayer vouchsafed by our Lord Jesus Christ. Abraham Lincoln said "I have been driven many times upon my knees by the overwhelming conviction that I had nowhere else to go." We have someplace else to go, and we should bow the knee every day in prayer along life's journey to that destination!

Originally printed in the *West Virginia Christian*, Vol. 24, No. 5, May 2017, p. 8. *Reprinted by permission.*

Vine's Complete Expository Dictionary of Old & New Testament Words
(W.E. Vine, Merrill F. Unger & William White, Jr.)

For those who do not know the Greek or Hebrew language (and those who do), this dictionary is vital. It is a must that every student of the Scriptures should have not only in the church library but in their personal libraries as well. At 2008 Polishing the Pulpit, I was fortunate to hear the Speaker of the International Gospel Hour, Winford Claiborne, discuss each morning various books for study. One of the sessions was "My Top Five Reference Books" and on this list was this dictionary. Brother Claiborne stated that Vine's dictionary was one of the very best, and I could not agree more. That this reference work is widely accepted is shown in the recommendations of Warren Wiersbe, F.F. Bruce and others.

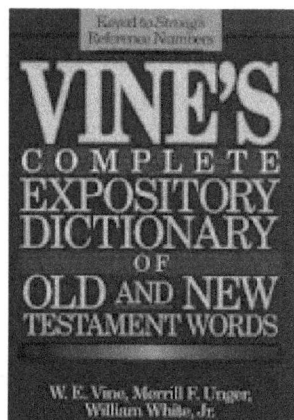

The Old Testament section of this book is from *Nelson's Expository Dictionary of the Old Testament* written by Unger and White. The New Testament section is from *W.E. Vine's Expository Dictionary of New Testament Words*. Nelson Publishing has provided both of these reference works in one volume and has standardized the layout of the material. At the beginning of the Old Testament section is a valuable article explaining the origins of the Hebrew language, its grammatical structure, and other important matters such as the various theories of text translation. Additional valuable material is provided for the New Testament section as well. It is important to know these matters not only for this reference material but also for the various translations of the Scripture. The reference text of the Bible used is the

King James Version and all words are grouped in alphabetical order by this version. The words are then classified into the various forms of grammar: noun, verb, adjective, etc. Then, the English transliteration of the word followed by how the word appears in the original language. In order to facilitate additional research and verification, the Strong's Reference Number is included. Then, the writer provides a definition of how the word is used and includes examples of where the word is in Scripture used in this manner. This structure is used to analyze more than 6,000 words.

One important point to note about this reference work—be sure you understand the cross-references in the book or you may get confused. For example, in the back of the dictionary is a Greek Word Index that has the words organized by the English transliteration of the Greek, then the Strong's number, a page number, and then a succinct definition of the literal meaning of the word. When I first used the dictionary I was under the impression that the page number was referring to the page in the dictionary. I would turn and turn but to no avail. After becoming frustrated, I then assumed that there must be a publisher error. Not so. The publisher, in addition to the Strong's reference number provides the page number of another valuable reference work, *A Greek-English Lexicon of the New Testament and other Early Christian Literature* by Bauer, Arndt, and Gingrich. (The Old Testament Index references the page numbers of *Hebrew and English Lexicon of the Old Testament by Brown, Driver, and Briggs*.) If I would have read a little closer about the structure of this book, I could have not only saved myself some frustration but have been able to use the cross-reference table to access other works in order to further validate the material. So, it is a good idea to be familiar with the structure of reference books! While the work is invaluable, it is not infallible. One should be careful to validate the use of words as they appear in the Bible with other reference works. The fact that this book has the words coded to the Strong's numbering system makes this easier to accomplish. I can recall someone counseling me to distinguish between what the word literally means and how the writer says the term is used in Scriptures. The Bible is perfect, but man is fallible.

The Current Issues
(Foy E. Wallace, Jr.)

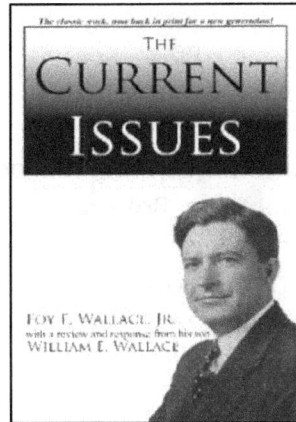

It takes courage for a person to change long held views; especially when flexibility has diminished with age. There are exceptions to this rule but often we "go down with the ship" of our opinions. One such exception I witnessed is in the life of a dear departed Christian, Bill Clevenger. Bill Clevenger was a WW2 veteran who served under General Patton. He had held the Non-Institutional (NI) position most of his life. Around 1998, Bill's health decline prompted him to move to Streetsboro where we attend church. He sought to worship with us stating "I want to worship peaceably and will not involve myself in the business aspect even though I don't agree with some of these practices." We welcomed Bill to our services which he attended faithfully and even led prayers. After a year or so, Bill came to our apartment for dinner after he hinted how much he would like to visit with us since he used to live in our neighborhood. We discussed freely our mutual concern for the church and had a wonderful visit. As time went by he requested that I visit him at his residence. Unfortunately circumstances repeatedly interfered, but Bill persisted and others began telling me how much Bill wanted me to visit him. Since I saw him at every service I knew something was on his mind. So a friend and I went to visit him as we were in town one evening. Bill was being called upon by Christian friends from the congregation he formerly attended, who were concerned about his worshipping with those who did not share their viewpoint. I decided it was a good time to approach him about this subject.

"Bill, have you ever heard the name of Foy E. Wallace, Jr.?" I knew based on books he had that that name would ring a bell. I asked him if he knew brother Wallace had broken from the new NI party. He had not. I went on to explain that Wallace had to make public statements orally and in print that he was not a part of this new party. Wallace, at first, was involved closely with those who would become heavily steeped in this mindset. Wallace was close friends with one of the leaders of the new party, even conducting his wedding. I told him that one of the breaking points between Wallace and NI party came over cooperative meetings. Both men fully supported these arrangements in the past by which a congregation would work with other congregations to pool resources to bring a preacher into a large venue of a major city. One of these famous cooperative gospel meetings was held in the Music Hall in Houston, TX from January 21-28, 1945. Wallace's friend, who became a leader in the NI party, not only arranged the meeting but also arranged to have Foy E. Wallace's sermons published in book form which became known as *God's Prophetic Word*.

The Current Issues is a booklet that Foy E. Wallace, Jr. published to set the record straight of his views on this new party that went about troubling churches with their newly restrictive doctrine. Wallace points out that both parties had fellowship on cooperative meetings but the new party had changed. Wallace points out that he held the same positions that his father, Foy E. Wallace, Sr. had also held. Wallace's main issue which the NI crowd seeks to claim his as one of their own was on Christian Colleges. Wallace was not opposed to Christian Colleges; he sent some of his children to Freed-Hardeman College. He was concerned that Christian Colleges would usurp the operation of local churches. This period of division was driven largely by personalities and much damage was done to the brotherhood. Some today are not even aware of the specifics of these issues. This book is a good reference work on this period of division from one that the new party sought to claim in their camp and his repudiation of such efforts.

Often I hear the process that gave rise to the NI party was that they drew their circle of fellowship smaller so that fewer fit in it. Then, they re-drew the circle even tighter and fewer fit. Eventually they drew it so tight that barely anyone fits into it. If they have not already done so, they will be as it is reported about two Yorkshire men conversing: "Everyone in the world is quite mad, except for me and thee. And sometimes I have my doubts about thee." Our plea is to let the New Testament be our guide, but some have a narrower viewpoint on matters than the Scriptures. As those who debated with this new party often pointed out—"It is just as much a sin to create a law where the Bible does not as it is to loosen a law that actually exists." This is a fair description of the NI position. I admire our mutual determination to have a *"Thus Saith the Lord,"* but they are sometimes too restrictive where the Bible actually provides more liberty.

Bill was captivated as I explained these events to him. Bill had become practically blind, but he wanted to read this book. So, I asked the church secretary, Nina Blackford, if she would be willing to read the book into a tape recorder for Bill to hear, which she graciously did. I didn't hear much more about the issue for some time. Then, during the summer of 2001, Bill came forward to express to our interim preacher, John Harris that he wanted it known that he had now rejected his former views and wanted to be in full unity with the congregation. Eventually our new preacher, Ralph Price, would come to work with us and become very close to Bill, even conducting his funeral in January 2006. Ralph later told me that he wanted to read the book that convinced Bill. While I had known of Bill's change, I did not know that *The Current Issues* had such an impact on his thinking.

This is proof that minds, regardless of age, can be reached.

God's Prophetic Word
(Foy E. Wallace Jr.)

In 1995, my wife and I were honored to meet brother Wilson Wallace, son of Foy E. Wallace, Jr. We traveled nearly 250 miles to converse with Wilson about his father. I told him how I had spent time at the church building waiting to walk to work (since we had only one car). During one of my stays at the building I leafed through the church library and came across God's Prophetic Word, which was placed there in the memory of Olive Hill. This interested me since Olive Hill was once my grandfather's girlfriend. Since I never met neither my grandfather nor Olive Hill, I was interested in this book since it was placed in her honor.

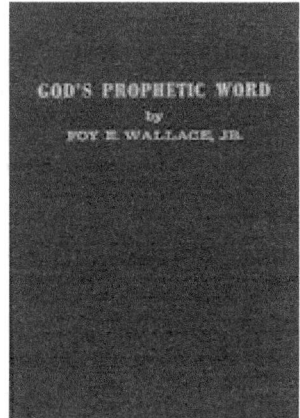

God's Prophetic Word contains three chapters to the proposition that the Bible is inspired of God, infallible, complete, and prophetic. The book proves there is no hope for the nation of Israel as "God's chosen people" without Jesus Christ. The author shows conclusively the church/kingdom was established as prophesied and was not postponed. Then the false eschatological view of premillennialism is refuted. The author shows that we cannot know that "Jesus Is Coming Soon" as the premillennialists assert based upon their misapplication of Matthew 24. Foy E. Wallace also supplies material refuting Seventh-Day Adventists and Anglo-Israelism. He concludes with a defense of pioneers who are misrepresented by premillennialists. A final chapter on prophecy proof-texts is extremely valuable. Although the book was put on the market in 1946 and the author went on to his reward on December 18, 1979, the book is still vital. It is indeed a classic. Testimony to the value of this book is further substantiated by the fact that another writer has labored to provide a scriptural index to God's Prophetic Word.

Wilson Wallace told me that one time when his father was away preaching in a gospel meeting, their house caught on fire. The firemen told his mother, Virgie Wallace, the house would surely be lost. She said if they could only save the contents of the library, it would be all right to let the rest of the house go. They were able to save books which no doubt reached well back into the 1800's. She realized the value of good books and so should we. I do not know who placed God's Prophetic Word in the library in honor of sister Hill; however, I am very grateful that they did.

Originally printed in *West Virginia Christian*, Vol. 7, No. 4, April 2000. Reprinted by permission.

The Gospel for Today –
An Extended Edition of the
Certified Gospel
(Foy E. Wallace, Jr.)

One may find it puzzling why a book of sermons would endure after many years. This usually speaks to two factors—the deliverer and the message. In this case, Foy E. Wallace, Jr. delivered a series of lessons in a gospel meeting in Port Arthur, TX in 1937 which were released in book form and entitled *The Certified Gospel*. Due to the book's enduring popularity and increased demand for the preaching of brother Wallace, it was expanded to its present format, *The Gospel for Today* which was released thirty years later. Today, over seventy years after the original release, it remains one of my personal favorites, even though the expanded version was released just a few months after I was born. I never had the privilege of knowing Wallace; however, my father inspired me from his recollections of days at the Nashville School of Preaching where he heard stories about brother Wallace and was able to watch him preach. I have been blessed to know his youngest son, Wilson and his wife Peggy. They are a delight to visit with and if you have the pleasure of their company to discuss his father, cherish it!

The message of the book is timeless—gospel sermons. We need more straight-from-the-book gospel preaching. Young preachers would do well to obtain brother Wallace's preaching books. Now, brother Wallace packed so much material in his sermons that one may likely find multiple sermons from just one chapter of the book. Brother Wallace was known for preaching

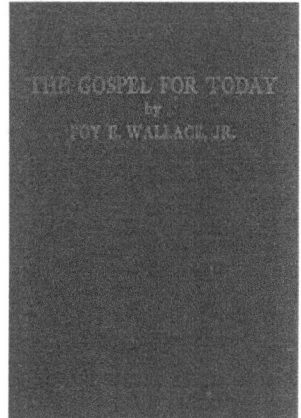

well over an hour or more. People travelled well over 100 miles just to hear him speak one night! There are sermons here we need to continually ring forth from our pulpits—"The Certified Gospel," "Who Wrote the Bible," "How and When the Church Began," "What to Do to Be Saved," "What Must the Church Do To Be Saved," "The Sin of Sectarianism," "Bible Baptism" and others.

My personal favorite from this work is "Why Send for Peter?" I wish every member of the church would read this sermon or their preacher would preach it to them or both! In this lesson brother Wallace deals with several miraculous manifestations including the appearances of an angel to Peter and Cornelius and the outpouring of the Holy Spirit at Cornelius' house. Brother Wallace points out the significance of these events and we do well to remember these. For example, Wallace writes concerning the angel which appeared to Cornelius and God's plan that men preach the gospel, not angels or the Holy Spirit directly:

> But why did the angel not tell him [Cornelius] what to do to be saved? Because that is not God's plan. Angels cannot preach the gospel to men. Cornelius might have said to the angel: "Now, I am ready to do what God commands, why send for Peter, when you are here already; just let Peter stay in Joppa, and let me stay in Caesarea, and avoid three days delay—just tell me what God would have me do." If ever the gospel plan should vary under any circumstances, would this not have been the one time when it should have varied enough for an angel to tell a man what to do to be saved? (Page 164).

Brother Wallace expands the lesson to point out some additional important points of which we must not lose sight:

> We have now learned the purpose of all three of the miracles in this case. First, the appearance of the angel to Cornelius—that was miracle No. 1, and its purpose was to

inform Cornelius where to find the preacher. Second, the vision at Joppa—which was miracle No. 2, and its purpose was to show Simon Peter that he should go and preach to the Gentiles. Third, the outpouring of the Holy Spirit upon the household of Cornelius—Miracle No. 3, the purpose of which was to convince the whole Jewish church that the Gentiles were acceptable to God as gospel subjects. (Page 168).

One will not agree with everything brother Wallace writes. He was not perfect and he made mistakes—we all do. We should keep these matters in mind but never let his great accomplishments and writings go unnoticed. People have and still do criticize the man when his name is brought up, but let them show forth their works for the kingdom and see how these set in the balance with brother Wallace's labors for the Kingdom. Sadly, many of us may find ourselves more akin to Belshazzar than Foy E. Wallace, Jr.

Originally printed in the *West Virginia Christian*, Vol. 17 No. 2, February 2010, p. 8. Reprinted by permission.

The Neal-Wallace Discussion on the Thousand Years Reign of Christ (Foy E. Wallace, Jr.)

With the popularity of the Left Behind series that teaches the false doctrine premillennialism, have you ever wondered why churches of Christ were not swallowed with the pernicious doctrine? One of the main deterrents against this error was Foy E. Wallace Jr. who was the editor of the Gospel Advocate. Wallace fought against this error and those who were trying to take the churches of Christ down this road to perdition. If you think that one can believe in premillennialism and be a faithful Christian, then you have not read the works of Foy E. Wallace, Jr. or you are blinded from the truth. Everyone should read this debate.

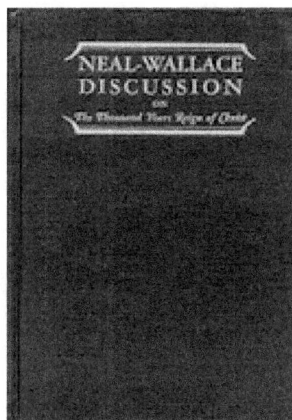

One of the great benefits of religious debates is the ability to gather the facts of two points of view and see the pros and cons tested against one another. It can be brutal for the opponent who is wrong; however, the truth is the victor and that is what the purpose of debates are. This discussion in January 1933 in Winchester, KY is a premier example of truth winning and winning decisively.

The proposition was pushed by Charles Neal who dared anyone to sign on the dotted line in opposition to his debate proposition—"The Bible clearly teaches that after the second coming of Christ and before the final resurrection and judgment, there will be an age or dispensation of one thousand years during which Christ will reign on the earth." The editor of the Gospel

Advocate signed the proposition, which began one of the more thrilling debates that can be read.

Wallace did not hesitate to use humor to force his points. My father tells of staying up late at night to read the debate and come across a funny incident. It would be so funny that he would wake up my mother to relay her the story. Needless to say as funny as the story was, it was not funny to my mother at the time! One of the examples where the humor shines is Wallace's attack of prophecies having to have a literal rather than literal or symbolic fulfillment relates to a prophecy about John the Baptist.

In Luke 3:3-6 is this prophecy from Isaiah 40:3-4 about John the Baptist:

> *"And he came into all the country about Jordan, preaching the baptism of repentance for the remission of sins; As it is written in the book of the words of Esaias the prophet, saying, The voice of one crying in the wilderness, Prepare ye the way of the Lord, make his paths straight. Every valley shall be filled, and every mountain and hill shall be brought low; and the crooked shall be made straight, and the rough ways shall be made smooth; And all flesh shall see the salvation of God."*

Here is what Wallace states to drive the point home that not all prophecies were fulfilled literally:

> "According to the statement in Brother Neal's book, John the Baptist would literally pull down the hills and fill up the valleys; for according to him, 'every prophecy that the Bible says has been fulfilled has been fulfilled literally.' John the Baptist was not a preacher at all. He was a road builder, operating a steam shovel, going out to pull down the hills and to build up the valleys, constructing a literal highway. That alone shows the fallacy of his statements that every prophecy is fulfilled literally."

I have a photocopy of a letter Foy Wallace wrote to a friend about the second debate Neal agreed to have in Chattanooga, TN. During this debate Wallace basically began refuting Neal's positions before he could present them. This so defeated Neal that he quit the debate. Neal's mentor for this doctrine was R.H. Boll. Boll refused to debate Wallace and it is evident that it was because the arguments used by Wallace were true. The premillennialist movement was basically stopped in its tracks. Indeed the church is better because of men like Foy E. Wallace, Jr. He may be dead, but his work lives on. All his works are available on CD. Anything by Foy E. Wallace, Jr. is worth studying.

Originally printed in the *West Virginia Christian*, Vol. 10, No. 1, January 2003, p. 5. Reprinted by permission.

Lectures on Church Cooperation
& Orphan Homes
(Thomas B. Warren)

Thomas Warren presented these lectures at the Burbank Gardens Church of Christ in Grand Prairie, TX in 1957 when the noninstitutional movement was creating much disruption in the brotherhood. There was much discussing and debating whether churches could coordinate their efforts through one congregation to sponsor a program. Ironically, some who originally practiced church cooperation were now claiming it was a sin to do so. Another point of debate with this anti-movement was whether or not churches could support orphan homes.

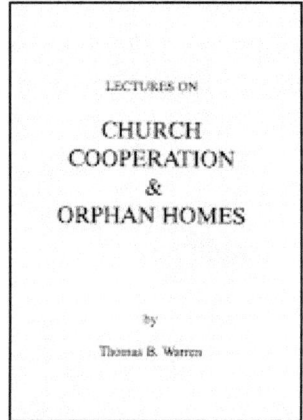

In these lectures Thomas Warren presented a systematic treatment of church cooperation and orphan homes. He used what in logic is referred to as the constituent argument to prove the objectors incorrect. If it were not for the fact that the matter was so serious, it would be laughable, Thomas Warren mentioned hearing a man pray at one of the debates "Lord, save us from logic." One wonders if the man gave any thought as to what the alternative to logic would be. The constituent argument simply means that if all the relating elements of a matter are sound, then the whole of the matter is sound.

To demonstrate that the constituent element has been used all along (whether one realized the name for it or not) Warren quoted Foy E. Wallace's Bulwarks of the Faith. It should be noted that this book and another of Wallace's books, God's Prophetic Word, were the products of a church cooperation effort in Texas organized by some who were now saying that method was sinful. Ironically, some of Wallace's early books were published by one of the chief antagonists on the anti-church cooperation party. This forced Wallace to take repeated stands against those of the noninstitutional party since the new party would claim him (for status) in their allegiance. The quote from Wallace Warren used was:

> "....to launch the mighty plea to abandon party names, party creeds, party organizations, and upon the right creed, the right name, the right doctrine, the right worship, such as taught in the New Testament itself, to restore the primitive apostolic church, the which could be neither Catholic nor Protestant, but Scriptural, and therefore divine. There is no other basis of Christian unity—scriptural unity. And there is no other way to establish the identity of the primitive apostolic church. The wrong creed, the wrong doctrine, the wrong worship, the wrong organization and the wrong name could not possibly result in the right church. But the right creed, the right doctrine, the right worship, the right organization and the right name, for a like reason, cannot be the wrong church." (As quoted on page 27.)

Warren then proceeded to examine all the elements relating to church cooperation and orphan homes. He demonstrated that all elements are scriptural thus proving the whole is scriptural. Dr. Warren also anticipated objections raised to his arguments by preparing a thorough response.

In closing, this writer would like to point out that saying the anti-orphan home group is opposed to helping orphans (or similar such statements) is grossly unfair and sinful. The noninstitutional group objects to the method the orphans are cared for and encourage members to do all they can to assist those without having to disrupt the church treasury. While I respect their sincerity in the matter, they are mistaken. I could tolerate worshipping with a group that held this view; however, based on my experience there is serious doubt as to whether or not they could tolerate one holding the opposing view. It is one thing to hold an opinion on a matter, but it another thing altogether to make the opinion a law. This is adding to the word of God and is as sinful as taking away from the word of God.

Originally printed in the *West Virginia Christian*, Vol. 15, No. 12, December 2008, p. 8. Reprinted by permission.

The Bible Only Makes Christians Only And The Only Christians
(Thomas B. Warren)

There are those who are comforta- ble with stating that we are only Chris- tians but become rather squeamish when it is also stated that we are the only Christians. This great book from the late Thomas Warren addresses this vital subject. In the words of Thomas Warren:

> Such people seem to hold that while it is a mark of humility to say that members of the church of Christ are Christians only, it is evidence of self-righteous- ness and arrogance to say that they are the only Christians. But it is neither self-righteous nor arrogant to point out that members of the church for which Jesus died are Christians only and the only Christians. This is the case because the Bible clearly teaches such.

The book starts out with Jesus' love for those who love and obey the truth. It then proceeds to establish that the Bible is the standard and the only guide to salvation. It discusses Bible au- thority, how it is ascertained, and deals with two basic extremes in relation to Bible authority and the fallacies of both—liberal- ism and anti-ism. I greatly appreciate Warren's point in refer- ence to inference. He prefers to refer to this concept in a differ- ent manner, stating we are bound because God implied an ac- tion: *"The crucial question is: 'Has God—in the New Testa- ment—implied it?' The question is not: 'Has Joe Jones, Bill Smith,*

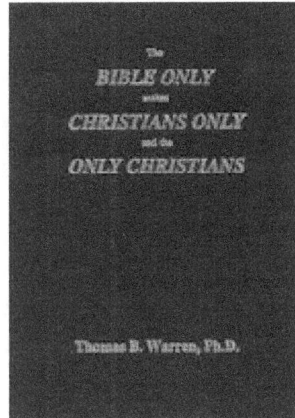

or Tom Warren inferred it?'" This distinction is important for us to understand as it relates to Bible authority.

The book explains that one cannot claim to be baptized into Christ while believing he was already saved prior to baptism. The book explains the law of inclusion and exclusion as it relates to the church. It presents very effective charts to illustrate the Bible is the seed which will produce a consistent fruit—New Testament Christians. It stresses that God is looking for militant faithfulness to His word and the church. Warren also deals with the Christian unity that Jesus prayed and died for not the union of false teachings as espoused by the ecumenical movement to tie various denominations together. Thomas Warren points out:

> The church...was not merely a social club, not merely a church among many other equally valuable churches—but that the church (like the Gospel) was (is) unique among all religious bodies.

One should not be ashamed of the implication stating the Bible makes the only Christians; the alternative is impossible since one cannot obey God correctly while following the Scriptures incorrectly. This book provides a very logical structured case for these great truths.

Thomas Warren was a very capable Bible scholar. He was chairman of the Bible department at Freed-Hardeman College from 1964-1971 and professor of apologetics at Harding Graduate School of Religion from 1971 to 1979. He was the founder of the Spiritual Sword and served as its editor from 1969 to 1989. He entered into debates with some of Christianity's current critics and defended the truth. Thankfully, he produced numerous articles and books that are still available for us to obtain and read. I am in the process of obtaining all his books for my personal library since I have been so impressed with the depth of this man's knowledge and presentation of the truth. Indeed, he was a great leader among churches of Christ and defender of

New Testament Christianity. Thomas Warren died on August 8, 2000 at the age of 80.

Originally printed in the *West Virginia Christian*, Vol. 11, No. 11, November 2004, p. 8. Reprinted by permission.

Have Atheists Proved There Is No God?
(Thomas B. Warren)

The existence of evil and human suffering is perhaps the strongest argument atheists have advanced to create doubts in the minds of Christians. The atheists seek to exploit the existence of human suffering in the face of an omni-benevolent God as a contradiction, and since human suffering is undeniable then God must not exist. Indeed, this is a challenging subject and Thomas B. Warren's book is devoted to tackling this very issue head on. The book is a product of the final chapter of Warren's doctoral dissertation in Philosophy entitled "God and Evil: Does Judeo-Christian Theism Involve a Logical Contradiction?" which he defended and was awarded the terminal degree from Vanderbilt University. Those familiar with dissertations and defending such before the scholars can imagine the amount of preparation and thought that went into this question. While the book is based on a dissertation for scholars, it is written at a level that all can profit from studying.

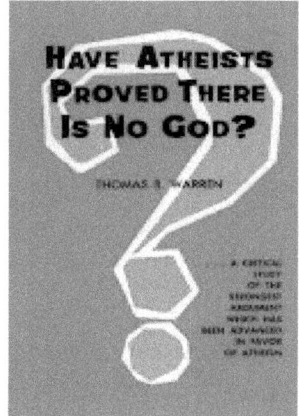

The book begins with a survey of the attacks atheists launch against Christianity on the problem of evil. It includes excepts of quotes from prominent antagonists to Christianity including J.L. Mackie who stated that there is no rational proof for the existence of God, David Hume who argues that the existence of a good God and existence of evil demonstrate a logical contradiction, and others from antiquity who have dealt with the problem of evil and suffering.

Warren goes on to delineate the divine attributes of God as all-powerful, all-knowing, all-good, and all-just; and demonstrates that there is no contradiction between God's attributes and the existence of evil. Then, Doctor Warren goes on to explain that the world is an ideal environment designed to accomplish God's purpose, which is to provide the human race a life of freewill so one's soul may choose to serve God. If one subscribes to the false concepts of predestination, total hereditary depravity, etc., then a contradiction does indeed exist between a loving God and human suffering. However, when one realizes that man has been given free moral agency, placed on an earth designed for the free exercise of this agency, and has the opportunity to prove himself by obedience to the gospel as a soul destined for heaven, then the contradiction has been removed. Dr. Warren defends what he calls "Biblical Theism" against the attacks made by atheists using J.L. Mackie's line of attack using the problem of suffering and existence of God as a framework for the refutation.

Thomas Warren goes on to deal with the subject of natural calamities; which often plague people with doubts. Indeed, it is difficult at times to see the good in disasters larger than the person such as a tornado or hurricane; however, that does not mean that good does not overcome. The writer reminds his readers that it is imperative that one remembers that this world is NOT our home. The world is a temporary dwelling but heaven and hell are eternal abodes based on what one does with the time given on this earth. This truth cannot be overstated nor should it be underestimated!

Warren also deals with all types of suffering—animal and human suffering. One word of caution...a person who is suffering may be naturally overwhelmed with emotions that cloud their ability to look at these items objectively. It is imperative that we study these matters before the difficult days come, because the difficult days will come!

Logic and the Bible
(Thomas B. Warren)

This book seeks to establish the premise the logic and the Bible are not mutually exclusive. In fact, one must have a good command of correct reasoning; i.e., logic, in order to be able to properly interpret the Bible. Tragically, some bemoan this even though they repeatedly use logic, improperly, to ridicule the use of logic. Thomas Be. Warren points out that logic, or correct reasoning, is critical to hermeneutics or the correct method of interpreting the Scriptures.

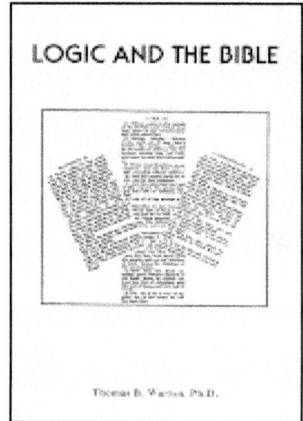

Warren draws upon his education with a Ph.D. in Philosophy from Vanderbilt University and vast experience to draw a direct correlation between the tools of logic and the Bible. He defines and explains how the laws of logic; e.g., law of rationality, laws of thought, and laws of inference and/or implication must be properly understood in order to properly apply the teachings of the Bible. He convincingly demonstrates that these laws of logic were used throughout the Bible and by Jesus himself.

For example, Jesus used the laws of rationality, implication and inference in a direct confrontation by Jewish religious leaders at the temple in Matthew 21:23-27. Warren points out that Jesus used correct reasoning (or logic) to turn the religious leaders' offensive into a hasty retreat. Jesus was not the only one to use logic, and in fact, the Bible demands that we use proper reasoning in order that we may know the certainty of the truth, c.f., 1 Thessalonians 5:21 and 1 John 4:1.

Warren deals quite extensively with the principles of implication and inference in the book. One must remember that properly reasoned arguments from the Scriptures are binding. Additionally, one must remember that the authority does not reside in the inferring but in the implication of the matter.

Thomas Warren quotes philosopher David Hume who stated that no one ever turns against reason until reason turns against him. It is important that we recognize that logic or correct reasoning is an ally of the Truth. It is an effective tool that we should utilize in saving the souls of men. Thomas Warren has used the tools of logic to meet the challenges of at least three major opponents: Anthony Flew, Joe Barnhart and Warren Matson. One should read these works and see how Warren uses the tools of Logic, coupled with the word of God, to defeat the atheist and humanist of the day.

One tool of logic that has been of use to myself is the law of contradiction; which basically upholds that two opposing views cannot both be true. One view must be true and the other false...both cannot be true at the same time or they are not really contradictory. An effective use of this tool is baptism—for salvation already obtained or to obtain salvation. Baptism cannot be because of salvation already obtained and for the purpose obtaining salvation at the same time. Both views cannot be true...one must be false. When one reads with an open heart passages such as Mark 16:15-16, Acts 2:38, Acts 22:16; 1 Peter 3:21 and others, there is only one view that is in harmony with the Scriptures—baptism is for the purpose of washing one's sins away in order to obtain salvation. To argue that baptism is for salvation already obtained is to either disregard the plain teaching of Scripture, the abandonment of reason, or both.

The proper use of logic is a skill that every Christian should seek to add to their arsenal in the Christian warfare. Dr. Warren's book will assist in sharpening our minds to properly reason the Scriptures for ourselves and for others.

The Warren-Flew Debate
(Thomas B. Warren & Antony G.N. Flew)

This debate occurred in Denton, TX at North Texas State University on September 20-23, 1976. Both Warren and Flew possessed doctorates and were trained in philosophy and the utilization of logic. The exchange is monumental for several reasons, but for one it meets the assertion that Christianity does not make logical or rational sense. In this debate, Thomas Warren uses the same tools of logic and rationality employed by atheists and agnostics to respond to and defeat their attacks against Christianity.

It would be good for one to know that Flew had signed a debate proposition that was unique among atheists which reflected his atheism and his conviction for it. Flew affirmed in the debate that "I Know That God Does Not Exist." This is different than other atheist debates who attempt to shift the burden of proof to those who are theist—they must prove God exists or atheists win by default. In the debate, they both were supposed to argue their points of view in the affirmative; i.e., in the second half of the debate Warren affirmed "I Know That God Does Exist" and Flew denied in the negative.

Prior to reading the debate, I failed to notice that Warren's book *Have Atheists Proved There Is No God?* was available to Flew prior to the debate. Had Flew read the book where Warren answers the best attack atheist can muster and outlines the case for biblical theism? Yes, he had...thoroughly it appears. Brother Garland Elkins, longtime friend of Warren, testifies:

Brother Warren told me that during his debate with Mr. Flew he walked over to his table and saw that Mr. Flew had a copy of brother Warren's book entitled, Have Atheists Proved There Is No God? (See the book review written for this book prior.) Brother Warren said that the book was very worn around the edges indicating that Mr. Flew had used it much in his studying.—Garland Elkins, "A Renowned Atheist Renounces Atheism," Yokefellow, Vol. 32, No. 1, January 2005, p. 2.

One wonders how much Warren impacted Flew. Brother Roy Deaver, who assisted brother Warren at the debate, makes an interesting observation about the shock Flew may have experienced when confronting true New Testament Christianity (as opposed to Catholicism or Denominationalism) being similar to what the skeptic Robert Owen had experienced when he encountered the same with Alexander Campbell. Deaver observed:

So far as he [Flew] was concerned 'Christianity' meant Catholicism and denominationalism. He had never before encountered simple New Testament Christianity. And, he had never before encountered an opponent of Dr. Warren's caliber. Dr. Flew, son of a Methodist minister, knows full-well that truth cannot be established upon the basis of feelings (emotionalism, subjective experiences). It must have been quite a shock to him when brother Warren said: "Dr. Flew, we fight that kind of thing just as much as you do. On that point you are just speaking to the wrong crowd."—Roy Deaver, "The Warren-Flew Debate," Biblical Notes, December 1976.

I found Dr. Warren's exchange with Flew about personal "religious experience" intriguing. Keep in mind that Flew is the one who brought up various religious people claiming a vision or some other experience as proof for Christianity or God, not Warren, who rejected such "experiences." To me, it seems as if

Flew's own past experiences were wrapped in this argument (as some religious do seek to establish their credibility on emotionalism). After Flew launched into this, when he was supposed to be in the negative criticizing arguments affirmed by Warren, brother Warren replied:

> Dr. Flew spent a great deal of his time about religious experience. Did you hear me say anything about "religious experience"? Did I make any argument thus and so that "someone has had a religious experience and therefore God exists?" I said nothing at all about that. Dr. Flew, I fight that as well as you do. There are people all over this country who claim "Oh a miracle occurred, a miracle occurred here and there." "Well, let's see one." "No, it happened over yonder. Somebody else knows how and where it happened."
>
> It's just like every evolutionist knows somebody else who knows how to prove it. Dr. Flew can't prove it. "There is somebody over in some other university." Now if you go over to that university, he'll point you to some other university. "There is some learned man in Munich or Austria." Or "there is somebody in New Zealand or Australia." Or "there is somebody in California or Harvard that knows how to do it." But when you get there, they don't know how to do it. "There is somebody in the last century." "Darwin did it." Well, Darwin didn't think he did. Dr. Flew sometimes argues as if Darwin gave a deductive argument, but that won't stand.
>
> No, I did not make the argument on "religious experience" Dr. Flew. You are talking to the wrong crowd of people when you are talking about that. And I suggest that you stay with the affirmative arguments. I am at a complete loss to know why you ignore the arguments I do make and invent other arguments and reply to them! It is sort of like Jones says "x is false," but Jones says "Ah, that is not right, y is

true." When there is no connection between "x" and "y."

One should take note that Antony Flew was not unqualified for the debate. If one does much reading among respected philosophers, Flew's name readily comes to the surface. Roy Deaver commented on Flew's credentials and evident failure in the debate, and it is interesting reading since Deaver's role was to read Flew's books to assist brother Warren in reply:

Dr. Flew knows full-well what a sound argument is. He knows that argumentation is not assertion and is not insinuation. He constantly chides and ridicules religious people for refusing to make a sound argument. He constantly calls upon them to face up to the task of proving their position. The "Law of Rationality" holds that "We ought to justify our conclusions by adequate evidence." Dr. Flew respects this law. Dr. Flew (of all people) did not refuse to make a sound argument because he did not know what a sound argument is!

Literally hundreds of people have expressed to me their disappointment because Dr. Flew refused to make an argument. He raised questions. He chided. He insinuated. He indicated that he would eventually get around to actual argumentation. But, he never did. He did a lot of talking and philosophizing, but he never did get down to the task of trying to prove his point. (Dr. James Bales observed: "A philosopher often spends his time throwing dust into the air, and then complains because he cannot see.") One person said: "Dr. Flew would approach the microphone as if he were really going to do something this time, and then...just fizzle."

It seems to me that the weak and disappointing efforts upon the part of Dr. Flew really show the force, the power, and the value of the debate. If Dr. Flew COULD have made a sound argument the conclusion of which would have been "I know that God does not exist" Dr. Flew WOULD have done so. The fact that Dr. Flew DID NOT proves that he COULD NOT, and that HE KNEW THAT HE COULD NOT! Dr. Flew's failure to make an argument also indicated his profound respect for Dr. Warren. He knew that every word he said would be carefully and thoroughly examined by brother Warren, and that no error would be allowed to pass unnoticed. Dr. Flew could not make an argument which would stand up under the light of logical examination. — Roy Deaver, "The Warren-Flew Debate," *Biblical Notes*, December 1976.

In preparing for this review, I did additional research by watching the DVD of the Warren-Flew Debate plus an interview of Thomas Warren reflecting on the debate 20 years later. Both videos are available from World Video Bible School.

Brother Warren passed away on August 8, 2000. I am sure he would have been pleased but saddened, that Antony G.N. Flew finally acknowledged that God existed but failed to follow through on the implications of an intelligent God before he (Flew) passed away. For more information about Flew's renouncement of atheism, see his final book *There Is A God: How the World's Most Notorious Atheist Changed His Mind* which will be the subject of a future book review.

When Is An "Example" Binding?
(Thomas B. Warren)

Interpreting the Bible correctly is what "Biblical Hermeneutics" is about. Only by interpreting the Bible correctly can one truly know the will of God. Dr. Warren has done much work in the field of hermeneutics and has demonstrated the value of logic in order to properly reason from the Scriptures. In this work, Warren makes important distinctions that make a difference in our approach to pattern theology of command, example & necessary inference. For example, Warren points out that necessary inferences are really implications which are binding on man, not because man has inferred them, but because God has implied them. In this work, Dr. Warren makes another important distinction in regards to examples. He points out that a more precise description would be the use of the term "course of action." When we read of various actions & events in the Bible, how do we determine what is binding on us today? This is the focus of the book. Warren identifies five classifications of actions in the Bible and how to properly identify and understand them including: (1) Action which was permanently sinful, (2) Action which was optional and temporary, (3) Action which was optional and permanent, (4) Action which was obligatory and permanent, and (5) Action which was obligatory and permanent. In this work, Warren provides a detailed analysis of Acts 20:7 and how we know Christians are to observe the Lord's Supper upon the first day of every week only. Everyone should read the analysis of this passage so they have a

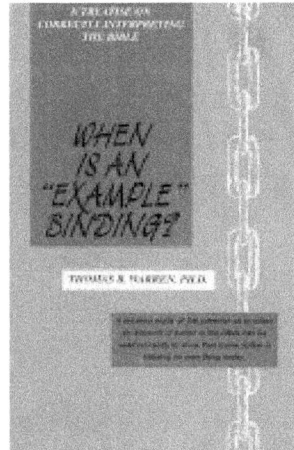

thorough knowledge of the use of immediate and remote contexts to understand the conclusions drawn.

Another important matter Thomas Warren reminds us is the binding authority of the Old Testament. Many realize that the law of Moses is not binding upon us today; however, Warren reminds us that there are principles of the Old Testament that are indeed binding on men today. For example, the case of Nadab and Abihu, in Leviticus 9, who used fire that God had not authorized to their destruction—God will be worship in the ways He has prescribed and we dare not add, subtract, or change those ways!

Reading books dedicated to logic and its application in interpreting the Scriptures have led some to consider this book (and Warren's other works) out of balance with emotions. This is a false attack. What Warren has done left for us is sound instruction on how to properly reason with the Scriptures. Warren's words should be kept in mind:

> It must be re-emphasized that all men, having been created by God with intelligent minds (able to recognize, to observe and to properly consider the evidence which God has given) are required by God to draw only such conclusions as are warranted by the evidence. It has been noted already that logical reasoning is not the answer to everything. Logic is necessary to a proper life, but logic alone is certainly not sufficient for such a life. Correct reasoning has its place and so does emotion. But both reasoning and emotion must be given content by the revelation of God, the Bible (Jer. 10:23; 2 Tim. 3:16-17). No purely intellectual life can be adequate any more than can a purely emotional one. Both are necessary, but both also need revelation from God. (Page 31).

Based on some the influence of post modernism and denial of absolute truth in society impacting the church, it is more important than ever to be able to reason properly. Regardless of the assertions of men that "there is no absolute truth for us to know," Jesus said "And you shall know the truth and the truth shall set you free." (John 8:32). Do not be deceived by the post modernists who are building houses on foundations of sand!

20th Anniversary Interview
with Thomas B. Warren
(Thomas B. Warren with Weylan Deaver)

In addition to watching the DVD of the Warren-Flew Debate, I did some additional research on events relating to the debate. I became more interested in The Warren-Flew Debate from a presentation by David Lipe at the Friends of the Restoration Luncheon at Freed-Hardeman University Bible Lectureship in 2008. Lipe spoke on "The Debates of Thomas B. Warren" and how he helped Warren prepare hundreds of charts (in excess of 500 charts on transparencies were made by both Warren and Lipe for the discussion with Flew). Brother Lipe showed how he made charts with handwriting so similar to Warren's that even Lipe's wife had difficulty discerning between the two. When flying to Texas for the debate, brother Warren was understandably anxious and kept checking on the charts in Lipe's care on the flight. It was the first and only time that Lipe flew First Class— one seat for Lipe & the other seat for the briefcases of charts! To hear brother Lipe's presentation on the Warren's debates, please see TheRestorationMovement.com/warren,_tb.htm.

World Video Bible School fortunately interviewed Thomas Warren as he reflected on the debate 20 years later (1996) with Roy Deaver's grandson, Weylan Deaver. There were several observations made by brother Warren as he reflected on this monumental debate that we should consider. (The debate can be ordered from wvbs.org/details.cfm?CourseID=170.)

Brother Warren previously had a career as a commercial artist which helped in drawing charts which he used effectively in his debates. Warren's charts were very effective and impressed Flew as well. This shows that experiences we may feel of no present or future value may actually work for the furtherance of the gospel.

Flew acknowledges that this was one of the two most well attended debates he conducted. In the interview, Warren reports that the operators of the North Texas State University Coliseum calculated the average attendance was 6,500 with the highest attendance being 7,000. Flew was greatly impressed by the interest in the discussion and even wrote of such in his final book. Imagine how this would have gone if Christians found other things of more interest? How many people will someday read *The Warren-Flew Debate* based on what Flew wrote about such interest in his last book renouncing atheism? Our attendance tells others where our loyalties truly are.

During the interview, Warren provides some insight on just how he met Flew. The Philosophical Association's annual meeting was held at a major university in Los Angeles, and Flew was to be a special speaker. Warren decided to attend. When he arrived he found the several in the audience distressed because Flew was chastising theists vehemently. Warren was in attendance with a university president of the Los Angeles area, and the president prodded Warren to get into it before it got ugly. Warren said that the president, not he, should do so; but the president said there was no way he was going to argue with that man! When Flew paused to take questions, he recognized Warren to ask a question. Flew's annoyance at Warren's questions quickly turned to near rage when Warren accused him of being "shifty" in his argumentation. Warren demonstrated how Flew was using "shifting" tactics of argumentation in an attempt to prove his points. Flew was so outraged at the attack of being "shifty" that he inadvertently knocked over the lectern when pounding on it. Afterwards, many praised Warren for his apologia. Sometime later, the church sought to have a debate over the existence of God, and selected Warren to represent them.

They asked brother Warren to recommend a disputant to debate, and Warren picked Flew, and Flew agreed. Warren says he did not know if Flew recognized him from the earlier encounter or not. At the debate, Flew acknowledged the hospitality of the hosts and some believe this certainly contributed to him listening more intently. Brother Warren states publicly that he considered Flew one of the most intelligent men he had ever met, just mistaken. One should take a lesson from this...if we win the argument but lose the soul then what have we gained? That is not to say that we will always convince our challengers, but we can certainly drive them further away or build sympathy for them (and thus their positions) in others by having an ugly disposition.

Warren warned us that we need to get busy with serious study to defend Christianity against the attacks of atheism and agnosticism. He pointed to a student of the Bible for 10-15 years being shaken by just one confrontation with an atheist because he was unprepared. As Warren points out "Prove all things" does not mean just to assert facts. One must be able to use facts to formulate valid arguments with true premises that prove the conclusions to be true. Logic is a tool for those who want to be rational and New Testament and Christianity is rational. Warren pleads for churches to stop "dilly dallying around" and read and study seriously! We should help train able men to get their doctorates and seek out opportunities to meet atheists and agnostics on the public polemic platform. An interesting observation comes from Winford Claiborne who knew and greatly admired brother Warren. Claiborne shared with us that at first he thought Warren's dwelling on logic and rationality was a bit overdone, but now with the threats posed by the post modernists and their emergents he knows that Warren was right! Brother Warren had equipped and prepared himself to debate several of the day's top atheists and foes of Christianity. Unfortunately, he had a heart condition which prevented his personal goal of confronting a list of top atheists and agnostics of his day from being fulfilled, but thankfully he was able to live longer to prepare and write several materials of assistance to us today. Brother Warren passed away on August 8, 2000.

The Minor Prophets
(Thomas B. Warren & Garland Elkins, Editors)

A study of the Minor Prophets is as much needed in our day as in any other time. The lessons on how to be pleasing to God by living a holy life are much needed in churches and our nation. The material in this section of Scripture, while often neglected, has some of the richest material for sermons & classes that needs to be taught in the churches today. I appreciate what brother Elkins and brother Warren stated in the Forward, "Though the 'minor prophets' were written long ago the principles that they set out therein are more up-to-date than tomorrow's Newspaper!" There are several predictive prophecies among the Minor Prophets that are enriching reminders that God indeed rules in the affairs of men. There are those who seek to deny the Bible is the Word of God; however, their assaults are feeble at best when compared to the evidence of predictive prophecy. The term "minor" does not denote their importance...just the length of the manuscripts are shorter than the longer (or major) ones.

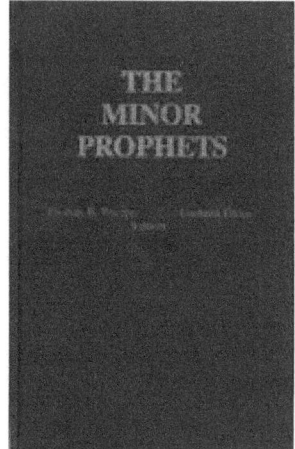

This book is the written record of the 1990 Power Lectureship in Southaven, MS with Garland Elkins and Thomas B. Warren serving as editors. Each of the prophets is addressed from three standpoints: introduction to the book, commentary, and then applications from the prophet. Another resource this book provides is an overview of the Minor Prophets by Rex A. Turner, Sr.; which makes the book invaluable if for no other reason. The descriptive catch phrases he assigns to each of the prophets are indicative of the type of message or messenger:

- **Joel**, The Pest Exterminator Preacher
- **Jonah**, The Gourd Vine Preacher
- **Amos**, The Country Preacher
- **Hosea**, The Preacher Whose Wife Was A Swinger
- **Micah**, The Preacher For The Church Across the Railroad Tracks
- **Obadiah**, The Preacher With A Message of Doom For The Nation Of Edom
- **Nahum**, Another Preacher With A Message of Doom – This Time for Assyria
- **Zephaniah**, The Preacher Who Held Several Degrees – Pedigrees, That Is
- **Habakkuk**, The Impatient Self-Righteous Preacher Who Dared to Remonstrate With God
- **Haggai**, An Old Preacher Whose Sermon Top Was, "Bag With Holes"
- **Zechariah**, The Young Preacher Who Saw Visions – Eight In Number
- **Malachi**, The Didactic-Dialectic Preacher

Before writing to advise that these are listed in the incorrect order, be aware that this is the list in *chronological* order. Also, the prophets served various kingdoms including the nations of Israel and Judah. Possessing a good understanding of the background for each of these prophets is vital to a fuller understanding of the message and power of the word of God in their day. While it takes effort to glean the background of each of these prophets, it is a very enriching study, which this book will provide. The lesson material from this section of Scripture is abundant for both class instruction and from the pulpit. The material in the book contains many lessons of application for us today, which is evident in that each prophet has its own lecture entitled "Great Lessons From..."

There are many books on the Minor Prophets. This one is edited by two of the most reputable men in our brotherhood who have assembled a lectureship that must have been wonderful to attend and just as profitable to read from.

The Spiritual Sword 1969 – 2000 on CD, Thomas B. Warren & Alan Highers, Editors

In October 1969 the Getwell Church of Christ launched one of the more effective journals to combat various forms of liberalism with Thomas B. Warren serving as the editor. Some may not realize this, but brother Warren had actually begun *The Spiritual Sword* back in 1958 to combat the rising tide of anti-ism. Unfortunately the paper lasted just over a year before it was discontinued largely over health issues of brother Warren. Brother Warren's health would return and provide him the basis to complete advanced degrees and have significant debates. Brother Warren's growing popularity provided a great catalyst for the return of *The Spiritual Sword* in October 1969. Ironically, Rubel Shelley was the preacher at Getwell Church of Christ and approached brother Warren with the proposition of publishing *The Spiritual Sword* with the Getwell Church of Christ as its publisher. Over the next twenty years brother Warren and the congregation in Getwell, TN published excellent articles on a quarterly basis on a common theme including certain false religions or systems. In 1989 brother Warren edited his final issue of *The Spiritual Sword*, seeking to free his schedule to devote more time to writing books. Brother Alan Highers was wisely chosen to sit in the editor's chair and has done so for nearly 20 years. The brotherhood has been blessed with a periodical that is highly esteemed by those seeking to "walk in the old paths" with balance rather than radicalism on the right or progressivism on the left. Back issues have been made available for several years; however, the continuing demand of the journal has led to

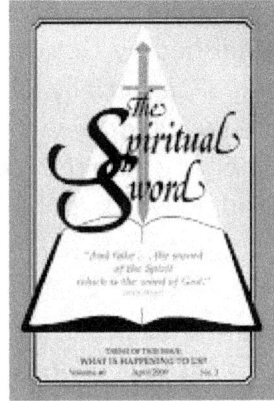

several of these issues becoming out of print. Fortunately, a CD is now available with issues in PDF format which makes the material more easily searchable and preserves the legacy of this excellent journal for future generations. Brother Warren also established The Spiritual Sword Lectureship which published some of the finest material on various subjects. Indeed, the materials published by Getwell should be read by every member of the church, especially deacons, elders and preachers. The issues we are facing today with postmodernism and its fruits such as "The Emerging Church Movement" could have been avoided if more read the works published by *The Spiritual Sword*.

Brother Highers took the helm of *The Spiritual Sword* with the October 1989 issue. Building on a solid foundation by brother Warren, Highers built a solid structure of periodicals that answers various errors and their adherents. Scholarly treatments on various facets of an overall theme are covered in each issue with documentation provided so a researcher may explore a given subject further. While *The Spiritual Sword* cites specific examples of digression (including names and places), it seeks to do so with a "matter-of-fact" approach rather than exhibiting a caustic mean-spirited attitude. Some may argue that point, but their objections stem mainly from the inability to refute the material.

The April 2009 issue of *The Spiritual Sword* is devoted to the theme "What Is Happening to Us?" The church has always been assailed by an array of foes. In this issue one can read about the major areas that are troubling the churches. Ironically, many of today's battles are not unlike the battles of years ago. Too many mistakenly thought the battles over baptism, instrumental music, objective truth, role of women, immorality, exclusivity of Christ and His church were fought and won. We must always remember that Satan never stops! What is the solution? We must never let the teaching of the fundamentals go out of style. Too many let the fundamentals escape their attention and have been swept into apostasy by later generations who did not have the blessing of fortifying instruction. If congregations are evangelizing successfully, then the need for the fundamentals will be more readily recognized. It would be a wise investment to obtain some of the older materials and re-read them. The CD version of *The Spiritual Sword* provides an inexpensive way to do some of that reading.

If the congregation where you attend is not reading this journal, it needs to. The church at Getwell offers a "Congregational Subscription Plan" where they will mail the issue to each address supplied by your congregation for $7 per address. The journal is published quarterly on heavy paper stock, which is suitable for later reference. This is an excellent method for elders to ensure the flock has fortifying materials in their homes. Perhaps a class period (or more) could be utilized to discuss the content of the most recent issue. This would encourage people to read the journal. The April 2009 issue would make an excellent starting point for such a plan. The brotherhood continually needs the religious writing of the highest caliber. *The Spiritual Sword* has fulfilled that level of service for over 40 years, and we pray for many more to come.

Seven Things A Loving God Hates
(Allen Webster)

Every soul is precious to God! Sadly there are those who do not believe God loves everyone but has already elected to save a few. God loves all mankind and Jesus came to the earth in order to establish a plan of salvation for all mankind (John 3:16; 2 Peter 3:9; 1 John 4:7-11). On the other side, there are those believe God so loves them that He will tolerate any and all deviant behavior; e.g., homosexuality. One must understand that while God is love, God is also holy and expects us to be holy as well (Leviticus 19:2; Romans 12:1). Some are under the mistaken impression that God cannot love and hate at the same time. God loves sinners (we are all sinners, Romans 3:23), but He hates sin. Another mistake some make is, while they understand God can both love and hate at the same time, they believe God's love will overrule His wrath toward those with unremitted sins and not condemn any to hell. Make no mistake—hell is a real place prepared by God to punish Satan and children of Satan (Matthew 25:41; Revelation 20:10-15). Some erroneously believe Satan's dominion is Hell. It is not his dominion...it is his final destination! How does God separate the sin from the sinners? Jesus Christ is the only solution for reconciling our sins before a loving and holy God (Romans 5:9-11). Jesus stood in our place when He was crucified, laid in a tomb and resurrected. In order for us to be saved, we must unite ourselves with His death, burial and resurrection and the only way to do that is to replicate the process the way He has

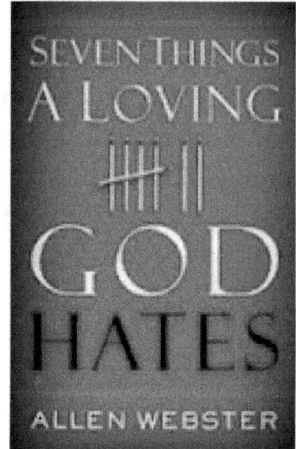

established—by immersion in water which is our unification with his death, burial and resurrection (Romans 6:1-6).

In "Seven Things A Loving God Hates," Webster begins with a thorough examination of the love of God. Then the writer moves to discuss several sins God hates based on Proverbs 6:17-19 which are a proud look, a lying tongue, hands that shed innocent blood, a heart that devises wicked plans, feet that are swift in running to evil, a false witness who speaks lies, and one who sows discord among brethren. Each of these subjects receives an excellent treatment with illustrations, scriptures and sound reasoning. Especially pleasing is the treatment of "hands that shed innocent blood" as it relates to the holocaust in our nation—abortion. I find it truly troubling that people are willing to vote for a candidate who supports the slaughter of the most innocent. I do not understand how people who vote for a candidate who supports abortion will be able to stand before God and try to rationalize their vote with Matthew 18:1-10. Some who do not favor a candidate opposed to abortion cannot bring themselves to vote for them (because of other issues) and decide not to vote at all. One who refuses to vote in order to avoid voting for a candidate that is pro-life needs to understand this may lead to the same result—election of a pro-abortion candidate. For those of us who vote—it is our opportunity to speak out against this heinous action. I would want to have either not been involved in our election process ever, vote for a pro-life candidate, but I would never want to vote for a candidate that favored abortion ever. I have heard some state that abortion will be our next civil war. Perhaps. I think that may be true but only if abortion is outlawed in the land because there will be nothing to stop those who are bent on killing children in the womb from killing those who want to stop them.

The book goes on to show that Satan really enjoys creating chaos in the world...anything to keep us from the God who truly loves and desires to save us. The book ends with a rally for us to fortify ourselves with God's love that we may be able to stand.

This book is an excellent study. It includes excellent questions and points for discussion at the end of each chapter; which makes it valuable for Bible class study. It is both profitable and enjoyable. Do not miss this book, but please do share it with others.

Originally printed in *West Virginia Christian*, Vol. 19, No. 1, January 2012, p. 8. Reprinted by permission.

The Enchanted Knight:
The Life Story of Hugo McCord
(Earl I. West)

This writer's first opportunity to hear Hugo McCord was as a student in 1987 in which McCord presented his translation of the New Testament to Freed-Hardeman College, now University. The fourth edition of his translation was printed in 2002 and includes books from the Old Testament. Unfortunately, Hugo's declining health will probably prohibit him from translating the rest of the Bible. The name of the translation, "The Everlasting Gospel," was supplied by Franklin Camp. The first personal interaction with brother Hugo began in May of 1997 when we began a written correspondence that led to a visit to their home in Portland, OR during the summer of 1998.

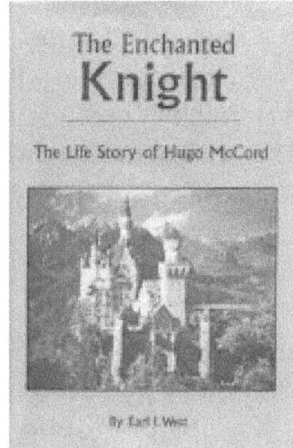

He holds the following degrees: A.A., B.A., M.A., B.D., and Th.D. He has been both a world traveler and located evangelist preaching the gospel for over 65 years. He has conducted research abroad including trips to the British Museum and Palestine. In 1951, he began working with the Central Christian College (which would eventually become Oklahoma Christian College). He has been the recipient of many honors (some humorous mock awards) from the brotherhood. He also has a delightful sense of humor and cherishes the humorous awards and displays them on the same wall of his study as his degrees and other awards.

Lois Henderson McCord (1910-2000) received the following dedication of the Enchanted Knight by Hugo: "Lois is my first, current, last, and favorite wife." They met at Freed-Hardeman as students and were married in 1932. My visit with her was during the decline of her health both physically and mentally. But even at 88 years of age she was very keen, hospitable, and delightful. Lois McCord passed on to receive her reward on July 12, 2000.

Hugo McCord's conversion is an example of the influence of the individual for the cause of Christ. B.B. Goodman, who was a traveling salesman who noticed Caruthersville, MS did not have a church of Christ, permanently altered the course of Hugo's life. This man contacted the only known member of the church in the area to secure a lot for a tent meeting in an attempt to establish a congregation. Arrangements were made to have L.L. Brigance come and hold a gospel tent meeting. There was one response, the twelve-year old son of the member who secured the lot—Hugo McCord. He left the Methodist Church and would eventually persuade his mother do the same two years later. If it was not for the efforts of one man—B.B. Goodman, then Hugo McCord may have never heard and obeyed the gospel. Only God would be able to calculate the influence the life of Hugo McCord has had for the cause of Christ.

Brother McCord is truly a life-long student of the Scriptures. If we think we have exhausted the Bible in our studies, then we have fallen into ignorant arrogance. We, as finite beings, cannot possibly exhaust the revelation of an infinite God.

Hugo McCord's translating work showed his resolve to listen to input and make changes when justified, but would stand firm when he had thoroughly studied the matter further and found the translation accurate. He did not seek to quarrel for the sake of notoriety, but he would state the truth at all costs including friendships. This illustrates a great lesson we all need to be reminded of—to avoid clinging to personalities as a substitute for the word of God. Some people are infected with what Hugo would call "preacheritis" where they would listen to a man more than they would check the facts to prove whether what the man said was true or not.

Someone once said "True courage is not the brutal force of vulgar heroes, but the firm resolve of virtue and reason." This is very fitting of the courage of Hugo McCord. We live in a day where some reject being role models because of being criticized for their public immorality; however, Hugo McCord would resist being held up as a role model because of his godly humility. But even the apostle Paul wrote and Hugo translated "Be imitators of me, even as I also am of Christ." (1 Cor. 11:1). Hugo rightly stated to this author (referring to brother Wallace) that the lives of great men help us live better lives. Truly, Hugo McCord has left us a legacy worthy of study and imitation.

This writer would also like to call attention to the love and dedication of the McCord's son and daughter-in-law, Charles and La Vera. They have personally cared for the elderly Hugo and Lois since 1989 including selling their houses to purchase a house large enough for all in order to provide the care needed by their parents. This is truly a great example of what God must have meant by "Honor your father and mother."

Originally printed in *West Virginia Christian*, Vol. 9, No. 10, October 2002, p. 8. Reprinted by permission.

Eye of the Storm –
A Story of Elder Benjamin Franklin
(Earl West)

Each fourth Monday in the month of May is set aside by our nation to honor citizens who died defending our beloved country. This observance includes visits to cemeteries, parades, and honorary services in churches and other public places. Indeed, it is fitting that citizens of the United States should honor, remember and reflect on the great sacrifices that have been made for our freedom—freedom is not free.

While those honored on Memorial Day are honored for the participation in physical wars, there are those who have fought in a war that is greater in every detail—the war between the kingdom of heaven and the kingdom of Satan. The apostle Paul wrote of such a comparison to Timothy,

> *"You therefore, my son, be strong in the grace that is in Christ Jesus. And the things that you have heard from me among many witnesses, commit these to faithful men who will be able to teach others also. You therefore must endure hardship as a good soldier of Jesus Christ. No one engaged in warfare entangles himself with the affairs of this life, that he may please him who enlisted him as a soldier." (2 Timothy 2:1-4, NKJV).*

While those being honored on Memorial Day are worthy of such, there is another group that I fear is often overlooked—the spiritual soldiers who have laid their armor down and wait for the Resurrection.

Recently, this writer made a trip to the city cemetery in Anderson, Indiana and was honored to visit the grave of a different type of veteran soldier. The "name" of the person is famous; however, the "name" often is associated with another, more prominently known, figure in history. This person was the great nephew of Benjamin Franklin. More often than not, when the name "Benjamin Franklin" is mentioned in connection with the church, people look puzzled and wonder what the kite-flying revolutionary patriot had to do with the churches of Christ. Many fail to realize that there was a man named Benjamin Franklin (1812-1878) who was probably the most popular leader among churches of Christ after the death of Alexander Campbell. Benjamin Franklin fought extensively against the introduction of mechanical instruments in worship, and he was in the middle of the battle over the missionary society. Indeed, Earl West's biography about him is well titled—Eye of the Storm – A Story of Elder Benjamin Franklin. (Lord willing, this writer is planning a lecture on the life of Benjamin Franklin for the 2008 *West Virginia Christian* Lectureship.) The biography of this great restoration soldier will deal with the period where the issues of instrumental music, missionary societies, and slavery where tearing the brotherhood and nation apart. It chronicles the events that led to a faction broke away from churches of Christ and taking land and property with its digression.

How many of us are surprised to learn that there was a key figure in church restoration history named Benjamin Franklin? Of course, God remembers the sacrifices that this Christian made for the cause of Christ (Revelation 14:13), but do we owe these soldiers any less? Often there is a comment made about those hypercritics who know nothing about the military—"they are not worthy to lace the boots of the ones they criticize." Tragically, we have those among us who berate the spiritual soldiers of yesterday with false assertions of "they never preached Christ" or "they never preached on God's grace." Indeed, those who make these false assertions are "not worthy to lace the boots of the ones they criticize." Even more tragic is that an uninformed brotherhood is ill equipped to rebuff these false assertions. Some attempt to excuse their willful ignorance with "well, they were not inspired...they made mistakes." Indeed, all men have sinned except the one Man. We do not allow our children to exempt themselves from the study of history because of the imperfections and mistakes of the people involved. Do we?

As a suggestion, why not make the commitment to learn more about the men and women who fought on the battlefield of good versus evil? We should seek to learn about the spiritual veterans who have gone on to their reward such as: Barton W. Stone, Alexander Campbell, Thomas Campbell, Walter Scott, Raccoon John Smith, Moses Lard, Benjamin Franklin, J.W. McGarvey, Foy E. Wallace, C.R. Nichol, R.L. Whiteside, David Lipscomb, James Harding, A.G. Freed, N.B. Hardeman, H. Leo Boles, T.B. Larimore, Gus Nichols, Guy N. Woods, Joe Warlick, J.D. Tant, et al. If these names are unknown to us, then we need to invest time in the study of restoration history of the church. As my father often says, "we are standing on the shoulders of giants." Hugo McCord wrote in a letter that the examples of good preachers & defenders of the faith show us how to be good ourselves. With a look at the confusion and defections from the truth around us, the expression of George Santayana rings clear & true—"Those who ignore the lessons of history are condemned to repeat them." Why not encourage preachers to include articles in our bulletins about restoration history? Why not encourage the leadership at the congregation devote some lessons (whether from the class lectern or the sermon pulpit) on figures and events in church restoration history? Why not have a gospel meeting with the theme of restoration history? This writer has been greatly enriched by those who have devoted time to research and writing along these lines especially those who can make history seemingly "come alive."

Originally printed in the *West Virginia Christian*, Vol. 14, No. 6, June 2007, p. 6. Reprinted by permission.

The Search for the Ancient Order – A History of The Restoration Movement Vol. 1 – 1800–1865 (Earl West)

In the spring of 1996, I was blessed with the opportunity to travel to Ohio Valley College (now University) for a special Restoration History Workshop conducted by Earl West. At this workshop I was able to hear brother West lecture on key events and figures in the Restoration Movement. Then, I was thrilled to be able to travel a short distance to Bethany, West Virginia (formerly Virginia) to tour the mansion, study, cemetery and other key items relating to the lives of Thomas and Alexander Campbell. The tour climaxed with a visit to Bethany Memorial Church where Alexander Campbell preached for many years, which included a presentation of an overview of the Campbells by brother West. Thomas Campbell had not preached in the building; however, the foundation stones for the Memorial Church were from the stone building where Thomas had preached his final farewell sermon prior to his death. This was truly an exciting event to attend and I wish others would have had the opportunity to do so as well.

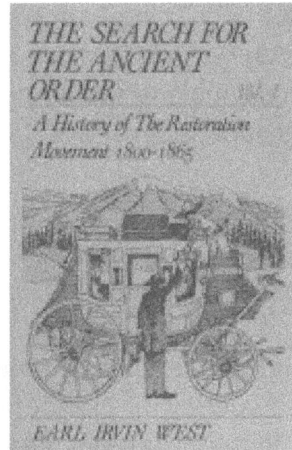

The Restoration Workshop was of great interest to me for several reasons, but none of these reasons probably would have materialized if it were not for men like Basil Overton, Earl West, my parents and others who have shared with me stories of the struggles and victories of those who led souls out of man-made denominations and back to pure Christianity. During his life, Brother West has written extensively on Restoration History. *In*

Search of the Ancient Order reminds one of Alexander Campbell's famed series on restoring New Testament Christianity entitled "Restoration of the Ancient Order of Things" in the famous (or infamous to the denominations), *The Christian Baptist*.

The first volume in the series takes a look at the early beginnings of the movement. It is important for people to realize that the plea to go back to New Testament Christianity preceded Alexander and Thomas Campbell. In fact, there were those in Europe making similar pleas. In the United States, there were also groups, such as the Christians with Barton W. Stone, who made the commitment to restore New Testament Christianity prior to the Campbells' arrival in America. Those not as familiar with Alexander Campbell may wonder why his name is held in such regard that those outside the church often stigmatize our movement with his name. The reason should be remembered. Alexander Campbell's name stands out because he stood up and was so successful in meeting the challenges of foes of New Testament Christianity whether from denominations, the Catholic Church, or even infidels. He is one of the richest scholars in the history of churches of Christ and his legacy is still one to be respected. One should also know that Alexander Campbell, just as Martin Luther pleaded for those who worshipped with him not to name themselves "Lutherans," resisted and spoke out against the use of his name for the movement with such terms as "Campbellite" or Campbellism." In fact, one of the reasons he ceased the name of his first journal, The Christian Baptist, was for fear that followers of him (rather than Christ) would call themselves Christian Baptists. So, he changed the name of his periodical to the monumental *Millennial Harbinger*.

This book deals with both the separate Stone & Campbell movements through the period where both recognized and unified on their commitment for a "Thus saith the Lord" in faith and practice. It deals with challenges of the movement including the missionary society and instrumental music into worship. It also discusses rise of educational institutions such as Bethany

College. Several biographical portraits (in words and pictures) are presented including Walter Scott, Moses Lard, J.W. McGarvey, Jacob Creath, Benjamin Franklin and others. In Search of the Ancient Order is a tremendous source book on Restoration History and every church library is incomplete without this important series.

Originally printed in the *West Virginia Christian*, Vol. 16, No. 3, March 2009, p. 5. Reprinted by permission.

Commentary on Romans
(Robertson L. Whiteside)

Guy N. Woods stated that there were over 3,000 books on the epistle of Romans. This speaks to the magnitude of themes for this great letter by the hand of the apostle Paul. I think of this book as part of the meat that has been provided for mature Christians to feed upon. Some mistakenly believe the Scriptures are all easily understood. Apparently they have not meditated on the epistle of Romans. They must not realize that the apostle Peter did not share that sentiment when he wrote:

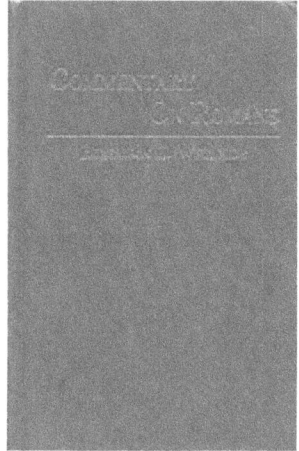

> ...and consider that the longsuffering of our Lord is salvation—as also our beloved brother Paul, according to the wisdom given to him, has written to you, as also in all his epistles, speaking in them of these things, in which are some things hard to understand, which untaught and unstable people twist to their own destruction, as they do also the rest of the Scriptures (2 Peter 3:15-16).

There are, obviously, some books on Romans that are good and some that are not so good. This work by Whiteside is one of the very best on the epistle to church at Rome. Even though printed in 1945, it is still one of the most praised works on the subject by faithful writers who attempt to build on Whiteside's work. In fact, I would almost say that unless someone referenced Whiteside on Roman in their book I would be reluctant to purchase it. This writer had made a feeble attempt to teach an adult class on the book of Romans. The study was as good as it was primarily because of this work. This reviewer is not alone in his assessment.

The Introduction of Whiteside's commentary was written by three eminently qualified scholars among churches of Christ—C.R. Nichol, Cled E. Wallace, and Foy E. Wallace, Jr. In the introduction they write of Whiteside:

> From the beginning of his study of the Bible he has respected the conclusions of godly and experienced students of the Bible, though he early realized that no man is infallible. He had to be sure of his own ground before he took issue with such men, he greatly admired the intellectual powers, the faith, and stalwart character, and humble bearing of that great man, David Lipscomb. To him David Lipscomb was the ideal teacher, the ideal Christian, and yet on more than one occasion in Bible classes in the Nashville Bible School, he took issue with the expressed views of Brother Lipscomb. On more than one occasion Brother Lipscomb accepted the views of Brother Whiteside.

That says volumes of not only the humility of David Lipscomb that he would be open to further study of the word of God by a student but also the student's ability to have an influence on the teacher.

The commentary is structured by chapters and verses with Whiteside's comments on each section of Scripture. There may be fancier formatted books on Romans; however, there are very few that measure to the depth of knowledge that Whiteside provides. This commentary is very readable and is not filled with a lot of religious jargon that is hard to understand or not worth the effort in attempting to figure out. This volume is an essential addition to the church library that needs material on Romans.

Originally printed in the *West Virginia Christian*, Vol. 11, No. 7, July 2004, p. 8. Reprinted by permission.

Difficult Texts of the New Testament Explained
(Wendell Winkler, Editor)

When preparing for a Bible class that is textual in nature on the New Testament, I nearly always refer to this book. The book is the permanent record of the fourth annual lectureship at Fort Worth in 1981. The book is a gold mine of information for a teacher who wants to be familiar with challenging Scriptures in the New Testament and wants the benefits of the study of seasoned men of the faith. When I am asked about difficult/challenging passage of Scripture I always refer the person to this book and suggest they purchase a copy for their private study. Often I have convinced others to make the purchases just by the table of contents alone.

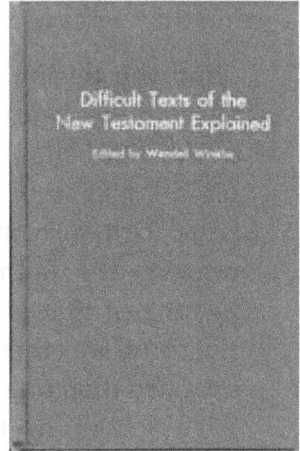

The book starts with a discussion that there are indeed challenging passages for us to understand and take effort to glean the message being conveyed. It provides material relating to tools, principles, methods, and approaches to studying difficult texts. There are articles dedicated to challenging subjects such as did Jesus turn water into fermented wine, reconciling the existence of God and human suffering, and predestination. The book is organized in order of the New Testament books for easy reference. It deals with additional subjects as they occur in the text including:

- Can Christians swear using oaths?
- Did Jesus teach situational ethics?

- Cutting off our hand to avoid sin—is this literal or figurative?
- Does eating the flesh of Christ and drinking his blood in John 6 refer to the Lord's Supper?
- Are we to use the holy kiss today?
- Did Paul repudiate inspiration in his writings?
- Are widows permitted only to remarry Christians?
- What does baptized for the dead mean?
- Must an elder have one or more children?
- Is there authority or Deaconesses in the church?
- What does the number 666 mean?

This is just a sampling of some of the subjects discussed in this book. It is definitely a book that should be on top priority for purchase for the church library.

Originally printed in the *West Virginia Christian*, Vol. 11, No. 5, May 2004, p. 8. Reprinted by permission.

Difficult Texts of the Old Testament Explained
(Wendell Winkler, Editor)

This book is the permanent record of the fifth annual lectureship at Fort Worth in 1982 and completes a fine two-volume set on challenging texts in the Bible that every Bible class teacher should review when preparing for a textual or difficult topical study.

This book contains a glossary of challenging words used in the Old Testament. I have heard of complaints of the use of vocabulary terms by teachers in the past. It is interesting that some of those making the complaints are often unable to define terms they use in the Bible. It is imperative that we understand what the Bible says right down to the very words that are employed. That is what is implied in verbal plenary inspiration.

The book also deals with alleged contradictions in the Bible. It has an article on archaeology in the Old Testament. It also includes a study on the providence of God. It discusses some challenging subjects in the Old Testament such as the atrocities found committed, multiple marriages and concubines, sins of Old Testament characters, the identity of the angel of Jehovah, and the challenges against the inspiration of the Old Testament by those who criticize the integrity of the Scriptures. This book is likewise organized in order of the Old Testament books for easy reference. It deals with additional subjects as they occur in the text including:

- The length of days in the creation of the world.
- The scientific reality of light existing before the sun.

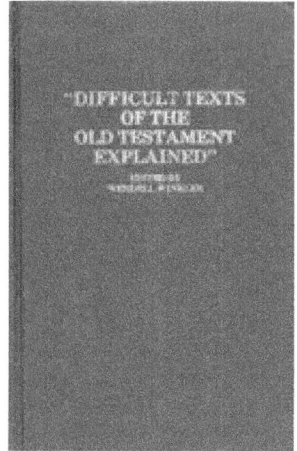

- The Sabbath observed all throughout the Old Testament.
- The mark of Cain and his wife.
- The flood—universal or local.
- The ark—large enough to handle all the animals.
- The hardening of Pharaoh's heart.
- The replication of the plagues by Pharaoh's magicians.
- The lie of Rahab the harlot.
- The fate of Jephthah's daughter.
- The contest between God and Satan over Job.
- The prophecy of the virgin birth.
- The story of Jonah and the great fish—fact or fiction.
- The repentance of God.

This is just a sampling of some of the subjects discussed in this book. The writers were very diligent students of God's word so their writings should be valuable for our edification. Both books on difficult texts on the Old & New Testament should be on top priority for purchase for the church library.

Originally printed in the *West Virginia Christian*, Vol. 12, No. 11, November 2005, p. 8. Reprinted by permission.

Biblical Backgrounds of the Troubled Middle East
(Guy N. Woods)

The recent events of September 11, 2001 will be etched in our memories for a long time to come. Some think that our country will never be the same and that the future of our children and society will be cloaked in fear because of this heinous act by Islamic terrorists. This writer does not subscribe to this pessimistic forecast. Men and women arose during a similar period of darkness to secure the blessings of freedom and prosperity for Americans after December 7, 1941. I am fully convinced that the same will happen here if America truly seeks God's blessings rather than just requesting God's blessing. It is one thing to say "God Bless America" but it is another matter to act in a way that God would bless America.

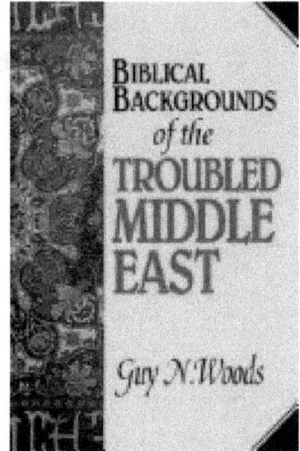

The conflict between Arabs and Jews is not new to most Americans; however, the background for this conflict is not understood by many. Some are surprised to realize that the conflict between Arabs and Jews goes back to Abraham, Sarah, and Hagar. The conflict has been one of the longest running conflicts except for the conflict between good and evil. Jerusalem is a focal point for much of the conflict. The main reason for this is that this piece of land is sacred to three major competing religions— Christianity, Judaism, and Islam. To appreciate the delicate and volatile relation of the Jews and Arabs, one only needs to know that the site of the Jewish Temple is now the location of an Islamic Mosque. So the Jews desire to rebuild the temple on the site ordained by King David that would require the destruction of an Islamic Mosque which is holy to the followers of Mohammed. This is only one aspect of the conflict.

Biblical Backgrounds of the Troubled Middle East traces the history of this conflict from the call of Abram in Ur of the Chaldees to the establishment of the nation of Israel. It traces the history of the nation of Israel through the division of the kingdom and the period between the testaments. It discusses the events of Jesus day and continues to the destruction of the Jewish nation by the Romans in AD 70. The book continues to explain historical events such as the establishment of Islam and its impact on the Arab world. The book explains the holocaust and the rise of Zionism, which led to the re-establishment of the nation of Israel in 1948. The Jews were allowed to take back the land that was once theirs but was now home to the Arabs of Palestine. Palestinians were driven from their homes because of the United Nations resolution permitting the Jews to take back land that they had once left. The book does a very concise but thorough treatment showing the complexity of this deep-rooted problem that will most likely never be resolved until Christ returns. The two groups will not live in peace with one another and both reject the one hope they have of reconciliation and peace—Jesus Christ and Christianity.

Gospel Advocate has recently reprinted this work by Guy N. Woods and is also making a cassette available on the same topic based on a Guy N. Woods teaching a Bible class on the same subject. Considering the renewed interest in this subject, I would suggest getting both the book and the cassette. Your congregation may have members that will profit from listening to the cassette if they are unable to read the book.

Originally printed in *West Virginia Christian*, Vol. 9, No. 2, February 2002, p. 8. Reprinted by permission.

How to Study the New Testament Effectively
(Guy N. Woods)

The importance of studying the New Testament cannot be under emphasized. Even if one studies the New Testament he can still stumble with its content. Therefore it is imperative that one not only studies but also effectively studies the New Testament.

One of the members of the church who is a sterling example of studying the New Testament effectively is Guy N. Woods. Brother Woods' credentials are so astonishing to this amateur student that he highly recommends each person who reads this review contact the Gospel Advocate and request the tribute issue in honor of brother Woods after he left this world. When I learned this book was available; I immediately purchased and read it with great satisfaction. "How To" books, in my opinion, are only as good as the one who writes them so I was very eager to read this work.

In this book Guy N. Woods emphasizes several important rules of Bible study. One of the rules he emphasized is the importance of understanding the context of the passages we are reading. He writes:

> An elementary rule of interpretation is to observe carefully the significance of that which goes before and that which follows the passage under study, before attempting to reach a conclusion as to its intended and proper meaning. Failure to follow this simple rule leads to many absurdities in the field of interpretation. More, it breeds disrespect for

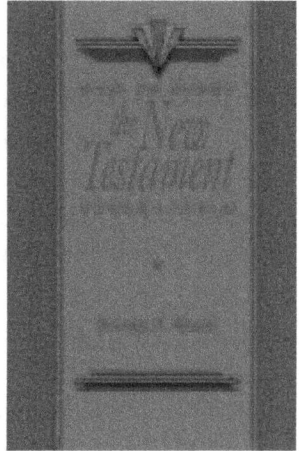

the word of God itself. The practice, all too common, of lifting a verse from its setting, and using it according to the whim of the speaker or writer, has led many people to the conclusion 'that you can prove anything by the Bible'. (Woods, p. 75)

Another principle that I would like to emphasize is the importance of studying in a strictly conditioned and controlled environment. Brother Woods would travel all over the country conducting meetings all the year. To facilitate his studying, he utilized a folding table that he could set his books and typewriter upon as to create the same working environment from place to place. Once his surroundings were more familiar his productivity increased. This is an important lesson for each of us. Having a designated place to study that is designed for that purpose would increase our productivity.

Guy N. Woods also emphasized the importance of having a good reference library. He stressed that it is not the volume but the quality of books that makes for an effective library. Recommending books has a times caused some people grief because sometimes a book is not sound in every section. Some will criticize a person if they recommend a book that has an obvious weakness and will try to ascribe the weakness to the person who recommended the book. This is sad in because it discourages those who know of excellent works makes them hesitant to recommend them for fear of having to defend the entire content of a book. If the popular translations are the product of people in denominations, subject to error, and we use and recommend them, then we should at least be as gracious to those who recommend a work that is by a denominationalist. Woods provides a complete chapter on books that he has found to be of tremendous value. I appreciate his willingness to recommend books that contain content he would not agree with. I refer to this list constantly and have discovered some of the books I have written reviews on from this very list. I highly recommend this book to not only help one to study the New Testament more effectively, but to equip one's self to do the job properly each day of our lives.

Originally printed in *West Virginia Christian*, Vol. 8, No. 7, July 2001, p. 2. Reprinted by permission.

Questions & Answers, Vol. 1
(Guy N. Woods)

Often when I am asked a question, the inquirer is looking for a brief answer rather than a lengthy discussion. Sometimes rather than answering the question directly, I attempt to point them to materials where they can find their answers. I do this not only to encourage the person to study on their own, but to familiarize them with good religious books they can read for profitable study. One of the books I go to repeatedly is Questions & Answers by Guy N. Woods.

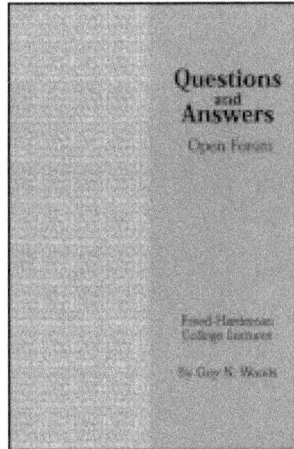

The book is a collection of questions that were asked of brother Woods and his answers to the questions during the Open Forum at Freed-Hardeman College (now University) Bible Lectureship. We sometimes get nervous when another person asks us a question, or maybe we get nervous about being asked a question when we teach a class. Imaging being asked any religious question on any subject in front of thousands of people! Imagine these questions being asked during a Bible lectureship in front of multitudes of preachers, professors, elders, etc. Brother Woods did this each year during the Open Forum for nearly 30 years! Unfortunately, I did not have the opportunity to hear brother Woods on the Open Forum. Fortunately, several of the Open Forum tapes exist when Guy N. Woods was moderator and can be ordered from Freed-Hardeman University Recording Services.

This volume is indexed both by scriptures and subjects for easier reference. I encourage members to purchase this work and keep in their cars to read when they have unexpected parking time. Some of the questions addressed in this book include:

- "Did the witch of Endor actually call up Samuel, from the dead, or did she deceive Saul by trickery?" (1 Sam. 28:1-25)
- "Did David introduce instrumental music into Old Testament worship with divine approval?"
- "Does Matt. 18:15-17 teach that a brother, who holds to, and has publicly advocated false doctrine, must be personally contacted before it is proper and right to refute his errors publicly?"
- Under what law was Cornelius worshipping before Peter's visit to him?" (Acts 10:1-48.)
- "Why is the birth of Jesus dated from 5 BC rather than AD 1, since the Christian era is supposed to have begun at his birth?"
- "Please give scriptural proof that Christian colleges have a right to exist."

Christians should seek out and read the writings of brother Woods. All of his writings are excellent and worthy of our attention. He has written commentary on books of the New Testament that are in the Gospel Advocate Commentaries. Because of my enormous respect for Woods' scholarship, I will not teach a class on a book he has written a commentary on before reading what he has stated on the subject. His commentary on James is still one of the best and I have several books on the Epistle of James by other authors in my possession at this time.

One should be extremely careful to know the author of a book they are reading; especially when the subject deals with controversial issues. This book is a prime example of one dealing with controversial issues. Woods' views were put to the test not only during the Open Forum, but he publicly debated over 100 times in his career. I encourage members to request the Gospel Advocate to send them a copy of the February 1994 issue dedicated to Guy N. Woods so they can read for themselves what a monumental scholar Guy N. Woods was. Brother Woods passed away December 8, 1993. He was eighty-five years old. Guy N. Woods donated his library to Freed-Hardeman. One would expect the number of books owned by a scholar to be large. (My guess would be over 1,000.) The actual number of books donated from his personal library to Freed-Hardeman University was over 7,000. Indeed, brother Woods has left us an example worthy of imitation!

Originally printed in the *West Virginia Christian*, Vol. 12, No. 7, July 2005, p. 8. Reprinted by permission.

Questions & Answers, Vol. 2
(Guy N. Woods)

Due to numerous requests for a follow-up to Questions & Answers, Vol. 1, Guy N. Woods published a second volume in 1986. (The first volume was published in 1976.) Guy N. Woods edited his second volume in an attempt to avoid duplication in the first volume and another book, Questions Answered by Lipscomb & Sewell (and published by Gospel Advocate). One should seek out all three books on Bible questions and answers.

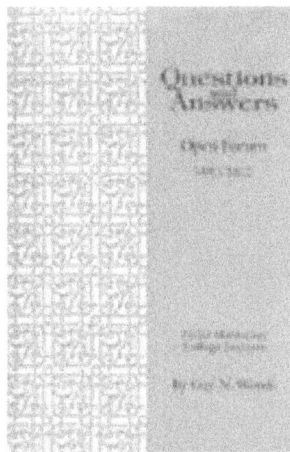

As discussed in the recommendation of Volume 1, Guy N. Woods conducted the Open Forum for nearly 30 years at Freed-Hardeman. Unfortunately, I never had the opportunity to hear brother Woods in person; however, I was able to hear Alan Highers who assumed the position as moderator of the Open Forum after Guy N. Woods retired from the position. Alan Highers also demonstrated great ability and poise as he conducted the Open Forum. Brother Highers has great respect for the late Guy N. Woods and stated in the Introduction of Volume 2: "It is truly the product of a lifetime of preparation and study, and an exceptional lifetime at that. The name of Guy N. Woods will take its place in future generations alongside McGarvey, Hardeman, Brewer and others, whose contributions to the Cause of Christ have endured long after the principals themselves have 'crossed over the river to rest in the shade of the trees.'"

This volume also has a subject and scripture index that makes the material easier to reference. Some of the questions answered by Guy N. Woods include:

- "Was there forgiveness of sins under the Old Testament covenant?"
- "Why is the 37th verse of the 8th chapter of Acts omitted from the American Standard Version of the New Testament?"
- "Why is it wrong to gamble?"
- "What is verbal inspiration?"
- "What is the difference in meaning, if any, in the words, 'Hebrew', "Israelite' and 'Jew?'"
- "Much is said regarding the qualifications of elders. What are the qualifications of preachers set out in the Bible?"
- "Is it scriptural and, or necessary as Christians to fast in the era which we now live? Would our prayers be more effective if we fast?"

Guy N. Woods was a prolific writer. His first article appeared in the Gospel Advocate in 1934 and it is estimated he wrote at least 937 articles for the Gospel Advocate alone. He also wrote nearly 200 articles for at least nine other periodicals. He wrote the Adult Gospel Quarterly for the Gospel Advocate for about 30 years. He also wrote 12 books and at least three tracts. It is astonishing when one contemplates the preparation and the work involved in writing these works. He was also scheduled for 50 gospel meetings a year. Guy N. Woods not only conducted 50 gospel meetings a year, but he was booked for over 200 meetings in advance. So, if a congregation desired to schedule Guy N. Woods for a meeting, he would not be available until after four years. (A reminder for those who want to schedule well-known preachers for gospel meetings—these men are in demand. Plan ahead!)

This book deals with controversial issues of which Guy N. Woods wrote:

> Difficult matters often obscured are frequently dealt with, and the answers, in consequence, will be sometimes

controversial. It is not expected that every reader will agree with each sentiment expressed; it is sincerely hoped that all who examine these pages will be stimulated to additional study and investigation in the search for truth, since it is the truth, and the truth alone, which frees from the bondage and thralldom of sin. (John 8:31,32)

Both Open Forum Volumes 1 and 2 should be in every church library and in each Christian home. Brother Woods passed away at the age of eighty-five on December 8, 1993.

Standing For Their Faith: A History of Churches of Christ in Tennessee from 1900 to 1950 (William Woodson)

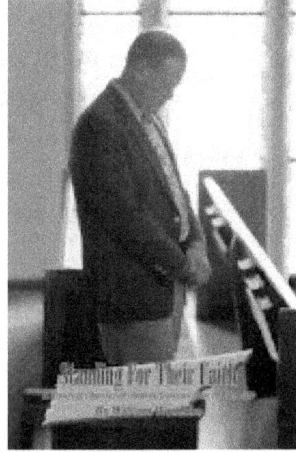

Someone once told me it was good that Christians had never heard of Alexander Campbell. This person was attempting to demonstrate that people are reaping the fruits of the Restoration pioneers' work to go get us back to the Bible, and not the pioneers themselves, for our authority in religion. While I understand the person's point, it is short sighted. It appears we are upon another division. One of the marks of the pending division is the use of mechanical instruments of music in worship—one of the major lines of demarcation in the first division of the 19th century! How has this resurfaced? My response is the lack of emphasizing the history of the Restoration Movement. A generation has a risen similar to the ones in the book of Judges—they were not taught the lessons of the past and are repeating the mistakes of past generations. Some have been taught but have apparently forgotten the issue of the past.

Standing For Their Faith, is a good reference work for the major challenges confronted in the state of Tennessee during the first half of the 20th century. The division between churches of Christ and the Christian Church was recognized in the U.S. Census of 1906. While the lines of division had been settled, the fight for the truth was still raging on. The issues of this period not only include instrumental music but also the Missionary Society and Premillennialism.

In relation to instrumental music, one of the statements quoted in the book is from H. Leo Boles at one of the Unity Meetings between the Christian Church and churches of Christ in Indianapolis of 1938. His speech included the point that the Christian Church had left the NT pattern, not the churches of Christ.

> Brethren, this is where the churches of Christ stand today; it is where unity may be found now; it is where you left the New Testament; it is where you left the churches of Christ, and it is where you can find them when you come back. On this ground and teaching, and only on this, can scriptural unity be had now; on these basic principles of the New Testament Christian unity may always be had. [Woodson, p. 83]

This point needs to be brought to the remembrance of some in our brotherhood. Apparently there are a growing number who want to compromise the NT pattern and fellowship religious bodies that use the instrument. In fact, some say the only barrier to fellowship is the belief that Jesus is the Son of God. There are several groups that are clearly not to be fellowshipped that believe Jesus is the Son of God; e.g., the Church of Jesus Christ of Latter Day Saints (Mormons). Fellowship (or union) on the basis of error then comes at the expense of unity with God's word that is totally unacceptable. The slippery slope slid down by the digressives of 1906 should be a warning to those who desire to pursue the same course of action.

This book also discusses the Hardeman-Boswell Debate in Nashville, TN. The Christian Church was thirsting for a challenger to debate instrumental music issue across the state. N.B. Hardeman met the challenge of the Christian church and quenched their desire to debate across the state.

William Woodson holds a doctorate in Church History. He has served as Dean of the School of Bible at Freed-Hardeman College (now University). He has also served as Dean of Biblical Studies at David Lipscomb University. This book is thoroughly documented and is an excellent primer on the background of the past events that will equip us to deal with future challenges on the horizon.

Originally printed in *West Virginia Christian*, Vol. 15, No. 6, June 2008, p. 3. Reprinted by permission.

Young's Analytical Concordance to the Bible (Robert Young)

One would be hard pressed to find a tool more effective and beneficial to studying the word of God than a concordance. As mentioned in the review of Strong's Concordance, Young's Concordance groups words by the Hebrew and Greek language rather than the English (as does Strong's Concordance). This grouping shows how the same term is used in various other contexts. If students of the Scriptures would learn to use the principle of checking the same word in other contexts, it would eliminate many errors. For each Greek and Hebrew term the transliteration and the original script is given plus a definition. There are over 300 thousand words referenced in this concordance.

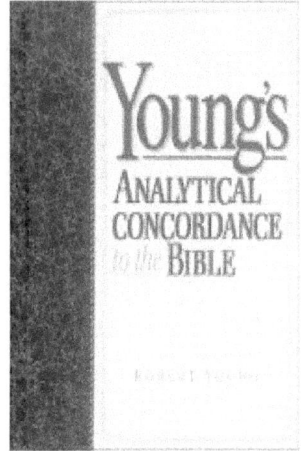

Robert Young (1822-1888) was a publisher who was proficient in various ancient languages. He was privately taught and served as an apprentice to the printing business. He also published a respectable translation of the Scriptures known as Young's Literal Translation. He was born in Edinburgh, Scotland and was a member of the Free Church (Presbyterian). His primary interest was in the field of Old Testament and language studies. One writer went on to describe Young's accomplishments as:

> Young was celebrated as an editor and translator of Jewish and Biblical writings in various languages, especially in Hebrew, Samaritan, Aramaic, Syriac, Arabic, and Gujarati, thus and in other ways contributing to the apparatus for textual criticism. He was also active in the region of comparative

linguistics and in Semitic philology. (The New Schaff-Herzog Encyclopedia of Religious Knowledge, p. 490).

My wife prefers to use Young's Analytical Concordance while I prefer to use Strong's Exhaustive Concordance. So, we have both volumes, and I find having both very beneficial to cross-reference.

Work Cited:

"Young, Robert," The New Schaff-Herzog Encyclopedia of Religious Knowledge, Grand Rapids, MI: Baker Book House, Vol. 13, 1964, p. 490.

Originally printed in *West Virginia Christian*, Vol. 7, No. 12, December 2000, p. 8. Reprinted by permission.

www.ingramcontent.com/pod-product-compliance
Lightning Source LLC
Chambersburg PA
CBHW062112020426
42335CB00013B/930